Nokalakevi • Tsikhegoji • Archaeopolis

Archaeological excavations 2001–2010

Anglo-Georgian Expedition to Nokalakevi

Edited by

Paul Everill

BAR International Series 2612

2014

Published in 2016 by
BAR Publishing, Oxford

BAR International Series 2612

Nokalakevi • Tsikhegoji • Archaeopolis

ISBN 978 1 4073 1243 9

BAR Publishing is the trading name of British Archaeological Reports (Oxford) Ltd.
British Archaeological Reports was first incorporated in 1974 to publish the BAR
Series, International and British. In 1992 Hadrian Books Ltd became part of the BAR
group. This volume was originally published by Archaeopress in conjunction with
British Archaeological Reports (Oxford) Ltd / Hadrian Books Ltd, the Series principal
publisher, in 2014. This present volume is published by BAR Publishing, 2016.

Printed in England

PUBLISHING

BAR titles are available from:

       BAR Publishing
       122 Banbury Rd, Oxford, OX2 7BP, UK
EMAIL   info@barpublishing.com
PHONE +44 (0)1865 310431
FAX   +44 (0)1865 316916
       www.barpublishing.com

Contents

PREFACE

Nokalakevi-Tsikhegoji-Archaeopolis is one of Georgia's important historical monuments, and a prolonged period of archaeological research has revealed very important cultural layers and archaeological artefacts. The monument represents the historical development of an important part of our country (Colchis, Egrisi/Lazika, Samegrelo/ Odishi) from the pre-Antique period to the Medieval centuries. The building of Tsikhegoji is associated with Kuji, who laid the foundation of a united Georgia with the Georgian king Parnavaz. The Archaeopolis ("old city") of Byzantine written sources was also located at Nokalakevi, and was the capital city of the kingdom of Egrisi/Lazika. For these reasons the newly elected president of Georgia launched his pre-electoral campaign at Nokalakevi. The first time I was able to visit this wonderful place and monument was in 2007. The fantastic architectural complex, the rich archaeological layers and the stunning environment around it are a delight to all its visitors.

The results of the Anglo-Georgian archaeological expedition from 2001-2010 are presented in this monograph. I am very happy and proud that such an important Georgian historical monument is being rigorously studied by an international expedition, staffed by professional personnel from a variety of academic institutions. Expedition scientists, led by David Lomitashvili, are undertaking intensive multi-disciplinary research using modern methodologies and technologies. Their frank, friendly and, at the same time, principled and professional approach enables specialists and students of significant, international scientific-educational institutions to participate in research at Nokalakevi. It is important to note that, alongside the scientific research, the main priority for the expedition is the delivery of educational programmes. Since 2001 more than 120 Georgian and international students have further developed their skills, and that is certainly an important fact in itself.

In conclusion I want to add that the publication of this work will be another step forward in the collaboration between Georgian and British scientists, and the development of science. This is clear from the volume and quality of scientific research that is included in the current work. I want to wish success to the Anglo-Georgian archaeological expedition and I hope that, in the future you will present many interesting finds and research to Georgian and international scientific communities.

Bidzina Ivanishvili

Prime Minister of Georgia

PREFACE

I am delighted to see this monograph of the first ten years of the Anglo-Georgian Expedition to Nokalakevi being published. The cooperation and high quality of work at Nokalakevi are a model of good, modern archaeological practice, as well as a vehicle through which a new generation of Georgian and British scholars come to know each other. Those who know Nokalakevi already know this. I hope this publication will make a wider circle of people aware.

I first visited Nokalakevi in the summer of 2007, thanks to an invitation from Ian Colvin. We met in Tbilisi on the evening that summer's contingent of students arrived to work at the site. Ian's enthusiasm drew me into promising to visit – which Kate and I did a couple of weeks later with our children. We were entranced, as everyone is, by the beautiful location of the site, and the wonderful swimming place at the foot of a Byzantine tunnel. But what impressed us most was the friendly, hard-working and stimulating atmosphere of the dig. That of course could be said of many digs – but the coming together of British and Georgian traditions on this lovely bend in the river give the place a unique flavour. That owes a great deal to the inspiration provided by David Lomitashvili, Ian Colvin, Besik Lortkipanidze, Paul Everill and their colleagues.

Over the next three years we got to know Nokalakevi and its staff much better, meeting friends such as Dato Lomitashvili and Nino Kebuladze in Tbilisi as well as Nokalakevi. I particularly remember our first visit after the terrible events of August 2008, when the appearance of the word "base" on maps led Russian forces to inspect the site. By good fortune, the dates of the students' visit had been changed, and they had all left before then. But it was a difficult time for the excavation, and when we visited, the local Georgian authorities remained very solicitous of the security of the site and its visitors. The important thing, though, was that work was resumed as soon as possible – the work that the Georgian team began in 1973, and kept going through the difficulties of the 90s.

And it is the work that matters. This is a fascinating site spanning the Byzantine and Hellenistic periods. There is much to be learned here, and continual opportunities to deepen Anglo-Georgian cooperation in archaeology. With other excavations, such as those at Pichvnari and Dmanisi, archaeologists are contributing both to the expansion of scholarship and to the deepening of links between Georgia and the United Kingdom. And we have our own souvenir – that first visit inspired one of our daughters to study archaeology herself.

I wish the Anglo-Georgian Expedition and everyone associated with it many more years of successful endeavour, and many more days in the shade of the cypresses.

Denis Keefe

British Ambassador to Georgia 2007-2010

FOREWORD

By Davit Lomitashvili, Ian Colvin and Paul Everill

The great richness of Georgia's cultural heritage remains largely undiscovered by western academics, with the notable exception of a handful of specialists. This is of course largely a result of 70 years of Soviet occupation, which impeded the free exchange of knowledge and closed Georgia to all but the most determined and resourceful non-Soviet academics. Within Georgia, however, the study of important sites and monuments was undertaken with great vigour for many years, supported by the vast coffers of the Soviet Union and driven forward by pioneering Georgian archaeologists, such as Giorgi Nioradze, Boris Kuftin, Germane Gobejishvili, Andria Apakidze, Aleqsandre Javakhishvili, Otar Japaridze, and Otar Lordkipanidze. The break-up of the Soviet Union in 1991 removed this veil from Georgia and opened its borders, but it also brought a decade of economic crises, civil wars, corruption and crime as competing factions sought to determine Georgia's future as a newly independent republic for their own benefit. Against this backdrop Georgian academics, now freed from the scrutiny of the KGB, struggled to continue their work. It was perhaps not until the peaceful Rose Revolution of 2003 that this chapter was finally closed, and democracy and stability were able to flourish in Georgia.

The story of the study of Nokalakevi, outlined in Chapter 2, should be seen in the context of the vast sweep of political and economic factors that shaped modern Georgia. When the site was first identified as the Byzantine fortress of Archaeopolis in 1833, the Principality of Mingrelia, within which the site is located, had not yet been formally annexed to the Russian Empire. A century later the first excavations were made possible by an agreement between the National Education Commission for the Georgian SSR, the Transcaucasian Museum in Tbilisi and the German Weimar Republic's 'Emergency Association of German Science'. The excavations that were undertaken between 1973 and 1991 were on a scale that is hard to conceive of today, with a total annual budget peaking at 350-450,000 Roubles, which supported long periods of excavation, conservation and restoration. In contrast the small investigations that took place between 1993 and 1998 were often largely undertaken by members of the S. Janashia Museum's (now part of the Georgian National Museum) Nokalakevi Expedition in their own time.

The Anglo-Georgian Expedition to Nokalakevi is the latest chapter in this story, and the Georgian language version of this monograph will be known as Nokalakevi 4. This reflects a continuity from the preceding publications of results from 1973 to 1977 (Nokalakvi 1); 1978 to 1982 (Nokalakevi 2); and 1983 to 1989 (Nokalakevi 3), edited by former head of the expedition, Parmen Zakaraia (1981; 1987; 1993). Apart from English language chapter summaries in Nokalakevi 1 and 2, and Russian summaries in all three, the information in these, now hard to find, publications is accessible only to those who can read Georgian. Consequently in this, the first significant publication of results from Nokalakevi to be produced in English, a short summary of previous work is provided.

The study of past societies, be it through their documentary or material remains, does not mean that the contemporary world can be ignored. The expedition has long exercised its social responsibility with regard to the people of Nokalakevi and the wider Senaki district. It is an important seasonal employer for the village, and accommodation for our student volunteers is rented from local families, both of which bring much needed money into an area with high unemployment. Food, goods and services sufficient to support an expedition of some 30 to 35 people are all procured locally. After working on site, English-speaking volunteers devote a great deal of time to language classes organised with schools from Senaki. These give children the chance to practice conversational English and to improve their proficiency. These popular classes are over-subscribed every year, and school children and teachers alike find them immensely valuable. The impact on the local economy of increased tourism also cannot be overstated. Money raised in Britain helped support much needed repairs to the local museum and the expedition dig house in 2005. Subsequent investment from the Georgian Ministry of Culture and the National Agency for Cultural Heritage Preservation of Georgia has seen the establishment of a secure archaeological park at Nokalakevi and repairs to local infrastructure. Increasing numbers of foreign tourists, for whom Nokalakevi might once have seemed too far off the beaten track, are being drawn there to enjoy the splendour of the standing remains and the beauty of the location.

The expedition has also contributed significantly to the teaching of Georgian archaeology students, both in the field and in the classroom. This latter group now benefits from the Georgian language translations of the Museum of London Archaeology Service 'Site Manual' and RESCUE: The British Archaeological Trust's publication 'First Aid for Finds'. Both these publications, the translations of which were organised by the expedition with the assistance of the authors, are now freely available for educational purposes and add to the body of modern methodological work accessible to young Georgian archaeologists. It is an achievement of which the expedition is rightly proud.

The archaeological work of course continues to shed light on the history of the site, and each year students from Georgia, Britain and a host of other countries learn modern excavation methodology at Nokalakevi. The Anglo-Georgian Expedition and the friendships that forged it grow year after year and, while presenting the results of the first ten years of our collaboration, we continue to undertake the excavations that will form the basis of 'Nokalakevi 5' in years to come.

Professor Davit Lomitashvili, Head of the Expedition
Ian Colvin, Director of AGEN
Dr Paul Everill, Co-Director of AGEN and Editor of this monograph

With thanks to Dr Besik Lortkipanidze, Dr Nikoloz Murgulia and Ana Tvaradze for their invaluable editorial support.

ACKNOWLEDGEMENTS

With thanks to the 142 staff, students and volunteers who worked with the Anglo-Georgian Expedition from 2001-2010, without whom this book would not be possible:

Abdul Alnuaimi (2007); **Giorgi Amashukeli** (2005-6); **Grahame Appleby** (2001-2); **Jo Appleby** (2001-2); **Becky Armour** (2005; 2010); **Nick Armour** (2001-5; 2010); **Giorgi Avtandilishvili** (2008); **Lisa-Marie Bak** (2009); **Liz Bates** (2002); **Henry Bennett** (2007); **Jessica Bennett** (2010); **Tom Bishop** (2003-4); **Richard Bliault** (2004); **Catherine Bohner** (2010); **Maka Bokeria** (2007-10); **Tomek Borowski** (2008); **Holly Brown** (2008); **Laura Burnett** (2001); **Rebecca Cassidy** (2008); **Nino Chkhartishvili** (2008-10); **Carol Colvin** (2008); **Ian Colvin** (2001-10); **David Connolly** (2004); **Amy Cove** (2007); **Lydia Critchley** (2008; 2010); **Jonathan Croese** (2008); **David Crowther** (2008); **Helen Curtis** (2007); **Misho Darjania** (2008); **Alice De Jong** (2010); **Alex Dennis** (2005); **Giorgi Dgebuadze** (2001); **Clara Dickinson** (2010); **Cliodhna Donnan** (2005); **Becky Dorran** (2009); **Kim Dowding** (2010); **Natia Dzigua** (2006-9); **Frankie Edwards** (2009); **Jamie Edwards** (2004); **Paul Everill** (2002-10); **Tamuna Gegia** (2002-4); **Andy Ginns** (2004); **Zura Giorgadze** (2009); **Kathryn Grant** (2006-9); **Rebecca Griffiths** (2010); **Ben Gruwier** (2010); **Davit Gurgenidze** (2005-6; 2009); **Jeanette Hall** (2010); **Alex Hanrahan-Soar** (2003-5); **Emily Hill** (2001); **Joshua Horrocks** (2008); **Naomi Humphreys** (2010); **Christina Jackson** (2006); **Natalia Jamburia** (2004-5); **Salome Jamburia** (2008-10); **Laura James** (2010); **Irakli Javakhia** (2007); **Robert Jefferies** (2004); **Giga Kakhishvili** (2009); **Luke Kane** (2007-8); **Sandro Kartsivadze** (2010); **Nino Kebuladze** (2002-10); **Steve Kemp** (2003-4); **Kerree Kendall** (2007); **Elene Kenia** (2008-9); **Revaz Kenia** (2007); **Vaniko Kenia** (2008); **Dave Kenny** (2005); **Abdulla Khamis** (2007); **Shorena Khetsuriani** (2008-10); **Eliso Kvavadze** (2009); **Larissa Kogleck** (2005); **Temuri Kubecia** (2009); **Maia Kublashvili** (2007); **Ross Lane** (2003); **Nicole Leckey** (2008); **Mary Leighton** (2001); **Christopher Lillington-Martin** (2005); **Beka Lomitashvili** (2009-10); **Davit Lomitashvili** (2001-10); **Giorgi Lomitashvili** (2004-10); **Irakli Lomtadze** (2002); **Besik Lortkipanidze** (2001-10); **Anna-Maria Luton** (2002); **Levan Makashvili** (2001); **Phil Marter** (2009); **Jane Matthews** (2001-2); **Zofia Matyjaszkiewicz** (2010); **Marika Mchedlishvili** (2004-7; 2009); **Ana Meunargia** (2007-8); **Giorgi Meurmashvili** (2008); **Ana Mgeladze** (2009-10); **Julia Morgan** (2005); **Lisa Morris** (2010); **Andy Muir** (2007); **Jan Muir** (2007); **Levan Murgulia** (2005-6); **Nikoloz Murgulia** (2003-10); **Benjamin Neil** (2002-10); **Tamuna Niniashvili** (2010); **Samantha Oakley** (2006); **Sally O'Brien** (2006); **Chris Oxbury** (2003-4); **Andrew Oxley** (2001); **Oliver Page** (2003); **Natalie Piekarski** (2006); **Ashleigh Plaskett** (2006); **Conor Roarty** (2006); **Harry Robson** (2007-9); Belinda van Roeden (2008); **Chris Russel** (2005-9); **Yasmin Saheid** (2005); **Clara Schonfeld** (2010); **Richard Scurr** (2010); **Andrew Shapland** (2001-2); **Davit Sharashenidze** (2008); **Lon Shepherd** (2010); **Mary Shepperson** (2002); **Toni-Anne Shields** (2007); **Levan Shotashvili** (2003-4); **Manana Shvelidze** (2007); **Nikoloz Skhirtladze** (2006); **Adam Slater** (2010); **Nikki Snape** (2008); **Judy Stanwell** (2001); **Megan Stoakley** (2004); **Maggie Struckmeier** (2004); **Qetalia Tamazashvili** (2009); **Geoff Taylor** (2005); **Jane Timby** (2007-10); **Petre Tsintskaladze** (2007); **Lali Tsomaia** (2008); **James Tuohy** (2008); **Lauren Turnbull** (2005); **Tanya Turner** (2008); **Ana Tvaradze** (2007-10); **Gemma Ward** (2009); **Jess Webster** (2004); **Matthew Wells** (2007); **Jess Wilkins** (2003-4); **Amy Williams** (2007); **Ellen Wright** (2010)

The Expedition is extremely grateful to those organisations that have provided financial assistance since 2001, in particular those which enabled its founding and first seasons, such as Oxford's Marjory-Wardrop and Craven funds, the British Academy's Black Sea Initiative, the British Institute at Ankara and Worcester College, Oxford. The expedition has subsequently received financial support from the University of Winchester, Friends of Academic Research in Georgia (FaRiG), and Archaeology Abroad. Their generosity has made the expedition possible.

Particular gratitude is owed to the following individuals and institutions: The Georgian National Museum, especially David Lordkipanidze and Zurab Tvaltchrelidze; National Agency for Cultural Heritage Preservation of Georgia; The Foundation for the Rescue and Preservation of Historical monuments of Georgia; University of Winchester Department of Archaeology; University of Southampton Department of Archaeology; University of Bradford Department of Archaeological Sciences; Professor David Braund (Exeter University); Professor Michael Vickers (Oxford University); Dr Mim Bower (McDonald Institute for Archaeological Research, University of Cambridge); Dave Kenny (English Heritage); Adrian Turgel; University of Cambridge Department of Archaeology and Anthropology, and particularly Jane Woods for her advice in the first two years of the expedition; the Cambridge Archaeology Unit; Archaeology South-East; David Connolly (www.bajr. org); the staff of the Nokalakevi museum, and particularly the late director Enrico Kokaia; Museum of London

Archaeology; and RESCUE: The British Archaeological Trust.

We also wish to thank the Ambassadors and staff of the United Kingdom Embassy to Georgia who have, throughout this period, provided support to the expedition. In particular we wish to single out Denis Keefe (HM Ambassador to Georgia 2007-10) and his family for their evident enthusiasm for our work; regular visits to Nokalakevi; and hospitality in Tbilisi.

Lastly, our greatest debt is to the government and residents of Nokalakevi and Senaki, whose friendship and hospitality have been overwhelming; and to the Senaki Police Department and officers of the Security Police who have ensured the safety of the expedition over the years.

To our dear Nokalakevi friends who have hosted and looked after our expedition and its guests over these years, and who have shared their houses with our volunteers we offer our heartfelt thanks.

CONTRIBUTORS TO THE VOLUME

Nick Armour BA MSc: Archaeologist and Conservation Officer, Planning Services, Huntingdonshire District Council, Pathfinder House, St Mary's Street, Huntingdon, United Kingdom; Co-Founder of the Anglo-Georgian Expedition and Site Director 2001-3

Dr Marine Bokeria: Palaeoethnobotanist; Herbarium Curator in Natural History Department, Georgian National Museum, Tbilisi, Georgia

Maia Chichinadze: Palynologist; PhD student at Ilia State University, Tbilisi; Assistant, Institute of Palaeobiology, Georgian National Museum, 3 Purtseladze Street, Tbilisi, Georgia

Ian Colvin: Historian, Cambridge University; Co-Founder and Director of the Anglo-Georgian Expedition

Dr Paul Everill MIFA FHEA FSA: Lecturer in Applied Archaeological Techniques, Department of Archaeology, University of Winchester, Hampshire, United Kingdom; Co-Director of the Anglo-Georgian Expedition and Site Director 2004-present

Kathryn Grant AIFA BA MSc: Archaeologist at Archaeology South-East, a division of the Centre for Applied Archaeology, Institute of Archaeology, University College London; Senior Supervisor for the Anglo-Georgian Expedition

Ben Gruwier: PhD candidate in Biological Anthropology, Department of Anthropology, University of Durham, United Kingdom

Dr Rob Ixer FSA: Freelance archaeological consultant and lithic, ceramic and ore (archaeo)-petrographer. Honorary Visiting Senior Research Associate, Institute of Archaeology, University College London.

Laura James BSc: Research Staff at Cambridge Archaeological Unit, Department of Archaeology, University of Cambridge, United Kingdom; Trench Supervisor for the Anglo-Georgian Expedition

Tamila Kapanadze: Curator, Department of Medieval Archaeology, S. Janashia Museum of Georgia, Georgian National Museum, Rustaveli Avenue 3, 0105 Tbilisi, Georgia

Dr Nino Kebuladze: Head of Restoration-Conservation Group. Georgian National Museum, Rustaveli Avenue 3, 0105 Tbilisi, Georgia; Director of Finds Conservation, Nokalakevi Expedition

Dr Eliso Kvavadze: Palynologist; Chief Research Associate, Institute of Palaeobiology, Georgian National Museum, 3 Purtseladze Street, Tbilisi, Georgia

Professor Davit Lomitashvili: Senior Research Scientist, Georgian National Museum, Rustaveli Avenue 3, 0105 Tbilisi, Georgia; Member of the Archaeological Committee of Georgia; Head and co-Founder of Anglo-Georgian Expedition to Nokalakevi and Visiting Research Fellow, University of Winchester, United Kingdom

Dr Besik Lortkipanidze: Professor of the Georgian-American University (GAU), M. Aleksidze St. 8, 0160 Tbilisi, Georgia; Deputy Head of Anglo-Georgian Expedition in Nokalakevi

Dr Nikoloz Murgulia: Assistant-Curator, Department of Medieval Archaeology, S. Janashia Museum of Georgia, Georgian National Museum, Rustaveli Avenue 3, 0105 Tbilisi, Georgia; Deputy Head and Deputy Site-Director for the Anglo-Georgian Expedition

Benjamin Neil BA MSc: PhD candidate, Department of Archaeological Sciences, University of Bradford, Bradford, United Kingdom; Co-Director of the Anglo-Georgian Expedition and Osteologist

Chris Russel BA: Field Archaeologist at Archaeology South-East, a division of the Centre for Applied Archaeology, Institute of Archaeology, University College London; Trench Supervisor for the Anglo-Georgian Expedition

Adam Slater: Project Officer at the Cambridge Archaeological Unit, Department of Archaeology, University of Cambridge, United Kingdom; Senior Supervisor for the Anglo-Georgian Expedition

Dr Jane Timby MIFA FSA: Freelance archaeological consultant and ceramic specialist. Visiting Research Fellow, University of Reading, United Kingdom

Ana Tvaradze: Assistant, Department of Medieval Archaeology, S. Janashia Museum of Georgia, Georgian National Museum, Rustaveli Avenue 3, 0105 Tbilisi, Georgia; Senior Supervisor for the Anglo-Georgian Expedition

Meri Zamtaradze: Consultant, Department of Medieval Archaeology, S. Janashia Museum of Georgia, Georgian National Museum, Rustaveli Avenue 3, 0105, Tbilisi, Georgia

SITE OVERVIEW

Located within a loop of the picturesque river Tekhuri, on the northern edge of the Colchian plain, western Georgia, lie the impressive ruins of Nokalakevi (Figure 0.1). Occupying some 20ha, the site was known to early Byzantine historians as Archaeopolis, and to the Georgian (Kartlian) chroniclers as Tsikhegoji, or the fortress of Kuji – a semi-mythical Colchian ruler, or 'Eristavi'.

According to medieval chroniclers, in the fourth century BC Alexander the Great installed the tyrant Azon as ruler (*eristavi*) of Kartli, east Georgia. Kuji of Colchis formed an alliance with Parnavaz, the nephew of the former *mamasakhlisi*, to overthrow Macedonian rule. Tsikhegoji, Kuji's capital, is therefore central to this story of an ancient unified Georgia. In reality Alexander did not campaign in Georgia, but stories of Kuji, like the British King Arthur, perhaps derive from a kernel of historical truth.

Nokalakevi is situated in Samegrelo, 15km from the modern regional capital at Senaki. Located on the Martvili road, the early Byzantine fortress would have commanded an important crossing point of the river Tekhuri, at the junction with a valuable strategic route that still winds through the neighbouring hills to Chkhorotsqu in central Samegrelo (Figure 0.2). Nokalakevi-Archaeopolis played a pivotal part in the major wars fought between the Byzantines and Sasanians in the South Caucasus during the sixth century AD. It was one of the key fortresses guarding Lazika (modern west Georgia) from Sasanian Persian and Iberian (East Georgian/ Kartlian) attack, and was part of a complex chain of forts and towers established along the northeastern frontier of the Byzantine Empire. During the war of AD 540-562, the Persians' failure to take Nokalakevi-Archaeopolis from the Byzantines and their Laz allies eventually cost them control of Lazika (Figure 0.3).

The earliest surviving fortifications at Nokalakevi date to the 4th century AD, and were strengthened in the 5th century. Significant additional fortifications were added in the 6th century AD, including a remodelling of defensive works around the eastern gate (Figure 0.4). These multiple phases of fortification led to the site being referred to as the 'Fortress of Triple Walls' in some Georgian chronicles. The early Byzantine defensive fortifications of Nokalakevi-Archaeopolis are augmented by its topographic position next to the river Tekhuri, which, to the west of the fortress, has carved a gorge through the local limestone. Furthermore, the steep and rugged terrain to the north of the site made the citadel that was situated there largely unassailable. A wall connected this 'upper town' to the 'lower' town below, where excavations have revealed substantial stone buildings of the 4th to 6th century AD (Figure 0.5).

Beneath these early Byzantine period layers is evidence of several earlier phases of occupation and abandonment from the 8th to 1st centuries BC, which includes a Hellenistic period (4th to 1st centuries BC) settlement and later necropolis. Current evidence indicates a prehistoric origin for settlement at the site, which is hardly surprising given the wealth of resources and easily-defendable character of the topography. Whether this lies in the Iron Age, the Bronze Age, or even earlier is yet to be determined and, given the size of the site under study, may not be established for some time.

Whatever the origins of settlement at Nokalakevi, by the 8th/7th century BC there was clearly a significant population engaged in complex ritual activity unique to the region. Double-headed zoomorphic figurines (Figure 0.6) dating to this period have only been found at Nokalakevi and at Vani, 40km to the southeast in Imereti. These finds indicate a unified socio-cultural system that spanned the Colchian plain. The settlement appears to have flourished again in the Hellenistic period, before the Laz kings and their Byzantine allies built the mighty fortifications at Nokalakevi that can still be seen today.

Figure 0.1: Location of Nokalakevi in western Georgia (identified by the star) and political geography of the region

Figure 0.2: 3D Model of the site, looking north, produced from RTK GPS survey data in 2009, showing the winding route of the Tekhuri and the road to Chkhorotsqu to the west

Figure 0.3: The Persian attack on Nokalakevi Archaeopolis in AD 551, illustrated by Phil Marter

Figure 0.4: Photograph of the eastern fortifications viewed from the hill to the north

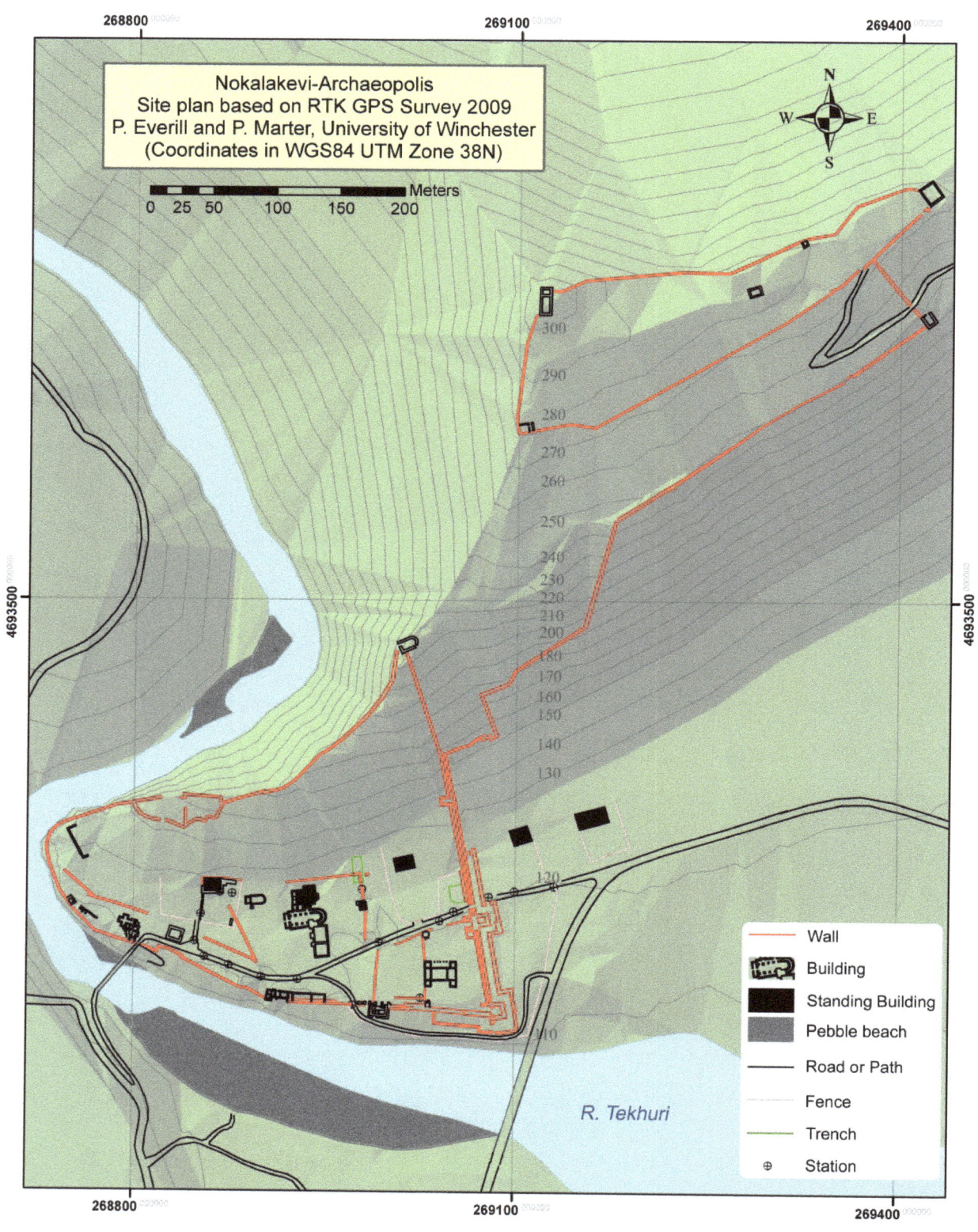

Figure 0.5: Nokalakevi-Archaeopolis Site Plan

Figure 0.6: An example of the double-headed zoomorphic figurines from Nokalakevi, dating to the 8th/7th centuries BC

CHAPTER ONE

Historical overview of Colchis-Egrisi-Lazika

By Ian Colvin, Besik Lortkipanidze, Nikoloz Murgulia

Introduction

This chapter considers the history of Colchis-Lazika on a local and regional level, and sets it against the backdrop of relevant global events. There are several reasons to include this here. One is that many western readers will be unfamiliar with Georgian history and need a detailed introduction in order to fully appreciate the archaeological results from Nokalakevi. Another is that, although Georgian scholars have constructed a history of Georgia that depends heavily on inferences from surrounding events, these are not always explicitly stated and the result is sometimes a history of Georgia divorced from the better documented events of the surrounding states and empires. Yet very often what we know of events in Colchis-Lazika, we know of only because of the outside interest or intervention of these states, empires and invaders. It is rare, until quite late, that we get an insider's view of events within Georgia. It is all the more important that we bear in mind the outside source of information and its potential biases, and make more explicit the link between inferences and assumptions.

It is important to begin by briefly defining the terms used when describing the region. Colchis and Lazika are terms used by the Graeco-Roman sources on which historians depend for the second half of the 1st millennium BC and the 1st millennium AD. The native Caucasian sources (Georgian and Armenian) use the term Egrisi (from which the name Mingrelia derives). Because Colchis and Lazika are more familiar to the greater majority of academics outside of Georgia these are the terms used in the following chapter. Readers delving further into the primary and secondary literature should bear in mind that in Georgian scholarship Egrisi is often the preferred term.

Colchis is used very inexactly by the ancient sources. Some ancient authors, such as Xenophon, considered Colchis to extend as far as Trebizond, while others, like Strabo, confined it more closely to territories approximating modern west Georgia. In later, Byzantine period sources it is generally used as a synonym for Lazika. Yet Lazika's boundaries varied considerably over the course of this period: in the second century AD it was but one among several kingdoms in West Georgia, while by the sixth it was the preeminent one. Furthermore there are grounds for thinking our sources use the term inconsistently: sometimes (e.g. Procopius VIII.2.21ff., 13.21) they use Lazika (or Colchis) to mean all the territories subject to (or claimed by) the Laz kings; at other times they appear to allude to a Laz heartland whose boundaries were much closer to the later principality of Mingrelia. This latter application of the term seems the most plausible explanation for Procopius' claim (*Wars* II.29.17-19 & 23; VIII.2.29f, 13.2) that all the habitations of the Laz were north of the Rioni-Phasis, that the region south of the river was 'uninhabited', and that the Laz preferred to keep the Persians away from the region north of the river (Colvin forthcoming).

In what follows Colchis is used to refer to the territory and kingdom in the years BC and Lazika for the Christian era. Used in a geographical sense, they represent the territories from Apsarus to the borders of Abasgia and the crest of the Greater Caucasus, and from the Black Sea to the Likhi ridge.

Prehistoric and proto-historic Colchis

Human settlement in the South Caucasus stretches far back into prehistory. At Dmanisi in east Georgia archaeologists have uncovered human remains belonging to the most ancient Europeans yet discovered, remains that have been dated to 1.8 million years before present. By the end of the Neolithic in the region, around the 6th millennium BC, the inhabitants of the South Caucasus and the Armenian Highland had domesticated cattle and pigs, and were cultivating cereals and grapes. This Shulaveri-Shomu culture is distinguished by mud-brick round houses, decorated pottery, female figurines, and the use of obsidian tools, especially long prismatic blades. Some scholars consider proto-Georgian tribes are identifiable on modern Georgian territory by this period. By the second millennium, palaeolinguists consider that proto-Kartvelian (i.e. proto-Georgian) had split into the three main branches of Kartvelian: Svan, Megrelo-Chan, and Kartvelian. Svan is spoken in the western Greater Caucasus mountains, while historically Megrelo-Chan speakers extended beyond their modern heartland of Mingrelia and the Gali region along the south-eastern Black Sea coast towards Trabzon, and into the Pontic mountain chain of the interior. The Karts occupied the central South Caucasus along the valley of the middle and upper Mtkvari river, and southwest towards the valley of the Chorokhi.

From the second half of the 4th millennium (early Bronze Age) to the last quarter of the 3rd millennium, or later in some parts, the so-called Kura-Araxes/ Early

Transcaucasian culture sprawled across an extensive territory to the east and southeast of Colchis. The inhabitants of a vast area – from the Greater Caucasus in the north to Lake Urmia in present-day Iran, through Armenia and across into eastern Turkey – shared a common material culture. Colchis, however, while clearly in contact with neighbouring territories boasted its own distinctive material culture, which in places (particularly the highland regions) had more in common with the cultures of the central and western North Caucasus, the Koban and the Kuban basins (Burney and Lang 1971). This was not, however, without internal variations between regions such as the mountains and plains, or the coastal zones and the interior (Braund 1994, 92).

From the time of the Assyrian king Shalmaneser I, calculated by Kuhrt (1995) as 1274-1245/1263-1234 BC, the Assyrians began to conduct campaigns into the area today known as the Armenian Highlands (Diakonoff 1984). During the reign of Tukulti-Ninurta I (1244-1208/1233-1197 BC), the Assyrians several times campaigned through the Armenian Highland in the direction of the Black Sea ('the Upper Sea'), thus approaching the very borders of Colchis. It is unclear whether or not Colchian tribes were among the '40 kings of the Naïri' (highlanders) who were defeated and on whom tribute was imposed (Melikishvili 1966, 31; Diakonoff 1984, 56). Tiglath-Pileser's campaign of 1112 BC drove deep into the Armenian Highland in the direction of the River Chorokhi (Turkish Çoruh). Here Tiglath-Pileser (r. 1114-1076 BC) encountered and defeated (he reports) a coalition of 22,000 warriors led by 23 kings (whose countries are listed by name). He then drove another army led by sixty kings of Naïri 'as far as the Upper Sea at arrow-point', i.e. the Black Sea. The unfortunate king of Daiene (which was located in the valley of the Chorokhi) was brought to Assur in chains. This was an Assyrian incursion reaching the edge of Colchis' sphere of direct interest but not, it seems, penetrating the Rioni basin itself. Around the end of the 12th century BC a series of misfortunes befell all the great powers of the Near East and for a period of nearly two centuries the cuneiform sources all but disappear. When they reappear, the Near East shows a very different configuration. It is not currently possible to say what effect, if any, these events had on the Colchians.

Early historical Colchis

The first indisputable mention of Colchis occurs only in the eighth century BC, in Akkadian sources. In this period the kingdom of Biainili or Van, known to its Assyrian neighbours as Urartu, was coming to dominate the tribes of the Armenian Highland. It challenged the neo-Assyrian dominance of the Near East, and, crucially for Colchis, was expanding northwards, encountering neighbouring tribes and statelets. The significance of Urartu to the Assyrians—whose archives show considerable interest in events affecting their neighbour; the adoption of cuneiform writing (which survives in rock-cut inscriptions

and clay tablets) by the Urartian state; and its expansion to the north, finally cast a pale glimmer of light on the neighbourhood of Colchis. The earliest Greek sources, though written several centuries later, also begin to provide some evidence for this period.

Thus the Urartian king Argishti I (c. 780-756 BC) defeated the Diauehi (the inhabitants of later Tao-Klarjeti in the Chorokhi River valley, to be associated with the Daiene of Tiglath-Pileser's campaign) and incorporated them into his empire. Argishti was succeeded by his son, Sardur II, who conducted campaigns against Colchis over several years in the mid-eighth century – on one occasion seizing and burning the royal city of Ildamusha. Not long after this the Cimmerian steppe nomads suddenly appeared in the Near East. Indeed the earliest mention of the Cimmerians is in Homer's *Odyssey* IX.14, which may refer to the ninth century BC (Sumilirski and Taylor 1991: 555). The arrival of these horse-riding nomadic warriors caused major disruption in the region. They first arrived in the South Caucasus, crossing the mountain passes of the Western and Central Caucasus (Diakonoff 1984: 90). Shortly before 714 BC they subjected the Urartians to a heavy defeat, according to Assyrian intelligence reports. The Assyrian king Sargon II (r. 721-705 BC) was quick to take advantage of this shift in the strategic balance, launching a devastating invasion of Urartu in 714 BC. While Urartu recovered from this defeat in the following century, the two states seem to have come to a more peaceful policy of coexistence by the mid-7th century. This détente resulted in almost a century of Assyrian hegemony in the Near East, with Assyrian imperial control extending across the Fertile Crescent from the Gulf to the borders of Egypt.

At the beginning of the 7th century BC a second nomadic group, the Scythians, followed the Cimmerians across the Caucasus, crossing by the eastern passes and settling in the steppes of what is now Azerbaijan. Some also reached Colchis, as finds of their distinctive iron 'akinak' daggers, Scythian arrow-heads (with a distinctive hooked barb), and iron battle-axes suggest. In the same way that Cimmerian groups had continued on into the Near East to play their part in wider Near Eastern history, the Scythians now joined the Medes in a revolt against Assyrian domination in 674-672 BC.

The Georgian historical narrative associates the invasions of these steppe peoples with the destruction of a unified Colchian state, which purportedly existed from the 13th century BC (or so, in other words the legendary kingdom of Aeetes and the Golden Fleece legend), though some scholars (for example, Braund [1994] and Diakonoff [1984]) are sceptical of the existence of such a state. The same period sees the transition from the Late Bronze to the early Iron Age in Colchis, accompanied by a population increase and the establishment of new settlements. Nokalakevi was among those created in the interior and layers excavated there have yielded large quantities of pottery, materials for making beads, and evidence of metal-working all dating to the 8th-7th centuries BC. Among the ceramics are numerous fragments of two-headed clay animal figurines. These finds are echoed, with variations, in layers from the same period at Vani, an apparently 'sister' site on the other side of the Colchian plain.

Graeco-Roman and Persian influence

Greek colonisation of the Black Sea began early in the first millennium BC, with colonies founded initially in towns on the northern coast of Asia Minor. The earliest extant Greek texts show that in the 8th century Colchis and the Caucasus had already been integrated into the world of Greek myth and imagination. Homer's reference (*Od.* 12.69-72) to the saga of the Argonauts (concerning the voyage of Jason and a host of Greek heroes to a mythical Colchis to recover Phrixus' golden fleece) shows it was well-known to his audience in the mid-eighth century when his poems crystallised in their current form. The evidence of myth is notoriously slippery and difficult to use to illuminate anything other than the stories Greeks told. There may, of course, be a kernel of truth at the heart of these myths, but we cannot be sure that they reflected a Colchian reality of any sort – despite the hold they had on the imagination of Greeks, (later) Colchians, and indeed modern scholars.

While first contacts with Colchis may have begun earlier, Greek colonies on the Colchian shore were only founded from the 6th century BC. Historical sources and archaeological excavation identify five colonies—Pityus, Dioscurias, Gyenus, Phasis and Pichvnari. Two further sites, Tsikhisdziri and Batumistsikhe, have been suggested as sites of Greek colonies on the basis of archaeological finds, but the material evidence is ambiguous at best. Greek pottery, finewares and storage containers from this period are to be found in coastal settlements, in towns along the Rioni, and further inland. As Braund (1994) has noted, the nature of Greek settlement has been much discussed but conclusions are not always rigorous due to a lack of evidence concerning their character, and relations with neighbouring peoples and states. Braund also warns that the presence or absence of Greek pottery does not necessarily relate directly to the presence or absence of Greek colonists (Braund 1994, 73).

The effects of these settlements can, however, be observed in the archaeological record—most directly on the coast, or inland at river ports. This period is a very rich one for west Georgian archaeology. Sites like Vani, Pityus, Sebastopolis-Dioscorias and Pichvnari show plentiful material remains, including the stunningly wealthy burials of Vani. Nokalakevi too has a rich layer of material in the 6th-4th centuries BC. Set further inland and away from the route of the Rioni, it has more local wares and fewer imports, but there are clear indications of the growth of the settlement at this time.

While the sixth century saw the arrival of Greek influence in Colchis both on the coast and inland, it also saw a renewal of influences from the south and east. The seventh and sixth centuries BC saw the successive overthrow of the Neo-Assyrian, Babylonian and Median empires, and the establishment of a new world power: the Achaemenid Persian Empire, which united the Near Eastern world from the Indus to Egypt and the Aegean, and from Arabia to Central Asia. This Persian hegemony and the stability that it brought helped draw the Caucasus into the Near Eastern world. Herodotus, writing at the end of the 6th century, gives a list of 20 satrapies established by Darius I. Parts of the south-eastern Black Sea coast and its hinterland appear in his 13th Satrapy, 'Pactycia, together with the Armenians and their neighbours as far as the Black Sea'. And the 18th and 19th satrapies include other South Caucasian peoples, 'the Moschi, Tibareni, Macrones, Mosynoieci and Mares' (Hdt III.90-95). These include parts of what might be termed Greater Colchis, and Kartvelian tribes (Melikishvili 1959). However Herodotus makes it clear that the Colchians and their neighbours to the north and west were not part of these 20 satrapies, and were at the very least semi-autonomous:

> "a voluntary contribution was undertaken by the Colchians and the neighbouring tribes between them and the Caucasus—the limit of the empire in this direction, everything to the northward being outside the range of Persian influence. In their case the contribution consisted (and still does) in the gift, every fifth year, of a hundred boys and a hundred girls" (Hdt III.97)

The Macedonians' eventual supplanting of the Persians, following the conquests of Alexander the Great (356-323 BC), inspired its own legends. Among these are that Alexander himself conquered the Caucasus, though in reality he never visited the region. Still later Georgian traditions describe how Parnavaz and Kuji, threw off the yoke of Alexander's 'Greek' lieutenant, Azon. It is to this tradition that the site of Nokalakevi is intimately connected. The Egrisian ruler Kuji – who in the Georgian legend acts with the Kartlian King Parnavaz to eject the Greeks – supposedly founded Tsikhegoji, literally translating as the 'fortress of Kuji', identified as today's Nokalakevi.

The fragmentation of Alexander's empire under his successors, the Diadochi, gave plenty of scope for independent action by satraps in the more distant regions. While there is relatively little information on what happened in Colchis, there is a wealth of information on the neighbouring kingdom of Pontos – partly because it was later to challenge Rome for hegemony in the region, absorbing both Colchis and the Crimean Bosphorus.

So much is known about this world because the Romans became interested in it when Mithridates VI Eupator, King of Pontus, sought to exclude them from it, threatening their interests in Asia Minor and in Greece itself. This brought Lucullus, and later Pompey, into the region during the great period of Roman empire-building. It effectively

NEAR EAST IN THE 3RD-1ST CENTURIES B.C.

Figure 1.1: Map of the region in the Hellenistic Period

brought the Seleucid system that had been semi-defunct for a while to an end and the resulting power vacuum sucked the Romans into the Eastern Mediterranean and the Caucasus. At the same time the Parthians inherited the Seleucids' eastern domains, extending their influence towards the Euphrates and the South Caucasus. While the sources for this period are predominantly Romans and Greeks writing grand political history, they do at least provide a snapshot of the Caucasus at this time.

The Romans, having defeated the formidable Mithridates in 65 BC, settled the situation by allowing his son, Pharnaces II, to rule a much diminished kingdom consisting of the Bosporan Chersonnese and eastern Pontus. Pompey granted Colchis to a different king, Aristarchus, who was overthrown by Pharnaces in 47 BC, during Caesar's civil war with Pompey. This act of revolt against Rome, along with the conquest of Armenia and part of Cappadocia, and the defeat of a Roman army under Calvinus, led to his defeat by Julius Caesar at the battle of Zela. In 37 BC Mark Anthony appointed his ally, Polemon I, as King of Pontus (including Colchis) and his rule saw some stability return to the region – perhaps aided by the latter's decision to support Octavian before the Battle of Actium in 31 BC. After the death of Polemon in 8 BC, the crown passed to his second wife Pythodoris.

However, her son and successor, Polemon II, was persuaded by Nero to abdicate the throne in 62 AD. Subsequently both Pontus and Colchis were incorporated into the Province of Galatia (63 AD) and later into Cappadocia (81 AD).

These centuries of violent political change left their mark on Georgia's archaeology. In West Georgia the important sites of Vani and Kutaisi both contain destruction layers followed by an abrupt reduction in the level of material culture. At Nokalakevi the archaeological sequence ends almost entirely for four centuries beginning again only in the fourth century AD.

After this period Rome's focus in the region was predominantly Armenia, Caucasian Albania and Iberia (Figure 1.2) and the rivalry with the Parthians over control of these kingdoms. Because Parthia was not contesting Rome's hegemony in Colchis there is much less written about the country in the extant sources. At the beginning of the second century AD, Arrian's account of his tour of inspection of the region gives us a detailed view of the Province of Cappadocia. Arrian, as governor of Cappadocia, clearly had a particular responsibility for the Roman garrisons along the east coast of the Black Sea and, one presumes, also for keeping an eye on the allied kings of several Colchian tribes. Another of Arrian's accounts, his *Order of Battle against the Alans*, concerns an expedition against the Alans in the north, to which some of those allied kings contributed troops. This illustrates how the Romans sought to regulate this frontier and the role that their allies in the region were expected to play.

The Parthians were replaced in 226/7 AD by a vigorous new Persian dynasty, the Sasanians, who reasserted claims to hegemony in Armenia, Iberia and the south Caucasus. This coincided with a period of crisis within the Roman Empire, which included threats on various frontiers as well as a series of usurpations. Raiding bands of Goths and Scythian 'Borani', ('northerners'), took to the sea and sacked coastal settlements around the Black Sea coast, including Colchian Pityus and Sebastopolis, and into the Aegean (Braund 1994, 262; Zosimus I, 31ff = Georgica I p266-267). In one such raid, having failed to take Phasis, the Borani may have continued inland. Dundua (1979) describes two substantial hoards found near Archaeopolis, at Eki and Sepieti, which were deposited after about AD 222, possibly in response to the threat posed by the raiders (Braund 1994). Roman garrisons appear to have been withdrawn, either under pressure of civil war, of war with the Sasanians, or perhaps of the growing power of the Laz kings, and for a brief period in the mid-3rd century the Sasanian Shahs claimed overlordship over Machelonia in Colchis (if their inscriptions are to be trusted). Clearly, initially at least, the Romans were in no position to exercise their claimed hegemony, however by the time of Diocletian the Roman recovery was fully underway. After the defeat of Narses by Galerius in 298 AD the terms of the Treaty of Nisibis cemented Roman hegemony in the South Caucasus for a generation. It was during this period that the South Caucasus, including the petty kings of Colchis, converted. Unfortunately there are no contemporary accounts of the conversion of the Laz, but historical sources describe the conversion of east Georgia in 326 AD.

West Georgia in the early medieval period, 4th-7th centuries AD

The political, economic and even social history of Colchis (known to the early Byzantine world as Lazika) in the early medieval period is best understood in the context of its strategically important position between the two great empires of the Near East, and at the boundary where the settled world of the Near Eastern civilisations meets the nomad-dominated Eurasian steppe. In the early medieval period two great powers dominated the settled lands of the Near East. From Constantinople the East Romans – Byzantines – ruled an empire centred on the Balkans, Anatolia, Syria-Palestine and Egypt that, at times, stretched as far as Italy, North Africa, and Spain. Their chief rivals were the Sasanian Persians, an Iranian people whose empire stretched from Mesopotamia to Afghanistan, and at times included much of the Arabian peninsula. Both states held ideological claims to world power. Yet each recognised their imperial neighbour as unique – the only people whom they were prepared to accord a degree of equality of status. Thus in formal letters their rulers described each other as brothers, or in a Sasanian phrase as 'sun and moon', comparing the empires to 'two lamps' or 'eyes, the one brightened by the light of the other'. Uncomfortably situated between these two great empires, the state of their diplomatic relations could dramatically affect events in Lazika. Sometimes relations between the powers were friendly – as briefly under Yazdegerd I (r. 399-422) and Theodosius II (r. 408-450) at the start of the fifth century, or under Maurice (r. 582-602) and Khusro II (r. 590-628) at the end of the sixth. More commonly they viewed each other with deep suspicion even during long periods of truce. And for much of the fourth, sixth and early seventh centuries they were formally at war.

One of the key factors affecting their relations, and thus indirectly affecting Lazika, was the state of affairs in the Eurasian steppe: the rise and fall of a succession of nomadic confederations periodically convulsed the peoples of the steppe. Thanks to the Black and Caspian seas, the world of the Eurasian steppe nomad meets the settled Near East at three locations: on the Danube, in the Caucasus and in Central Asia (Transoxiana). Disturbances on the Danube or in Central Asia affected Egrisi indirectly as they altered the balance of power between the two major Near Eastern empires. At times when their Danube frontier was threatened by a major confederation like Attila's Huns in the mid-fifth century or the Avar khaganate in the late sixth and early seventh centuries, or by the side effects of these – the flood of Germans, Slavs and rival nomads seeking to flee these aggressive, expansionary empires – the Byzantines were more willing to compromise with their Sasanian rivals on their mutual frontier, including in the Caucasus. The Sasanians likewise reacted to trouble on their Central Asian frontier – with the Hephthalites up until the 550s, and thereafter with the Western Turks – by seeking to avoid confrontation with their Byzantine neighbours, or with their subjects in the South Caucasus. The rulers of both powers recognised that two-front wars were generally disastrous and tried to avoid them.

But the steppe world also impinged directly on the settled South Caucasus across the narrow passes of the Greater Caucasus range. A particularly devastating incursion of

steppe peoples into the settled world occurred at the end of the fourth century when in AD395 Huns crossed the mountains and devastated Iran, Syria and Asia Minor as well as the South Caucasus (Maenchen-Helfen 1973, 51). This raid underlined the importance of the South Caucasian kingdoms and the passes they controlled. One of the key demands that led to conflict between the Byzantine and Sasanian powers in the fifth and sixth centuries was the recurrent Sasanian demand that the Byzantines provide men or money to them to compensate them for the expense of maintaining garrisons in these Caucasian passes, the so-called Caspian Gates. According to the Sasanians, these forts protected both powers from nomadic invasion. But the Byzantines considered a regular contribution demeaning, fearing it would be seen as tribute, and they sought to avoid these payments whenever they could — especially in the rare periods when settled conditions on the Danube or disturbances on the Sasanian frontiers in Central Asia and the Caucasus allowed them to face down the Sasanian threat of war. The loss of face involved in making these payments is reflected in the euphemistic terms the emperors and Sasanian diplomats used to refer to them: 'loans', 'gifts', or 'customary contributions'. And the emperors chose to pay large multi-year payments for fixed periods of peace rather than suffer the shame of making an annual payment.

The literary sources demonstrate how both the great powers and the South Caucasian rulers used these routes across the mountains for passage of ambassadors, gifts, subsidies and payments by which the support and goodwill of neighbouring peoples could be purchased, and for access to mercenaries from and allies among the powerful North Caucasian steppe tribes. Both empires recognised the advantage that control of the passes gave them in military and diplomatic terms and sought to maintain or extend their hegemony over the neighbouring South Caucasian kingdoms. For Lazika—a small kingdom in a key strategic location—all this affected its rulers' ability to maintain a degree of independence from its greedy imperial neighbours. While the Lazikans were not powerful enough to defeat either without help, they were sometimes able to win the support of one against the other, and they too might seek to draw on the military manpower of the nomads in extremis. If Lazikan kings were able to maintain a higher degree of independence than their Armenian neighbours, then it owed much to their skill in making the most of their location and playing off the two powers against each other.

Following the conversion to Christianity, any commentary on events in Lazika must be drawn out from very limited sources. The great powers – and consequently the sources – focussed on which of them would exercise hegemony over Iberia and Armenia. The few sources that touch on Byzantine deployments on the east coast of the Black Sea admit of more than one interpretation: either they show Byzantine garrisons withdrawn to a series of fortresses around Trapezus (Trabzon), or they show a continuity of their occupation of fortresses in the region. Most probably the Byzantines retained garrisons in Pityus and Sebastopolis, in the territory of the Abasgians and Sanigians (Figure 1.2), but withdrew their forces from Lazika itself, for it appears that by the mid-5th century they held no port on its coast. (Priscus fr. 33 = Exc. De Leg. Rom. 8 = Blockley 1983 p337 = Georgica I p254)

The lack of information is tantalising, for this period saw the growth of Christianity in the region. Though long present in the Pontos (Bishop Stratophilus of Pityus, a Byzantine enclave, was among the signatories of the first ecumenical church council at Nicaea in 325 AD) Christianity was by no means the norm at the start of the period. During the third century the Sasanians asserted themselves in the South Caucasus and may briefly have won influence in Lazika or West Georgia (the inscriptions from Naqsh-i Rustam and Paikuli contain disputed readings that may refer to West Georgia, if Machelonia is to be located there). But from 298 until 363 AD the Byzantines had the upper hand in the South Caucasus. Thus Constantine the Great's success in the Roman civil war of the early fourth century probably influenced the spread of Christianity through the kingdoms of the South Caucasus.

Then, in 363, a serious Byzantine setback during an invasion of Persia transformed the balance of power in the South Caucasus. For a quarter of a century the Sasanians challenged the Byzantines for hegemony in Iberia and Armenia. And finally, around 387, the Byzantines, pressed by severe problems in the Balkans, agreed to divide the region. Iberia and four-fifths of Armenia would fall to the Sasanians, leaving Lazika and only the westernmost portion of Armenia under Byzantine leadership.

It must initially have seemed improbable this new arrangement would endure. Had there been a lessening of the Byzantines' troubles in the West they would undoubtedly have sought to overturn the 387 settlement. But the division of the South Caucasus into two spheres of influence persisted and two brief wars between the empires, in 420-1 and 440-1, produced no change. It must have become increasingly apparent that the Byzantines would not re-establish their influence in Iberia and Armenia any time soon and gradually both powers and the South Caucasian peoples adapted to the new geopolitical balance and its consequences. With the surrender of Iberia, the Byzantines had given up control of the Darial, the best and shortest route across the central Greater Caucasus mountains. This loss heightened the importance to them of the passes in the western Caucasus and of the kingdoms that controlled them (a point underlined by the Hun invasion of 395 AD). It is interesting therefore that from the early or mid-fifth century their ally, the Lazikan king, appointed each ruler of the Svans and notified the emperor, whose despatch of regalia to Svania in turn confirmed him in office. This supports the theory that the Lazikan kings extended their influence over some of their neighbouring peoples around this time, possibly

with Byzantine support. But while Lazikan rulers used Byzantine recognition to buttress their position vis-a-vis their neighbours, increasing great power intervention could be a double-edged sword, as the Iberians, Caucasian Albanians and Armenians were discovering around this time (Blockley 1983 p359-361, 398 = Priscus fr. 51 = Exc de Leg Gent 22 = Georgica 261-262).

In 450-451 the Sasanian South Caucasus erupted in a great revolt prompted by the Sasanian promotion of Zoroastrianism among the populace. Unable to stand against the mighty Sasanians alone, the Christian Iberians, Armenians and Caucasian Albanians appealed for Byzantine help. The Byzantines, who were hugely concerned about the chaos in the West and the threat posed by Vandals, Visigoths and Huns, rebuffed them. When, a few years later, Lazika fought a three-year war with their ostensible Byzantine overlords (around the mid 450s or early 460s) the Sasanians were able to return the favour. King Gobaz I had appointed his son co-ruler and the Byzantines objected that this infringed the Emperor's right to appoint or confirm the Lazikan king. The Byzantines won Persian permission to send an army through sensitive frontier districts and the Persians closed their borders to Lazikan fugitives. Peace was eventually agreed on condition Gobaz resigned in favour of his son and travelled to Constantinople to give an account of himself (Blockley 1983 p337-9, 353 = Priscus fr. 33 = Exc de Leg. Rom. 8 = Georgica I p254-6).

Both revolts illustrate the complexity of the relationships between the two great powers and their South Caucasian clients. While the two powers were rivals, they might nevertheless cooperate in keeping their subject peoples in check. Yet it would be wrong to think this left these peoples and their rulers no room for manoeuvre. Gobaz, for example, was still in power a decade later when, in 466, he travelled to Constantinople as a result of another disagreement. With the help of the stylite Saint Daniel he refuted Byzantine accusations of rebellion and was reconciled to the Emperor (Dawes and Baynes 1996, 51). According to the saint's biographer the king established a relationship with Daniel that lasted until Gobaz's death. Less than two years after this visit (about 467-8 AD) Gobaz was requesting Byzantine troops to protect Lazika from a threatened Persian and Iberian attack, sparked by the actions of the Svans. Frustratingly, the outcome of the episode is missing in our fragmentary source. Some historians have concluded that the Lazikans went over to the Persians as a result of this crisis, for when the main Byzantine sources next mention Lazika in about 523 AD, its kings are described as Zoroastrians and friends of the Persians (Blockley 1985). There is, however, one intervening mention of Lazika in a contemporary Armenian source. This – together with Gobaz I's long connection with Daniel the Stylite – shows that the Lazikans did not submit to the Persians before 484. For in that year, when the Iberian king Vakhtang Gorgasali took refuge there at the time of the second Great Caucasian revolt against the Sasanians, Lazika was clearly still independent of

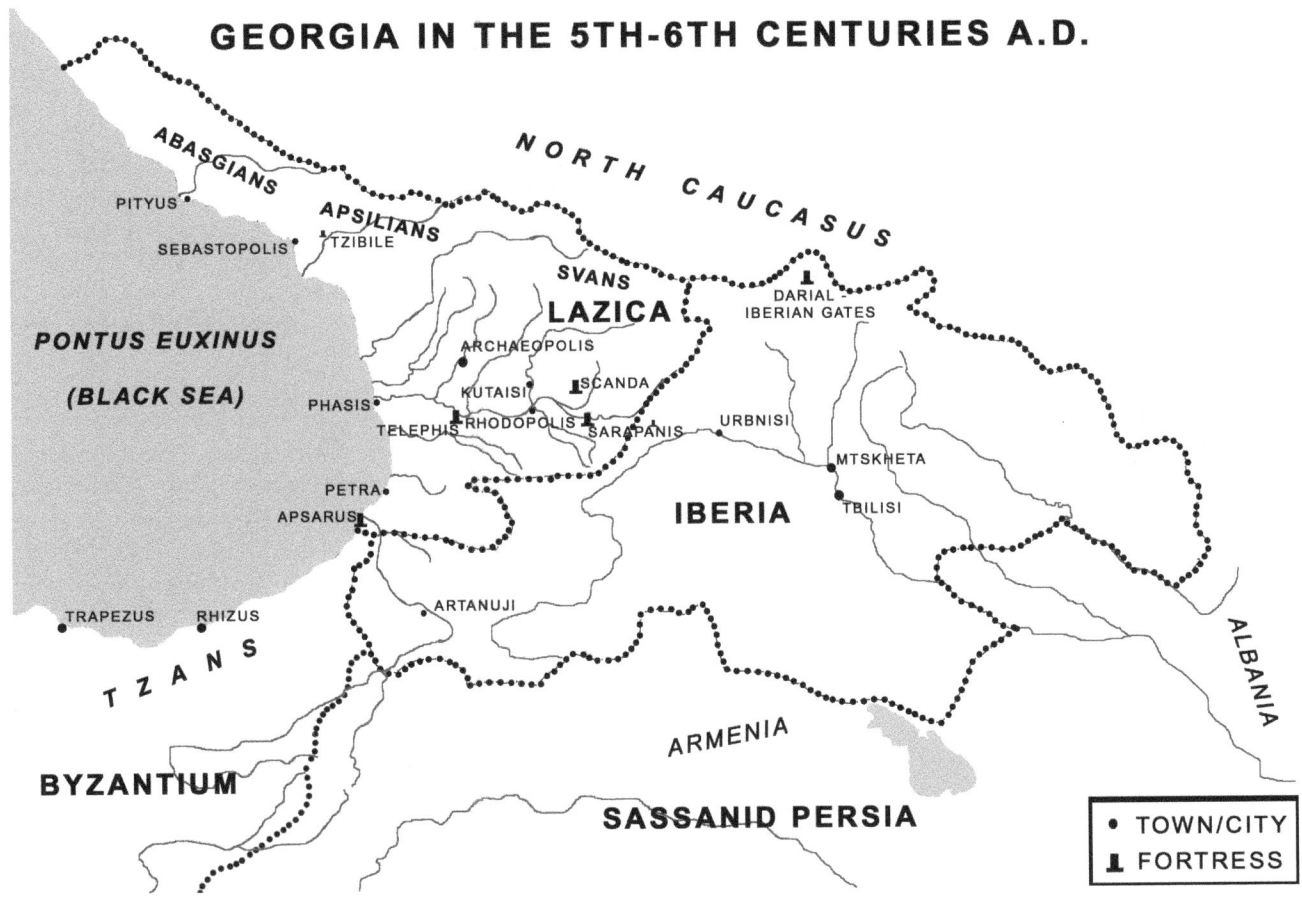

Figure 1.2: Early medieval Georgia

the Sasanians. That same year the Sasanians suffered a severe defeat at the hands of the Hephthalites, which was followed by nearly two decades of domestic turmoil. It seems inconceivable they would have risked war with the Byzantines by winning over the Lazikans during this period. However, in 498 the Great King Kavadh (r. 488-96 & 498-531) regained his throne with the Hephthalites' help. This marked a resurgence of Sasanian power and of their demands. War ensued in 502-5, and suggests the most plausible circumstances for a Lazikan change of side.

In 522 or 523 the Lazikan king and Persian ally Damnazes died and his heir Tzath, or Tsate I (r. 522 or 523-?) crossed over to Constantinople. He was baptised, crowned by the Byzantine Emperor Justin I (r. 518-527) himself, and married to a Byzantine noblewoman. The couple returned to Lazika laden with gifts. This winning over of a Sasanian vassal amounted to a declaration of war—which nevertheless was forestalled after initial skirmishes. Justin requested peace and the two emperors sent ambassadors to negotiate, but peace was not to be. The Byzantines dragged out negotiations until 525. Then, just when the Sasanians thought they were close to negotiating an acceptable compromise, the Byzantines chose to sabotage further negotiations. They deliberately insulted the Persian heir to the throne, whom the Persians had requested Justin should adopt in order to guarantee

his succession, and they promised to support a second Sasanian ally, Gourgenes the king of Kartli (r. ?-526/7 or 523 according to some Georgian historians), in revolt. The negotiations had stuck on two items: Byzantine payments and Lazika. The effects were felt immediately in the South Caucasus. A Sasanian army was mobilised that, in around 526 or 527 (or 523), drove Gourgenes and the rebels out of Kartli and into the borderlands of Lazika. Byzantine support – a general, Peter, with some Hun allies – arrived too late to help the Iberians. Instead Byzantine troops were installed in the Lazikan border fortresses, Skande and Shorapani. A separate Byzantine force raided Armenia.

In 528 it was Lazika's turn. The Sasanians benefited from the withdrawal of the Byzantine garrisons from Skande and Shorapani, supposedly owing to supply problems. They then won a victory over the Byzantines in a major battle, which prompted a reorganisation of the Byzantine command. At this point the sources turn away from Lazika to discuss events on the powers' southern border. But the Byzantines' despatch to Lazika of Bulgar reinforcements in 531 shows that Lazika remained divided between, and occupied by, the two imperial powers for the rest of the war. It was the death of the Sasanian Great King Kavadh that year and his heir's need for peace that brought about compromise. The Byzantines purchased a treaty in 532 with a large payment to the Sasanians, who in return surrendered the eastern forts of Lazika. Kartli remained under Sasanian suzerainty, and those Iberians who had fled their country were given the freedom to choose whether to return home unmolested or to stay and serve the Byzantine emperor. But the return of the Lazikan fortresses, and peace, did not solve Lazika's problems. Relations between the Lazikans and the Byzantine general in charge, first Peter and then John Tzibus, deteriorated. The Lazikans complained of the burden of supporting the new garrison (peace did not lead to a withdrawal of Byzantine troops); they complained about the trade monopoly the general introduced; and they complained that the Byzantine general had usurped the king's powers, leaving him the form of kingship without its substance. In Abasgia (Figure 1.2) the Byzantines went further.

In the mid to late 530s Justinian decided to intervene against the Abasgian trade in eunuch slaves and sent one of his court eunuchs, an Abasgian named Euphratas, to order them to stop the practice. Justinian sent priests and builders with him to found a church to the Virgin and instruct the Abasgians in Christianity. Whether part of Justinian's original plan or not, the two Abasgian kings were deposed soon afterwards and the Byzantines sought to annex the country, quartering soldiers on the populace as they had in Lazika. The Byzantine source claims that the removal of the kings and the ending of the trade in eunuchs were popular with the Abasgians. The annexation was not. But it was the arrival of war in the South Caucasus that brought a halt to these Byzantine efforts to integrate the region into their empire.

In 540 AD the Sasanians responded to growing tensions on the eastern frontier by invading a poorly prepared Byzantine east and sacked Antioch, the chief city of the region. The blow to Byzantine prestige was immense. The Lazikans, spying an opportunity to escape Byzantine interference, invited the Great King Khusro I (r. 532-579) to receive their submission and in 541 or 542, with the aid of a Sasanian army led by the Great King himself, they captured Petra and expelled the Byzantines from the eastern Black Sea coast.

In 545 the Byzantines agreed to purchase a five year truce from the Sasanians. This granted the Sasanians de facto control of both Lazika and temporary receipt of Byzantine tribute, without conceding a long-term agreement. Unsurprisingly, further discussions won no concessions from the Sasanians. The Lazikans, meanwhile, tired of their new masters. Procopius blames religious differences and a Persian plot to murder King Gubaz II (r.?-554 or 555) and resettle the Laz abroad for souring the relationship. Thus, in 548 Justinian I (r. 527-565) sent an army to Lazika at the Lazikans' request to help them expel their Sasanian oppressors.

The Persian garrison in Petra-Tsikhisdziri was besieged, but the approach of a Sasanian army forced the Byzantine besiegers to lift the siege. Despite two notable victories

for the allied Lazikans and Byzantines in 549 and the fall of Petra to assault in 550, the Sasanians succeeded in bringing the Abasgians over to their side and capturing Tsebelda in Apsilia (which lay between Abasgia and Inner Lazika) with the help of a Lazikan traitor. Both territories were recovered in 550. But in 551 the Sasanian general Mermeroes expelled Gubaz and the Byzantines from eastern Lazika and Svania and established Persian authority there. The failure of his attempt to seize the stronghold of Archaeopolis-Nokalakevi from Byzantine forces made the Hippis River (the Tskhenistsqali) the effective boundary between Sasanian-controlled and Gubaz's Lazika.

Stalemate ensued. The Sasanians were unable to take the well-supplied western fortresses by siege, but King Gubaz and the Byzantines apparently lacked sufficiently strong and motivated forces to go on the offensive. Tensions between these allies mounted. Gubaz denounced a succession of Roman generals as traitors, leading to their dismissal by the Emperor Justinian. When, in 554 or 555, a Byzantine army took flight before a surprise Sasanian advance and abandoned their position, some of the generals involved treacherously murdered Gubaz apparently to prevent his complaints reaching the Emperor's ears. The disastrous result of this murky affair (at trial the ringleaders claimed they were following Justinian's orders) was a temporary Lazikan boycott of the fighting.

It took Justinian's appointment of Gubaz's brother Tzath II (r. 555 or 556-?) as king and the arrival of Byzantine reinforcements from Italy (where the Gothis war had just been brought to a successful conclusion) to mend the Byzantine position in 556. A last major Sasanian advance against Phasis (modern Poti) was defeated, and the Byzantines counter-attacked and recaptured Rhodopolis-Vartsikhe in the east. Meanwhile a joint Lazikan-Byzantine force marched to Misimia (the Kodori gorge) to avenge the Misimians' previous massacre of a Byzantine general and his escort and to recover the gold the general had been conveying to Byzantine allies in the region.

The Sasanians agreed a truce the same year – the situation on their northeastern steppe frontier was deteriorating as the powerful Western Turk confederation replaced the decaying might of the Hephthalites. But it nevertheless took until 562 to agree a peace that recognised Lazika as a Byzantine ally in return for Byzantine payments to the Sasanians. While Lazika's status was agreed, that of Svania remained contested and was left out of the treaty pending further negotiations. In 572 the new emperor Justin II (r.565-574) refused to make the stipulated payments to the Sasanians and launched an attack in support of the rebellious Persarmenians.

The third great Byzantine-Sasanian war began disastrously for the Byzantines and then dragged on for nearly two decades, punctuated by periodic truces. Lazika, Svania and the wider South Caucasus saw sporadic and poorly documented fighting. Yet it was a Sasanian coup that brought the war to a sudden end. In February 590 the shah Hormizd IV (r. 579-90) was deposed in the face of the rebellion of his general Bahram Chobin. His son Khusro II Parvez (r. 590-628) fled to the Byzantines who helped him recover his throne and were rewarded with a most advantageous peace. Under the treaty of 591 the Sasanians ceded the Emperor control over the South Caucasus as far as Tbilisi and Dvin – the most extensive territorial settlement they had won in 200 years – and agreed to peace without payments.

This peace too lasted barely a decade. This time a Byzantine army revolt toppled the Emperor Maurice I (r. 582-602). Khusro took the opportunity to launch a war in support of his former protector's heir (or more probably a pretender who claimed to be him) against the usurper Phocas (r. 602-610). The sources for the early phases of this last great Byzantine-Sasanian war, during which Byzantine defence was hampered by civil war, are sparse, fragmentary and say nothing of operations in the South Caucasus before AD 624. Clearly, however, Lazika was not untouched by the collapse of Byzantine fortunes during the 610s. By 618 the Sasanians had conquered Mesopotamia, Syria-Palestine and Egypt, and had advanced across Anatolia to the Bosphorus.

Byzantine attempts to sue for peace in 615 were rejected; apparently Khusro had decided to wipe the empire from the map. Yet in 624 Heraclius I (Maurice's avenger, r.610-641) chose to counter-attack the Sasanians through the South Caucasus, where he remained in 625 and 626. Lazika must have provided essential lines of communication with Constantinople during these years. Heraclius' effort to win the support of the powerful Western Turks (whose empire now extended to the European steppes north of the Caucasus) bore fruit in 626 when their khagan occupied Caucasian Albania. The following year 627 AD the allies attacked Iberia, besieging Tblisi, which fell the following year. As winter came on, Heraclius led the Byzantine army south against the Sasanian heartlands in Mesopotamia, sparking a *putsch* that deposed Khusro and threw Persia into chaos. It consequently took until 630 to dictate a triumphant peace on Roman terms. The undefeated Persian armies of occupation were withdrawn back to the pre-war borders.

The Sasanians were never to challenge the Byzantines again. Instead a new force appeared in the Near East. In the 620s, while the two powers fought their last great war to the north, Muhammad united the tribesmen of northwest Arabia under his leadership and forged a new Islamic polity. His successor, the Caliph Umar initiated attacks on the Byzantine lands to the north and in 636 at the battle of Yarmuk (on the border between modern Syria and Jordan) the Byzantine forces were decisively defeated. The same year Sasanian forces were defeated by another Arab force at the battle of Qadisiya.

The overthrow of the old world order was completed over the following century. The last Sasanian Shah Yazdegerd III (r. 632-651) was captured and killed in Merv in AD 651. The Byzantine Empire was shorn of its richest provinces: Egypt, Syria-Palestine, Mesopotamia, Cyprus, and eventually North Africa. In the South Caucasus Armenia, Caucasian Albania and Iberia came under attack. In the midst of this cataclysm the sources turn their attention away from Lazika. Though there are several accounts of the Arab attacks on Caucasian Iberia, Albania and Armenia, it was not until the early eighth century that these incursions reached Lazika. A few sources mention the invasions of the early and mid-eighth century, including that of Arab general Murvan ibn Muhamed (Murvan the deaf) who attacked Georgia, including Lazika, in 735-738. During this century the centre of the West Georgian kingdom moved to Kutaisi, and the kingdom of Lazika was replaced by the kingdom of Abkhazia. These events marked the end of the Early Byzantine period, and of the present account.

Appendix: The fortification system of Lazika in the 4th-6th centuries AD

Recent research (Murgulia 2013) has analysed the system of fortifications of the kingdom of Lazika in the early Byzantine period, and the role of Nokalakevi within this system. From the beginning of the 4th century, the Laz rebuilt several old and important fortifications in the kingdom (for example Gonio-Apsarus, Pityus, Kutaisi, Scanda and Sarapanis) and also built several new cities (including Vardtsikhe-Rhodopolis and Mocheirisis). These cities played an important role in the development of the Lazikan economy, as they were located at the junctions of, and controlled, the main trade routes within and beyond the country.

The Lazikan authorities also maintained border defences in this period. As has been described above, the kingdom was surrounded by expansionist powers such as Rome and, subsequently, Byzantium in the west, Sassanid Persia in the east and aggressive nomad tribes in the north, all of which made it essential to defend borders and trade routes. Therefore, from the beginning of the 4th century, a strong fortification system was established which covered the whole territory of Lazika. Around 60 fortifications dating to the 4th-6th centuries have been discovered in western Georgia through archaeological survey since the mid-20th century.

The fortification system of Lazika in the 4th-6th centuries has been attributed to several subsystems according to their role (Murgulia 2013). These were: Black Sea coast defensive line; southern border defensive line; south-eastern border defensive line; eastern border defensive line; Mokhirisi region fortification system; Central Lazikan fortification system; and north-western border defensive line. Each of these subsystems were a response to different threats. For example, the castles of the Black Sea coast defensive line protected the kingdom from seaborne attack and, at the same time, they protected trade and merchants arriving in Lazika by the sea, and secured custom control of the border. The fortresses of the southern, south-eastern, and eastern subsystems controlled and defended borders. The main function of the north-western subsystem fortresses was to control and block the passes from the Greater Caucasus into Lazika.

The defence of the central part of the kingdom - which included Nokalakevi's hinterland – was one of the most important problems for Lazika. That region was circumscribed by the river Tskhenists'qali in the east, by the river Rioni in the south, by the Black Sea in the west, and by the river Enguri and the Egrisi ridge at the north. The central fortification subsystem of Lazika was located in the geographic centre of west Georgia. It was here that the capital of the kingdom – Nokalakevi-Archaeopolis – was located, and was able to control all parts of the region (for example modern Abkhazia to the north-west or modern Imereti to the south-east). The rulers of Lazika were able to maintain some independence from the Romans and, later, from the Byzantines by the foundation of the capital city in the interior of the kingdom. Furthermore, the central part of the kingdom had a very important strategic role for the region because of the trade routes that passed through it that contributed to the economic development of Lazika.

Nineteen fortresses formed the defensive system in central Lazika, with the most important being at Shkhepi, Menji, Abedati, Tamakoni, Khomakirde and Nokalakevi-Archaeopolis. The Black Sea coast defensive line was based on the fortification system created by Rome, known as the "Pontus Lines", in the 1st century A.D. The majority of those fortifications were built by the Romans to protect the eastern frontiers of the empire: Gonio-Apsarus, Batumi, Phasis, Gudava-Zighanes, Sebastopolis and Pityus. Petra was added in the 6th century A.D. by the Byzantine emperor Justinian (AD 527-565), in order to control the Laz economy.

The southern defensive line of Lazika was situated on the mountains in the modern region of Guria and protected the country's southern borders. The most important fortress of that system was Tolebi, which is identified with Telephis and was mentioned in the 6th century Byzantine written sources. The south-eastern fortification line was situated along the river Khanists'qali and united two fortresses – Dimi and Vardtsikhe-Rhodopolis. Dimi was situated near the end of the river gorge protecting the road from Armenia to Lazika, and was the main defence for the city of Vardtsikhe-Rhodopolis from the south. Rhodopolis was a strongly fortified city, which was itself able to block the road to any hostile approach.

The defence of the eastern borders was one of the most important considerations for the Laz rulers as Lazika's neighbour in the east was the Kingdom of Iberia, which, particularly after the mid-5th century, was under Persian political influence. The Likhi ridge provided a strong border

for Lazika, but there were several passes across it which were very well fortified by two castles – at Scanda and at Sarapanis. The economic centre of Lazika – in the region of Mokhiris – was fortified with several strong fortresses as well. The 6th century Byzantine historian Procopius of Caesarea wrote: "Now Mocheresis is one day's journey distant from Archaeopolis, a district which includes many populous villages. And this is really the best land in Colchis; for both wine and the other good things are produced there ..." (Procopius, *Wars* VIII.14.46). The fortifications of this region included the city of Kutaisi, the town of Mokhiris, and the castle of Ukhimerion (Uthimerios). The southern border of the Mokhiris region was protected by the Tolebi (Telephis) and Mtisdziri fortresses.

As mentioned above, the guarding of the Greater Caucasus passes into Lazika was a very important consideration for the local rulers. Procopius states that before the 520s the Laz did not pay tribute to the Romans and did not take part in their military campaigns. The only obligation they had to the Romans was the protection of the northern borders against incursions by nomadic peoples. It should be noted that such an obligation was first and foremost in the interests of Lazika. Therefore the Laz fortified the gorges which connected the North Caucasus to Lazika, and the most important of these fortresses were Skuri, Napichkhovo, K'urzu, Ts'arche, Rek'a and Ts'ebelda (Tzibile).

Each of the castles/ fortresses of the Lazikan defensive systems performed discrete roles and functions as described by Murgulia (2013):

1. The Post-Signal castles were built close (3-5 km) to each other in order to pass information to each other by signals of smoke or fire. Such information could, for example, be regarding the movement of enemy troops in the territory. The majority of the castles of Lazika had a Post-Signal function; they were small in size like a tower and were predominantly located on high hills or mountains;

2. The gorge-road blocking castles were predominantly built at the mouths of gorges, near the junction of uplands and plains. Any enemy had, therefore, to pass those castles before entering the plains, which were the most heavily populated and important parts of the country;

3. Administrative-Custom-house fortresses were the most important political and economic centres of the kingdom. They had two functions, and while it was necessary for merchants and envoys to reach them easily at the same time they had to have strong fortifications against attacks from armies of brigands. For this reason it would be more correct to call them fortified cities. The Laz capital at Nokalakevi-Archaeopolis, and Mokhiris, Kutaisi, Vashnari and Vardtsikhe-Rhodopolis can all be described as such.

Around 60 castles/ fortresses dating to this period (4th-6th centuries AD) of the Laz kingdom have been discovered in west Georgia. However, in the written sources, there is information relating to only about ten of them, and most of that is in connection with the battles in Lazika during the Byzantine-Persian war of the 6th century. Byzantines and Persians both tried to take the most important trade centres of Lazika: Archaeopolis, Petra, Mokhiris, Kutaisi, Rhodopolis and Phasis. The Byzantine written sources, while describing those battles, mention several other important fortresses – Telephis, Ukhimerion/Uthimerios, Onoguris and Tzibile. The remainder of the fortified sites are not described in these acccounts. This may be because the main function of the fortifications of the Lazikan defensive systems was to provide security for the country during peace. During large-scale military operations they served little function, but in peacetime they protected borders, roads and populated areas from attack by bandits or small-scale military incursion. This interpretation would seem to be the best explanation for why most of the fortifications were built near overland and river routes and why they do not appear in the written sources that describe the military engagements within Lazika. According to these sources, the Byzantines took care of the protection and security of Lazika as war with Persia seemed increasingly likely in the beginning of the 6th century AD. They rebuilt and strengthened several fortified sites in Lazika, including its capital Archaeopolis and a newly founded city at Petra. Evidence for this strengthening of fortifications is very visible at Nokalakevi, where the eastern gate was remodelled to a more defensive configuration, utilising very large limestone blocks. The style of fortification is entirely in keeping with the 6th century – in particular the period of the Byzantine emperor Justinian the Great (527-565) – and it is as a result of this additional fortification work that the Byzantine and Laz army within was able to withstand, and repel, an attack from a significantly larger Persian army.

Bibliography

Blockley, R. C. 1983. *The Fragmentary Classicising Historians of the Later Roman Empire: Eunapius, Olympiodorus, Priscus and Malchus*. Arca 10. Liverpool, Cairns

Braund, D. 1994. *Georgia in Antiquity: A History of Colchis and Transcaucasian Iberia, 550 BC-AD 562*. Clarendon Press, Oxford

Burney, C., and Lang, D.M. 1971. *The Peoples of the Hills: Ancient Ararat and Caucasus*. London

Menander Protector. 1985. *The History of Menander the Guardsman: Introductory Essay, Text, Translation and Historiographical Notes*. Translated by R. C Blockley. Liverpool: Cairns.

Colvin, I. Forthcoming. *Justinian's Wars in the Caucasus: Procopius and Agathias on Roman and Sassanian Rivalry in Lazica 518–565AD*. Unpublished D.Phil. thesis, University of Oxford

Dawes, E., and Baynes, N. 1996. *Three Byzantine Saints: Contemporary Biographies of St. Daniel the Stylite, St. Theodore of Sykeon, and St. John the Almsgiver*. Crestwood (NY), St. Vladimir's Seminary Press

Diakonoff, I.M. 1984. *The Prehistory of the Armenian People*

Dundua, G.F. 1979 Sakartvelos samoneto gandzebi. Tbilisi

Kuhrt, A. 1995. *The Ancient Near East, c. 3000-330 BC*. London, Routledge

Maenchen-Helfen, O.J. 1973. *The World of the Huns: Studies in Their History and Culture*. University of California Press, Berkeley

Melikishvili, G.A. 1959. On the history of ancient Georgia, GSSR, Tbilisi

Melikishvili, G.A. 1966. The Black Sea in Assyrian Cuneiform Sources of the 13th-12th centuries B.C., in *Questions of the History of Caucasian Peoples*. Tbilisi (in Russian)

Murgulia, N. 2013. The fortification system of the kingdom of Egrisi in the 4th-6th centuries. Unpublished doctoral thesis. Tbilisi, Saint Andrew the First-called Georgian University of the Patriarchy of Georgia

Sumilirski, T. and Taylor, T. 1991. Scythia and Thrace: The Scythians, in The Cambridge Ancient History: Volume 3 Pt 2: *The Assyrian and Babylonian Empires and Other States of the Near East, from the Eighth to the Sixth Centuries B.C.* Cambridge University Press, Cambridge

CHAPTER TWO

Previous archaeological work at Nokalakevi, 1973-1998

By Davit Lomitashvili, Besik Lortkpanidze, Tamila Kapanadze and Meri Zamtaradze

Introduction

The site of Nokalakevi has been the subject of investigation for nearly 200 years. It was first described by Frédéric Dubois de Montpéreux in the 1830s. Subsequently, Nokalakevi was described by A. Muravyov, K. Koch, M.Brosset, P. Ioseliani, D. Bakradze, T. Zhordania and others, and more detailed scientific description of the standing ruins was published by D. Chubinashvili, who investigated the site in 1928.

The first archaeological excavations at Nokalakevi took place from November 1930 to February 1931, funded by the Emergency Association of German Science (Der Notgemeinschaft der Deutschen Wissenschaft) in collaboration with the National Education Commission for the Georgian SSR and the Transcaucasian Museum in Tbilisi (Kirchhoff 2003: 338). The plans for the trial excavations were conceived by Joseph Sauer, but management of them fell to a young German Byzantinist, Alfons M. Schneider, supported by the Georgian specialists L. Muskhelishvili and G. Gozalishvili. Over four months the team of archaeologists and workmen traced the line of the fortification walls, and excavated a number of towers and, to the east of the Forty Martyrs Church (very close to today's Trench B), an area he interpreted as the ancient 'agora'. Schneider concluded from these excavations that the oldest monument on the territory of Nokalakevi was a small settlement with a fortress. He argued that in the 4th century BC a large city with strong fortifications sprang up on the site, the Tsikhegoji of the Georgian chronicles (*Kartlis cxovreba*). These original fortification walls were, in his opinion, destroyed by an earthquake at the end of the 6th century AD and rebuilt at the end of the 6th or the beginning of the 7th century. According to Schneider, these new walls were damaged by another earthquake and repaired with cobbles. Schneider believed that the cultural layer contained 4th to 8th century AD pottery. Furthermore, a hoard of 23 gold coins of the emperor Maurice (582-602 AD) was found in one of the towers (Figure 2.1). Schneider's expedition was the first to excavate a burial at Nokalakevi, which was found to the north of the Forty Martyrs Church beyond the precinct wall. It contained two small ceramic jugs, two bronze bracelets, five beads of glass-like paste and an irregularly shaped piece of bronze sheet. He dated this burial to the 2nd or 3rd century AD, though the grave goods now appear more typical of those of the Hellenistic period.

After the Second World War two small expeditions worked in Nokalakevi. V. Lekvinadze visited several times in the 1950s and dated the oldest buildings to the 3rd-4th centuries AD. The West Georgian Exploratory Archaeological Expedition headed by G. Grigolia visited the site several times in the 1960s and in 1971 unearthed a pot burial, containing a bronze bracelet, in the central courtyard of the Nokalakevi citadel. The archaeologists assigned this burial to the late Hellenistic period.

Previous excavations: 1973-1977

In 1973 the Department of Medieval Archaeology of the S. Janashia Museum of Georgia began excavations at Nokalakevi. The results of these excavations, 1973-1989, were published in three volumes in the 1980s and 90s (Zakaraia 1981; 1987; 1993).

The first year was mostly devoted to assessing the presence and character of archaeological remains, which revealed some interesting monuments. Among other buildings, a large bathhouse was found, later interpreted as the 'royal' bathhouse. During the 1974 season the south part of a stone-built palace was cleared. This work revealed that it had been constructed around the beginning of the 6th century AD and was converted into a wine-cellar in the 16th-17th centuries. Interesting results were also obtained from the excavation of the East gate and the discovery of the northeast portion of the outer wall. In the same year it was confirmed that the city had not only a 'land' gate but a 'river' gate as well. The former, an arched gateway, was in the east wall of the city, while the latter was actually a tunnel running down to the river at the western end of the city.

In 1975-1976 excavation of the eastern fortifications continued, which revealed that there were actually three parallel defensive walls (Figure 2.2). The inner wall was constructed of dressed limestone blocks and was preserved in places to a height of up to 4 metres. This wall was reinforced by square protruding towers, of which two protected the gate house and one situated half way up the hill slope protected the lower fortifications from being overtopped. A second wall was subsequently constructed between, and flush with, these protruding towers. Later excavations revealed that the first wall has a very substantial foundation; however the second wall lacks any proper foundations, its wide base resting close to the surface and its upper levels tapering. The third wall, of the large ashlar blocks mentioned above was clearly added last. The excavators dated the first wall to the 4th century AD, the second to the turn of the 4th and 5th centuries, and the third to the end of the 5th or the beginning of the 6th century.

13

Figure 2.1: Gold coins from the reign of Emperor Maurice discovered in 1930

Figure 2.2: The eastern walls of Nokalakevi in the early stages of clearing and conservation (Zakaraia 1981)

At the end of 1974 work was begun on the construction of a building for the management of the Nokalakevi State Farm. This was situated 100 metres to the east of the lower terrace fortifications. An archaeological watching brief on the work recorded a pot burial at the point of convergence of the trenches dug for the foundations of the north and the east walls. Further excavations in this area in the following years, up to 1977, revealed twenty-four more graves belonging to an ancient cemetery. Of these, two inhumations date back to the 5th or the middle of the 3rd centuries BC; six pot burials to the middle of the 3rd or to the 2nd century BC.

During the same period, an ancient basilica and another bathhouse were revealed on the lower terrace at Nokalakevi. This large aisled basilica seems to have been built in the middle of the 5th century as, after its destruction, probably at the beginning of the 6th century, a smaller basilica was erected a little to the north of its ruins to which a dome appeared to have been added later.

The second bathhouse is presumed to have served the townspeople because it was comparatively small in size and had only hot and cold rooms. It is situated in the south part of the city, on the high river bank and is dated to the 5th-6th centuries AD.

During these first four seasons excavations were confined to the lower part of the fortress, on the terrace above the Tekhuri river. In 1977, however, the completion of a road to the top of the mountain, allowed the expedition to start excavations in the citadel. Work began with the clearing of the towers in the fortification wall of fallen masonry. A number of articles in the first volume of reports from Nokalakevi-Archaeopolis are devoted to publishing the most important archaeological materials recovered between 1973-1977 (Abdushelishvili and Tsiuma 1981; Gvinchidze 1981; Kaukhchishvili 1981; Lekvinadze and Khvedelidze 1981). Coin finds belong almost exclusively to the late 5th-early 7th centuries AD (these are Byzantine coins of the Emperors Anastasius to Maurice 491-602AD). Glassware belongs exclusively to the 4th-10th centuries. Among these were fragments of goblets decorated with fused blue dots; vials with amphora-like bottoms; bottles with a ring fused on a collared rim, and a flat fluted handle; goblets with a honeycomb design; wineglasses with stems; icon lamps; and a cut-glass goblet with a fused base ring.

Noteworthy among the ceramics found at Nokalakevi at this time (Figure 2.3) were imported amphorae and red slip ware of the 4th-6th centuries, as well as locally produced wares of the same period. These were represented by pithoi with stepped stems; pithoi decorated with round circular strips; luteria; pots with circular lid-rests; censers with pierced bases; burnished pottery, etc. Of later ceramics from Nokalakevi, only fragments of painted dishes of the 9th and 10th centuries had so far been found.

Metalwork found between 1973 and 1977 includes a spearhead, two axes, a hoe, a copper bowl, the framework of a helmet and some arrow-heads. Fibulae were definitively dated to the 5th-8th centuries AD. The most interesting find was a significant portion of a bronze 'choros' (a light hanging introduced in Byzantine domed churches from the 12th century) with a cruciform personal monogram reading 'Evstrat', which was found in the two-storey palace.

Previous excavations: 1978-1989

Between 1978 and 1987 work continued both in the citadel and on the lower terrace. The remains of two churches were exposed in the central part of the lower city near the Forty Martyrs Church. The first of these was dated to the middle or the second half of the 4th century. It is rectangular in plan, with a semi-circular apse at its east end. It was replaced by a large aisled basilica erected directly over it in the middle of the 5th century. This was in turn destroyed after which another aisled basilica was built to its north. This, the extant Forty Martyrs Church, underwent several phases of repair and extension during the middle ages, finally becoming a domed church (Kapanadze 1987).

Two other new buildings were discovered in the terrace during this period. In the south-eastern part of the site, near the fortification walls, the stone foundations were uncovered, of a capital 'I' shaped building. This was interpreted as a 'palace'. Foundations of another building – a small basilica with apse situated to the west of the Forty Martyrs church – was interpreted as a church.

Work also proceeded with clearing and excavating the citadel, including the multi-phased tower at the north-west corner of the palace building. The tower at the east end of the citadel also consisted of several phases of construction. In the southwest corner another small gate was discovered and clearing along the southern wall yielded numerous finds and made it possible to get a clear notion of the system of the citadel's defences.

Excavation in the eastern and central part of the lower terrace produced finds from the main periods of occupation of Nokalakevi, namely the 8th-7th centuries BC, the Early Antique and Hellenistic periods, and the 4th-8th centuries AD. The earliest date for significant occupation at Nokalakevi, the 8th-7th centuries BC, was confirmed by excavation of stratified deposits in the eastern part of the city's lower terrace, between the castellated 5th century AD wall and the 6th century AD wall of large ashlar blocks. Find of this period included various coloured, precious and semiprecious stones relating to bead-manufacture; evidence of metal-working; and the discovery of a large number of fragmentary, two-headed zoomorphic figurines. Occupation of the site was especially intensive during the 6th-4th centuries BC. Finds included almost all kinds of local ceramic material, typical to this period – sherds of pithoi, cooking pots, jugs, bowls, drinking vessels etc. Two types of drinking vessel dated to the 7th-4th

Figure 2.3: Amphorae discovered at Nokalakevi in the 1970s (Zakaraia 1981)

centuries BC were found. The first type was characterised by a cylindrical upper body and a conical lower, in a grey fabric. The base is flat (diameter 75-105 mm) and the body is decorated with a wavy sparsely dotted design. The second type of drinking vessel had a wide body, narrowing towards the base. The foot of one of these vessels, of which only a fragment survives, is cylindrical, in others the foot has a 'waist'. The fabric is grey, brown or black. One fragment bears a wavy design. This type dates to the 6th to 4th centuries BC (Lomitashvili and Lortkipanidze 1987).

During this period of excavation graves were unearthed immediately outside the site of Nokalakevi and within the walls, as well as between the fortification walls. The graves were of two types: inhumations and pot burials and they date from the early Hellenistic period to the Byzantine period. The most common grave goods were of pottery and metal. Signet rings occur in large numbers as well as high status goods such as gold necklaces and ear-rings, silverware (Zamtaradze 1987).

The numerous finds of the 4th-6th centuries AD, unearthed between 1978 and 1989, were mainly of the same type as those discovered there between 1973 and 1978. Especially noteworthy finds include local imitations of Roman and Byzantine red slip ware of the 4th to 6th centuries AD. Excavations carried out over these ten years shed more light on later ceramic wares that were very different from types dating to the 4th-6th centuries AD. This later ware falls

into two distinct groups: one group shows deep dimples and incisions made in the thicker elements (for example the base and handles) before firing; the second group of later wares is of white clay, the walls of the vessels are thin, the sherds are hard, and the surface is burnished. Some examples were decorated with patterns in red slip. Both groups of late pottery are dated by analogies to the 7th-11th centuries (Lekvinadze 1987).

Other significant finds produced from this period of excavation include a ceramic tile (315x110x20mm). This was found in 1973 during the excavations of the 'royal' bath house, and upon it were two concentric circles in relief. Crude Greek letters had been incised onto the ceramic both within and beyond the circles, including a line of cursive characters. The letter forms were dated by Kaukhchishvili (1981) to the 6th-7th centuries AD. In 1977 four fragments of the round lid of a ceramic vessel were discovered at Nokalakevi. Separate Greek letters in relief were discernible on three of the fragments and the configuration of the letters also points to the early Byzantine period, approximately to the 6th-7th centuries AD (Kaukhchishvili 1981).

Relatively few coins were found at Nokalakevi during the excavations 1978-1989. These date from the 4th century BC to the 17th century AD. Colchian 'tetri' of the 4th century BC constitute the bulk of the numismatic material found at Nokalakevi. The presence of Byzantine coins could be indicative of political and economic relations between Lazika and Byzantium, or may simply reflect the presence of the Byzantine military from the second quarter of the sixth century AD. Together with the west-Georgian coin (kirmaneuli) which was the standard currency in the 13th to 15th centuries, there were also finds of Turkish currency, evidence of the expansion of Turkish influence into west Georgia (Abramishvili 1987, 1993).

Previous excavations: 1990-1998

The scale and duration of archaeological work in this period was significantly affected by serious political and economic instability in Georgia, which stemmed from the dissolution of the Soviet Union in 1991 and included civil war following a coup d'état (1993), and conflicts in Abkhazia (1992-3) and in South Ossetia (1991-2). The Senaki district of Samegrelo, within which Nokalakevi is located, was one of the epicenters of the civil war and is also located very near to Abkhazia. Therefore it was only possible to undertake small archaeological projects in Nokalakevi in 1990-1991 and in 1995-1998.

In 1990 archaeological excavations took place at three sites. The first was located to the west of the lower town of Nokalakevi, about 50m north of the tunnel that provided secure access to the Tekhuri. Excavations at this location revealed a square building orientated northwest-southeast, the southwest wall of which was 26.5m long. The walls that run northeast from this survived to a length of 7m, and were not more than 1.5m in height, and 1.2m thick. The walls define an area of more than 100 cubic metres. The main southwest wall includes two pipes which extend the full width of the wall, which led to the building being interpreted as a reservoir which supplied water to a 5th/6th century AD bathhouse 70m to the south, down a steep slope. Excavation of deposits within the building produced archaeological material from various periods, some of which was present as a result of colluvial movement including Hellenistic pottery, and two sherds of pottery dated to the 9th-11th centuries AD.

In the same year work took place on some of the interior fortifications located in the southeast of the lower town, near the first palace. Surviving walls were conserved to prevent their collapse, and a small excavation associated with this work produced only two small sherds of pot and two sherds of amphorae dated to the 4th-6th centuries AD.

In 1990 excavations also began to the northeast of the 'bell tower', in an area located immediately to the east of the current Trench B after the state had acquired it from the private owner. As is the case with much of Nokalakevi, material found in the upper layers related to the recent occupation of the site, and associated agriculture. There was also a great deal of mixing of material, resulting from colluvial movement down the slope immediately to the north. For this reason fragments of pipe-handled vessels from the 6th-4th centuries BC were found in the same

contexts as Hellenistic-period beads and ceramic, and glass and metal wares dating to the Early Byzantine period. Archaeological excavations continued in this trench in 1995-1998 and produced very interesting archaeological material - including sherds of pitchers, pots, amphorae, jugs and other ceramic vessels; military weapons; and a Byzantine coin – but chronologically very mixed.

In 1991 the work of the Nokalakevi Expedition was limited to undertaking archaeological surveys in villages of the Senaki District, such as Old Senaki, Betlemi, Ledzedzame, Khorshi and Eki. In the village of Khorshi the expedition discovered a three-nave church that had been destroyed above ground level. In Kvauti (a suburb of the village of Ledzedzame), the expedition surveyed the church of St. George.

In 1995 the expedition once again undertook excavations, this time in the west of the central area of Nokalakevi, on agricultural land to the north of the expedition dig house. This part of Nokalakevi was virtually unstudied however, while cultivating the ground, locals had unearthed dressed stones that may have indicated the presence of a building. Initial work involved the digging of test pits, but no structures were revealed. Instead this area was interpreted as the location for the processing of building material. However, excavations in 1996 did produce some structural evidence.

Excavation in 1996 was focussed on the Hellenistic necropolis, where work in the early 1980s had revealed a significant number of graves. A single trench was opened, and no further graves found. Being located at the bottom of the steep slope, archaeological layers were shown to be subject to the same colluvial movement that had produced very mixed upper layers in other areas of Nokalakevi. In 1996 excavations also began of a circular building located to the north of the "royal bath", which continued in 1997 and 1998. This building was interpreted as being an early Byzantine/ early medieval two door kiln. It was probably for firing local coarse wares and ceramic building material, however later it was used as a pit for slaking lime.

Conclusion

The excavations that took place from 1973 to 1998 were the first fully scientific archaeological studies of Nokalakevi, and utilised a multi-disciplinary approach. Much of this work was made possible by the significant funds provided by the Georgian SSR that also saw investment in a new expedition base, built specifically for that purpose alongside an existing building that housed a team of archaeologists throughout the year. Electricity and mains water were provided for the expedition and, consequently, the village as a result of lobbying by Parmen Zakaraia who managed to balance the concerns of the Georgian SSR, the Academy of Sciences, and the KGB, with his own academic and humanitarian priorities.

The excavations of the team from the S. Janashia Museum of Georgia during this time revealed several periods of more intense occupation of the site of Nokalakevi – the 8th-7th centuries BC, the 6th-5th centuries BC, the 4th-2nd centuries BC (the Hellenistic period), and the 4th-8th centuries AD (the early Byzantine period) – punctuated by periods of shifting focus for the settlement, decline, or outright abandonment. In particular the significant stone structures of the early Byzantine period were studied in great detail, providing a clear picture of the system of fortifications, and the churches, baths and palaces that occupy the lower town and, to a lesser extent, the upper citadel of Nokalakevi. The investment in conserving and protecting much of the standing remains in this period is also directly responsible for the continued health of the whole monument, and without this work it would undoubtedly be in a more ruinous state today. The greatly improved economic vitality of modern Georgia means that the future for this important site now looks, once again, to be secure.

Bibliography

Abdushelishvili, M. and Tsiuma, N. 1981. Anthropological materials of Hellenistic times from Nokalakevi, in Zakaraia, P. (ed) *Nokalakevi-Archaeopolis I. Archaeological excavations 1973-1977*. 'Metsniereba', Tbilisi: 200-219 (in Georgian)

Abramishvili, T. 1987. Coins from Nokalakevi and Nodjikhevi. In Zakaraia, P. (ed) *Nokalakevi-Archaeopolis II. Archaelogical excavations 1978-1982*. 'Metsniereba', Tbilisi: 274-287 (in Georgian)

Abramishvili, T. 1993. The Numismatic Material found at Nokalakevi. In Zakaraia, P. (ed) *Nokalakevi-Archaeopolis III. Archaeological excavations 1983-1989*. 'Metsniereba', Tbilisi: 270-272 (in Georgian)

Gvinchidze, G. 1981. Burials at Nokalakevi. In Zakaraia, P. (ed) *Nokalakevi-Archaeopolis I. Archaeological excavations 1973-1977*. 'Metsniereba', Tbilisi: 150-183 (in Georgian)

Kapanadze, T. 1987. Basilicas at Nokalakevi. In Zakaraia, P. (ed) *Nokalakevi-Archaeopolis II. Archaeological excavations 1978-1982*. 'Metsniereba', Tbilisi: 90-125 (in Georgian)

Kaukhchishvili, T. 1981. Greek Inscriptions from Nokalakevi. In Zakaraia, P. (ed) *Nokalakevi-Archaeopolis I. Archaeological excavations 1973-1977*. 'Metsniereba', Tbilisi: 197-199 (in Georgian)

Kirchhoff, J. 2003 *Wissenschaftsförderung und forschungspolitische prioritäten der Notgemeinschaft der Deutschen Wissenschaft 1920-1932*. Unpublished doctoral thesis. Ludwig Maximilians Universität München (in German)

http://edoc.ub.uni-muenchen.de/13026/1/Kirchhoff_Jochen.pdf (Accessed November 2012)

Lekvinadze, V. and Khvedelidze, L. 1981. Mass archaeological finds from excavations at Archaeopolis, in Zakaraia, P. (ed) *Nokalakevi-Archaeopolis I. Archaeological excavations 1973-1977*. 'Metsniereba', Tbilisi: 120-149 (in Georgian)

Lekvinadze, V. 1987. Mass Archaological Material of the 4th to the 11th centuries discovered on the site of Nokalakevi in 1978-1982. In Zakaraia, P. (ed) *Nokalakevi-Archaeopolis II. Archaeological excavations 1978-1982*. 'Metsniereba', Tbilisi: 237-248 (in Georgian)

Lomitashvili, D. and Lortkipanidze, B. 1987. Early Antique table ware (drinking vessels) from Nokalakevi. In Zakaraia, P. (ed) *Nokalakevi-Archaeopolis II. Archaeological excavations 1978-1982*. 'Metsniereba', Tbilisi: 203-210 (in Georgian)

Zakaraia, P. (ed) 1981 *Nokalakevi-Archaeopolis I. Archaeological excavations 1973-1977*. 'Metsniereba', Tbilisi (in Georgian)

Zakaraia, P. (ed) 1987 *Nokalakevi-Archaeopolis II. Archaeological excavations 1978-1982*. 'Metsniereba', Tbilisi (in Georgian)

Zakaraia, P. (ed) 1993 *Nokalakevi-Archaeopolis III. Archaeological excavations 1983-1989*. 'Metsniereba', Tbilisi (in Georgian)

Zamtaradze, M. 1987. Burials unearthed at Nokalakevi in 1981-1982. In Zakaraia, P. (ed) *Nokalakevi-Archaeopolis II. Archaelogical excavations 1978-1982*. 'Metsniereba', Tbilisi: 211-236 (in Georgian)

CHAPTER THREE

The AGEN excavations 2001-10: Methodology

By Paul Everill

Introduction

As has been described elsewhere (see Chapter Two for discussion of the work undertaken up to 1998) archaeological work at Nokalakevi has taken many forms since the first excavations in 1930. Since the withdrawal of state funding for the previous expedition (1973-1998), resulting from the collapse of the Soviet Union and subsequent economic and social turmoil, three international collaborations have operated in Nokalakevi, including a small Swiss-Georgian Expedition which excavated four test pits in 2006/7, and an ongoing Norwegian-Georgian conservation and restoration project which began in 2010. By far the largest and longest-lived of these is the extant Anglo-Georgian Expedition which, in 2012, became the longest running, explicitly international, collaborative excavation to date in western Georgia (overtaking the British-Georgian Pichvnari Expedition, led by Amiran Kakhidze and Michael Vickers, which operated very successfully from 1998-2009). The longevity of the Anglo-Georgian Expedition is, in itself, a great success and reflects the strength of a collaboration underpinned by personal friendships and shared goals. In terms of professional output, the work of AGEN has undoubtedly added greatly to the body of evidence regarding human activity at Nokalakevi from pre-history to modern times, which is discussed in the following chapters. However, ten seasons of excavation from 2001 have also witnessed a considerable number of Georgian and British trainees, and it may be that this is ultimately the more significant legacy of the expedition.

The principal objectives of the Anglo-Georgian Expedition from 2001 can be outlined as follows:

1) The collaborative study and conservation of the important historic site of Nokalakevi-Archaeopolis-Tsikhegoji; its standing and buried remains; its situation in a wider geographical and historical context; and its prehistoric origins. To achieve this, the expedition depends on the contribution of archaeologists, historians, osteologists, ceramicists, conservators, palaeobotanists and other specialists. The expedition is founded on, and continues to encourage, the collaborative exchange of knowledge and expertise between Georgian and British specialists, including those from other disciplines who have an interest in working in and around Nokalakevi.

2) The training of archaeology students from Georgian, British and other universities is a key objective of the expedition. A programme of on- and off-site training has been conceived to ensure that student participants experience as great a diversity of tasks as possible, above and beyond the basic requirements of their university degree programme.

Between 2001 and 2010, students from six British universities have undertaken work at Nokalakevi as part of the fieldwork requirement of their degree programmes alongside non-student volunteers from USA, Australia, Holland, Belgium and Poland. Georgian archaeology students have also been trained in the methodology utilised at Nokalakevi, as a concerted and deliberate effort to provide young Georgian archaeologists with the skills required for modern professional practice. Initial discussions between the Georgian and British directors, prior to the first field season in 2001, determined that the deeply stratified archaeological deposits of Nokalakevi warranted the use of a recording system that was best able to cope satisfactorily with a complex urban site. This factor, combined with the previous work experience of the British archaeologists and the desire to train students in modern methodology, led to the adoption of the Single Context Recording (SCR) system. SCR, as utilised by the Museum of London Archaeology Service, forms the basis of the dominant methodology currently applied in British urban, developer-funded, archaeology. SCR sytematises the reduction of deeply stratified archaeological deposits without reference to section recording, although sections may be integrated where deposits are particularly complex. The expedition was the first to introduce this methodology to Georgian archaeology and was able to arrange for the MoLAS *Site Manual* (MoLAS 1994) to be translated into Georgian. Subsequently RESCUE: The British Archaeological Trust's handbook *First Aid for Finds* (Watkinson and Neal 1998) was also translated into Georgian. Both these manuals are now used in the teaching of Georgian archaeology students. However, as will be discussed, the expedition has found Single Context Recording to be inadequate for the broader research and training goals of Nokalakevi.

The development of British methodology

The British urban archaeological tradition stems largely from Martin Biddle's work in Winchester (1961-71), and Philip Barker's work at sites such as Hen Domen (1960-1988) and, particularly, Wroxeter (1966-1990). Both men, working in parallel, though not in isolation, perfected so-called 'open area' excavation as a significant step forward from the then prevalent tradition of box trenches known in Britain as the 'Wheeler-Kenyon method' (derived initially from the excavations directed by Sir Mortimer Wheeler in the 1930s and developed, by his student Dame Kathleen Kenyon, in the 1950s). The idea of utilising a grid of box trenches was to allow the recording in detail of a series of sections, giving 'vertical' data pre-eminence over horizontal plans. This emphasised the sequence of stratification which, many thought, could not be appropriately illuminated by layers. However, at Maiden Castle Wheeler himself had abandoned box trenches in order to shed more light on complex horizontal stratigraphy. Certainly both Biddle and Barker considered their 'open area' excavation to be a continuation of Wheeler's drive for greater stratigraphic clarity utilising 'continuing' sections derived from a series of temporary baulks across the site, to be drawn and removed at regular intervals (Martin Biddle pers. comm.). However Barker also suggested that the focus on vertical sections on some sites often led to a paucity in the recording of horizontal plans. The move away from box trenches and towards the use of large, 'open area' excavation was pioneered in the 1930s and 40s by van Giffen in Holland, Hatt and Steensberg in Denmark, and Bersu in Germany and Britain. It was further developed in Britain in the 1950s by Hurst and Golson working at Wharram Percy, and Frere at Verulamium (Barker 1982: 16-21). Biddle himself describes being particularly influenced by the work of Hurst and Frere and, through them, back to Steensberg (Martin Biddle pers. comm.). However, it is fair to say that the work of Biddle and Barker perfected and popularised this methodological approach, which insisted on the accurate recording of deposits in both plan and section.

The extensive excavations at Winchester and Wroxeter tackled incredibly complex sequences of deposits and engendered new ways of working and, perhaps more importantly, new ways of organising and interpreting the data produced. However, the projects were quite different in character. Biddle's excavations combined a 'rescue' and research focus, having negotiated time ahead of development in order to undertake the work. The scale of the operation, while not unusual in today's commercial environment, was literally ground-breaking then. The sheer number of excavators and deposits demanded academic and organisational rigour and a firm hand on the rudder. Biddle's future wife, Birthe, an exemplary archaeologist in her own right, became an invaluable member of the Winchester team in 1964. In contrast, Barker's excavations at Wroxeter – though no less rigorous – dealt with shallower sequences, perhaps allowing the time to set 'best practice' methodological yardsticks. His focus on the theory of excavation led to the publication of the methodological bible, "Techniques of Archaeological Excavation", in 1977 (2nd edition: Barker 1982), which set a new benchmark for the standard of archaeological work, but one that was, admittedly, time-consuming. Barker's approach was initially ridiculed by traditionalists for its apparently slow pace, before he silenced all his critics by revealing incredible sequences

of late/post-Roman timber buildings that contradicted established opinion on the lifespan of Wroxeter Roman city (White 2006). Such evidence would simply never have been found through the excavation methods that came before.

Biddle's great success was in the use of Open Area excavation – perhaps the first application of it on a 'rescue' site of that size – but also the organisational rigour that he employed, some of which he learnt from Wheeler (Collis 2011). His projects, like Barker's at Wroxeter, attracted domestic and international students of archaeology, who returned home taking with them this approach to archaeological excavation which became known as the Winchester Method, or La Méthode Winchester in the USA and France (Everill and White 2011; Collis 2011). The removal of permanent baulks, and the widening of the area under excavation, was consequently a product of the desire to reveal the greatest extent of the layers that characterise an urban site, as much as it was a recognition that the use of permanent baulks often acted to obscure important, structural relationships.

However, other methodological developments emanated from Winchester that ultimately ran contrary to the ideals expressed by both Biddle and Barker. A young Bermudan named Edward Harris gained his first excavation experience under the Biddles, as an Ordinary Digger on the Cathedral Green site, Winchester, in 1967. In 1968 he worked as a Principal Digger and demonstrated great potential as an excavator during the work at St Swithun's tomb, which led to him being asked to take on an Assistant Supervisory role in 1969 (Martin Biddle, pers. comm.), when he was first required to undertake site recording. Harris worked at Wolvesey Palace, Winchester, in 1970-1, before working in Bergen, Norway, where he began formulating his ideas on stratigraphic recording. By early 1973, under Biddle's patronage, Harris was employed by the Winchester Research Unit to work on the Lower Brook Street excavation archive. Originally conceived in February 1973, from doodles while working late one evening interpreting the complex stratigraphical data, the Harris matrix, or simply the stratigraphic matrix, allows the schematic presentation of incredibly complex sequences of contexts as an aid to interpretation. This in itself provides a useful tool to archaeologists, however Harris took his ideas a step further and, with others, laid the foundations for Single Context Recording which had, at its heart and effectively governing the process, the stratigraphic matrix. The innovation of planning individual contexts in isolation was first suggested to Harris by Laurence Keen, then Director of the Southampton Archaeological Research Unit, who had regular contact with the Winchester Research Unit and had already trialled the idea (Edward Harris pers. comm.). The concept was adopted along with the first use of a rolling stratigraphic matrix on site during the 1975 rescue excavation at New Road, Winchester, making it the first site to make use of the embryonic Single Context Recording system. This project was supervised by Patrick Ottaway (working for the Winchester City Rescue

Archaeologist, Ken Qualmann) who had been encouraged by Harris to trial this new approach – an experiment supported by Qualmann (Patrick Ottaway pers.comm.). Harris and Ottaway published an article outlining "A recording experiment on a rescue site" in Rescue News (Harris and Ottaway 1976), however later publication of the excavation contains conventional section drawings and no reference to SCR (Qualmann *et al* 2004). Shortly after the start of work at New Road, Harris approached Brian Hobley, then Chief Archaeologist at the Museum of London's Department for Urban Archaeology, asking if he would also trial this new system. The large excavation at the General Post Office site in London, which also began in 1975, was selected for this purpose and site supervisor Andy Boddington reported it to be a great success (Edward Harris pers. comm.). When Steve Roskams arrived at the site the following year, he worked on developing the system with the GPO team, which ultimately led to the creation of the DUA *Site Manual* in 1980 (Steve Roskams pers. comm.). Harris, during his PhD in London from 1976 to 1979, maintained regular contact with the DUA team while continuing to develop his theories on stratification that would be published as *Principles of Archaeological Stratigraphy* (Harris 1979).

Single Context Recording, therefore, is ultimately a composite of several innovations, first brought together by Harris before the system was developed through application by the Department for Urban Archaeology. The DUA merged with the Department of Greater London Archaeology to form the Museum of London Archaeology Service in 1991. Others had developed their own stratigraphic flow diagrams and recording systems at around the same time (e.g Steve Roskams and Henry Hurst at Carthage in 1974 [Steve Roskams pers. comm.]) and consequently the DUA system stems from the work of several people. However, clearly Harris was the driving force behind the first expression of what would now be called Single Context Recording, the key elements of which are:

1) The Stratigraphic/ Harris Matrix
2) Individual units of stratification
3) Pro-forma recording sheets
4) Single context plans

Under this system section drawings were rendered almost a resource of last resort, and plans were to consist of single contexts in isolation. The plan drawings themselves became subject to their own stratigraphy, being overlain during post-excavation analysis according to the matrix, so that the phases could be re-constructed and interpreted. Harris wrote, in his first publication on the implementation of a matrix in 1975, "when studying stratification, many excavators rely on the section as a way to work out the relationships between the layers of a site; the layer plan is usually ignored in stratigraphic analysis, partly because the standing section or baulk works on an excavation against the recovery of the plan of each layer" (Harris 1975: 110). He goes on to add, "the section of the face of the baulk,

cannot, except on the simplest sites, reflect either the vagaries of individual layers or represent any but the most local of stratigraphic sequences. Arguments of chronology or of the sequence of a complex stratigraphic situation based on sectional analysis must be suspect or completely fallacious" (Harris 1975: 110). He was, of course, partly correct in that assessment, though his criticisms seem to be of the old Wheeler-Kenyon method, the problems with which had already been amply demonstrated. Both Biddle and Barker (and others including, in fact, Wheeler himself) had advocated, for a number of years, that both the vertical and horizontal record should be considered, and in combination would provide the accuracy Harris appears to have sought through the application of a synthetic stratigraphic matrix.

That said, the use of proforma recording sheets, rather than notebooks, and individual stratigraphic units (the term 'context' is used in Britain, but other terms are used elsewhere) provided a simple method for ensuring that every context – each one representing a temporal event in the sequence – is recorded fully (and comparably) regardless of subjective significance. The issue of temporality is key to the successful analysis of a site's stratigraphy. Rather than grouping deposits, determined as belonging to the same period by their associated finds, the application of individual units of stratification correctly identifies that each relates to a specific event. Consequently a stratigraphic matrix becomes a readable storyboard of all of the events that led to the formation of the site. However, in reality, carefully observed section drawings are an important component of the overall site archive, if their local limitations are acknowledged. Equally it would be disingenuous to suggest that a stratigraphic matrix represents an infallible, final word on a site, and clearly a matrix includes significant elements of interpretation.

Biddle and Barker continued to favour the use of phase plans and section drawings over the emerging Single Context Recording system. Barker argued that the separation of the drawn record into individual contexts made it harder to reinterpret the evidence in post-excavation (Everill and White 2011: 176-7). He also wrote that "where, in my experience, such a [matrix] has been used it has not altered the interpretation arrived at from the study of the ground and the plans and sections. It is more an instrument for aiding clear thinking and coherent publication than for primary interpretation" (Barker 1982: 203). Certainly the huge quantity of incredibly detailed drawings from Barker's excavations were a hallmark of his approach that recognised the crucial importance of careful and patient excavation and recording. However, the great strength of Harris' broader approach was in the organisation of the data and the systematising of a methodology that supported the birth of the British profession, underpinned by common approaches to recording. The use of individual stratigraphic units and pro-forma recording sheets crucially enabled the more effective administration of the archive.

AGEN Methodology

The appeal of SCR to many British archaeologists in the 1970s and 80s, was the apparently efficient and non-hierarchical system that it produced, within which individual, experienced excavators have responsibility for the area that they are excavating and are expected to work with minimal supervision. This was welcomed, in part, as a rejection of the very hierarchical site organisation favoured by excavators like Wheeler and Biddle. However on most research projects, which are often less constrained in terms of time, the majority of those on site have little or no previous experience and require close supervision, training and management. For this and other reasons the expedition has, since 2001, moved away from a strict adherence to Single Context Recording and towards the combined horizontal and vertical approaches utilised by advocates of Open Area excavation. The expedition does, however, assign unique numbers to individual contexts, and recording is undertaken on a series of registers and sheets that form a modern paper archive. Site drawings are produced on permatrace, and a rolling stratigraphic matrix has been constructed as an aid to interpretation and discussion, though it is not the engine that drives the recording process as it would be in a pure Single Context Recording system. Operating in a non-commercial environment the expedition is able to place more emphasis on training and best practice. It has been possible to select a methodology that best suits the combined goals of research and teaching, in which the need to pause excavation to undertake phase planning, for example, does not impact negatively. Like Biddle and Barker, we have opted to utilise 'phase plans', which show more clearly the relationship between different contextual elements of structures and associated features, and we also utilise multi-phase plans at the start and/ or completion of each field season in order to map annual progress. In consequence the methodology employed at Nokalakevi is one that stems from the excavations of Biddle, Barker and others, incorporating some of the methodological innovations of Single Context Recording.

The use of experienced (five years or more) commercial archaeologists as British trench supervisors (working in collaboration with Georgian trench supervisors with several seasons' experience of working at Nokalakevi with this methodology) ensures that the on-site training of students is led by archaeologists with current and extensive archaeological experience, gained from a wide variety of site types and periods. From 2001 to 2010 all British trench supervisors (this author [Trench B: 2002-03], Andy Ginns [Trench A: 2004], Kathryn Grant [Trench A: 2006-09], Chris Russel [Trench B: 2009], Adam Slater [Trench A: 2010] and Laura James [Trench B: 2010]) and Site Directors (Nick Armour to 2003, and this author from 2004) were first recruited from UK commercial organisations. Georgian archaeologists Nikoloz Murgulia (Trench A supervisor) and Ana Tvaradze (Trench B) have worked at Nokalakevi since 2003 and 2007 respectively.

The implementation of a modern excavation methodology was supplemented in 2009 with the undertaking of an RTK GPS survey of standing structures (including the excavated foundations in the lower town and the three phases of fortification walls) and topography. This survey provided the most detailed plan of the site to date, and was the first to locate the site with UTM Zone 38N coordinates. The author and Dr Phil Marter spent a total of 15 days mapping the 20ha site, during which 3,145 points were measured (Everill *et al* 2011). The GPS survey undertaken in 2009 is valuable for a number of reasons. First and foremost it has allowed the current expedition to produce a modern, digital plan of the site that is tied into an accurate global position. The flexibility of this digital resource will enable future survey work to be added to the data available, as new remains are revealed, and even enable far broader landscape analysis to be undertaken. This work could extend beyond the site and its hinterland, incorporating other archaeological sites in the region.

The following two chapters summarise the results of excavations undertaken by the Anglo-Georgian Expedition to Nokalakevi from 2001-2010. The excavations are described with reference to individual contexts and structures, with individual numbers assigned to each and every fill, cut, layer, skeleton and masonry. Within the text, context numbers are referred to in bold for ease of identification. Each context is described in the annual interim reports, therefore in the following two chapters only key contexts and interpretation will be discussed.

Bibliography

Barker, P. 1982. *Techniques of Archaeological Excavation* (2nd Edition). London, B.T. Batsford Ltd

Collis, J. 2011. The urban revolution: Martin Biddle's excavations in Winchester, 1961-1971. In Schofield, J. (ed) *Great Excavations: Shaping the archaeological profession.* Oxford, Oxbow Books: 74-86

Everill, P., Marter, P., Lomitashvili, D., and Murgulia, N. 2011. Mapping Archaeopolis: GPS survey at the multi-period site of Nokalakevi. *Bulletin of the Georgian National Museum. Series of Social Sciences #2* (47-B): 117-130 (in Georgian)

Everill, P. and White, R. 2011. Philip Barker's Wroxeter. In Schofield, J. (ed) *Great Excavations: Shaping the archaeological profession.* Oxford, Oxbow Books: 167-180

Harris, E. 1975. The Stratigraphic Sequence: A question of time. *World Archaeology* 7 (1): 109-121

Harris, E. 1979. *Principles of Archaeological Stratigraphy.* London, Academic Press Ltd

Harris, E. and Ottaway, P. 1976. A recording experiment on a rescue site. *Rescue News* 12: 6-7

MOLAS 1994. *Archaeological site manual.* London, MoLAS

Qualmann, K., Rees, H., Scobie, G. and Whinney, R. 2004. *Oram's Arbour. The Iron Age enclosure at Winchester Volume 1: Investigations 1950-99.* Winchester, Winchester Museums Service

Watkinson, D. E. and Neal, V. 1998. *First Aid for Finds.* RESCUE & UKIC

White, R. 2006. Excavating Wroxeter at the end of the twentieth century. In Ellis, P. and White, R. (eds) *Wroxeter Archaeology. Excavation and research on the defences and in the town, 1968-1992.* Transactions of the Shropshire Archaeological and Historical Society 78: 165-9

CHAPTER FOUR

AGEN Trench A Results: 2001-2010

By Paul Everill, Nick Armour, Davit Lomitashvili, Nikoloz Murgulia, Kathryn Grant, Benjamin Neil and Adam Slater

Introduction

Trench A was first opened on the 18th July 2001 and originally measured 9m x 10m, including an area to its southeast that had previously been opened along the inner wall in 1995. It was extended to its current size of 13m east-west x 13.5m north-south, excluding the, by then, redundant area of the 1995 trench, in 2004. Its southwest corner is located at 269050.35 E/ 4693255.22 N (WGS84 UTM Zone 38N). The trench is orientated parallel to the fortification walls and consequently lies NNW-SSE, with the northeast corner located at 269058.18 E/ 4693271.10 N. It is situated about 5m to the north of the main, eastern, gate, and immediately to the west of the 6th century AD steps and their associated foundations (Figure 4.1).

The archaeological study of the area around Trench A was started in 1995 by the S. Janashia Museum expedition to Nokalakevi with the intention of clarifying early (pre-Antique) industrial areas and associated ritual finds. This study included the excavation of a test trench of 5m x 3m in an area directly abutting the inner curtain wall to the east of Trench A. This test trench was excavated through 1.20m of rubble and unstratified material to reveal a foundation that ran the length of the trench to a width of 2.65m from the wall. The foundation was made of small unshaped limestone rubble bedded into a friable sandy lime mortar. This foundation was found to measure approximately half a metre in depth, but these excavations proved inconclusive in terms of its precise function. The opening of Trench A in 2001, directly adjacent to this earlier trench, was intended to clarify the relationship of this foundation with surrounding deposits, and to assist in its interpretation.

Trench A has provided, since 2001, a complete sequence through the various occupation, abandonment and colluvial deposits in this part of the eastern lower town of Nokalakevi. By 2010, the Expedition was revealing deposits from the 7th-6th centuries BC, and expecting up to a further metre of occupation deposits to extend the sequence into the late Bronze Age/ early Iron Age. Annual reports were produced which discuss the progress in detail (Armour and Colvin 2004; Everill 2007; Everill and Ginns 2005; Everill et al 2011; Grant and Everill 2009; Grant et al 2010; Lomitashvili et al 2005, 2006, 2007, 2010, 2011, and forthcoming; Neil 2006).

The excavation process will be described in more detail below, but the significant phases revealed by Trench A can be outlined as follows:

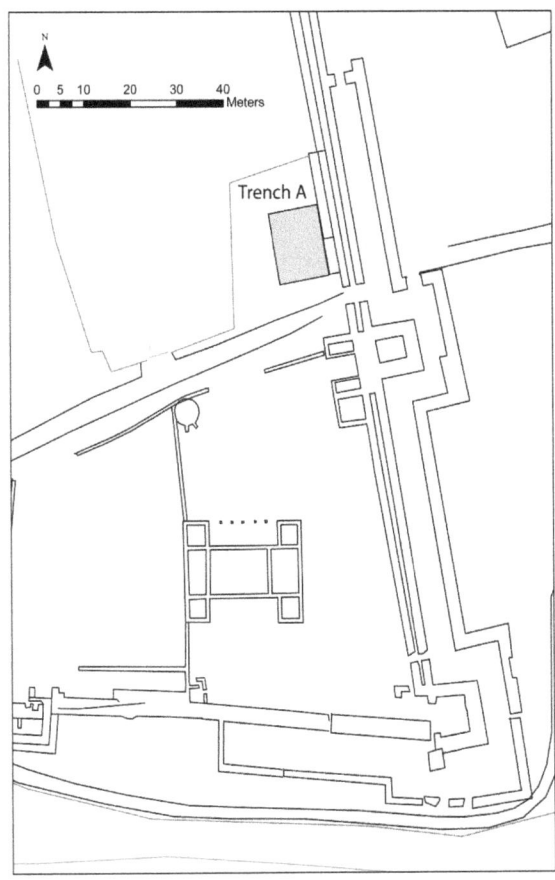

Figure 4.1 Location of Trench A by the east gate

1) Modern overburden, containing very mixed deposits including finds from the Hellenistic period through to the 20th century.
2) Large sections of masonry that had fallen from the fortification walls sealing the underlying deposits.
3) Deposits relating to various phases of wall construction from the 4th to the 6th centuries AD
4) Hellenistic period burials, including flexed burials with associated jewellery, cremations and inhumations within amphorae and cooking vessels
5) Hellenistic period structures (4th - 2nd centuries BC)
6) Early Antique period deposits (6th - 4th centuries BC)

2001 Season

Excavations began on the 18th July 2001 when a mechanical excavator was used to remove spoil from previous excavation and overburden remnants of the conservation projects of the 1970s and 80s. An area of 10m x 6m was opened immediately to the west of the trench excavated in 1995 (Figure 4.2). Initial cleaning by hand revealed that, even with reduction of the modern layers, there were still many centimetres of mixed deposits to remove. It also revealed that much of the area was covered by the fallen remains of the fortification walls. Consequently the first contexts removed were those of mixed layers **100** and **101** which were found to cover the whole area and contained fragments of pottery from the Hellenistic period to the 20th century and also a quantity of modern bottle glass. With the removal of layer **101** the full extent of the fallen masonry (**103**) was revealed (Figure 4.3), lying across the area *in situ* from the northwest corner to the southeast. Further deposits were removed from either side of the fallen masonry, layer **102** from the northeast and layer **105** from the southwest. Both these layers produced modern materials along with early pottery and tile.

Beneath layer **105** was a dark greyish brown silty deposit (layer **106**) from which was recovered a fragment of a cross. Carved from limestone, this find represented the left arm of a cross (210mm long; 85mm deep; 150mm wide on left side narrowing to 100mm wide on right side) and included a fragment of a Greek inscription of the Byzantine period. Professor Tinatin Kaukhchishvili (pers comm) suggests a reading of '[(?G)Y(?)AYR.ETI (M or N) / DOY' (interpretation/translation: *Aurelius gave (or honoured) ... the slave (of God)*) and suggests a date of the late 3rd to early 4th century AD, which, if correct, would

make it the oldest Christian inscription found in western Georgia. An alternative reading has been provided by Charlotte Roueché (pers comm.) of 'STAURETIM.../DOU...'. Roueché suggests a restoration of *STAURE TIMETHO BOETHI /DOULOI (SOU) .... X.* (translation: *Honourable Cross, help your servant ... X*). From the letter forms Professor Cyril Mango (pers comm) suggests a possible alternative date of the 6th century AD. A photograph of the find appears in Chapter Seven.

With these deposits having been removed it was possible to assess the fallen wall (**103**) which, although fragmentary in places, appeared to be remarkably intact and lying as it had fallen. The wall had clearly impacted heavily into the underlying stratigraphy, a fact that made continuing excavation of the area difficult as deposits had been crushed and folded into each other. Having extensively cleaned the site it was decided at this point to halve the excavation area and to concentrate on the stratigraphic relationships between the steps, wall, foundation and deposits.

In the northeast of the trench was layer **104**, which included modern material culture. Underlying this to the west was deposit **110**, an almost sterile abandonment layer that in turn covered layer **108**. The latter covered the whole trench and was interpreted as an occupation or cultural layer due to the considerable number of finds recovered from it. This layer was cut for the foundation of the extant

Figure 4.2: Excavation in 2001 showing the 1995 trench and 6th century AD steps to the left, looking south

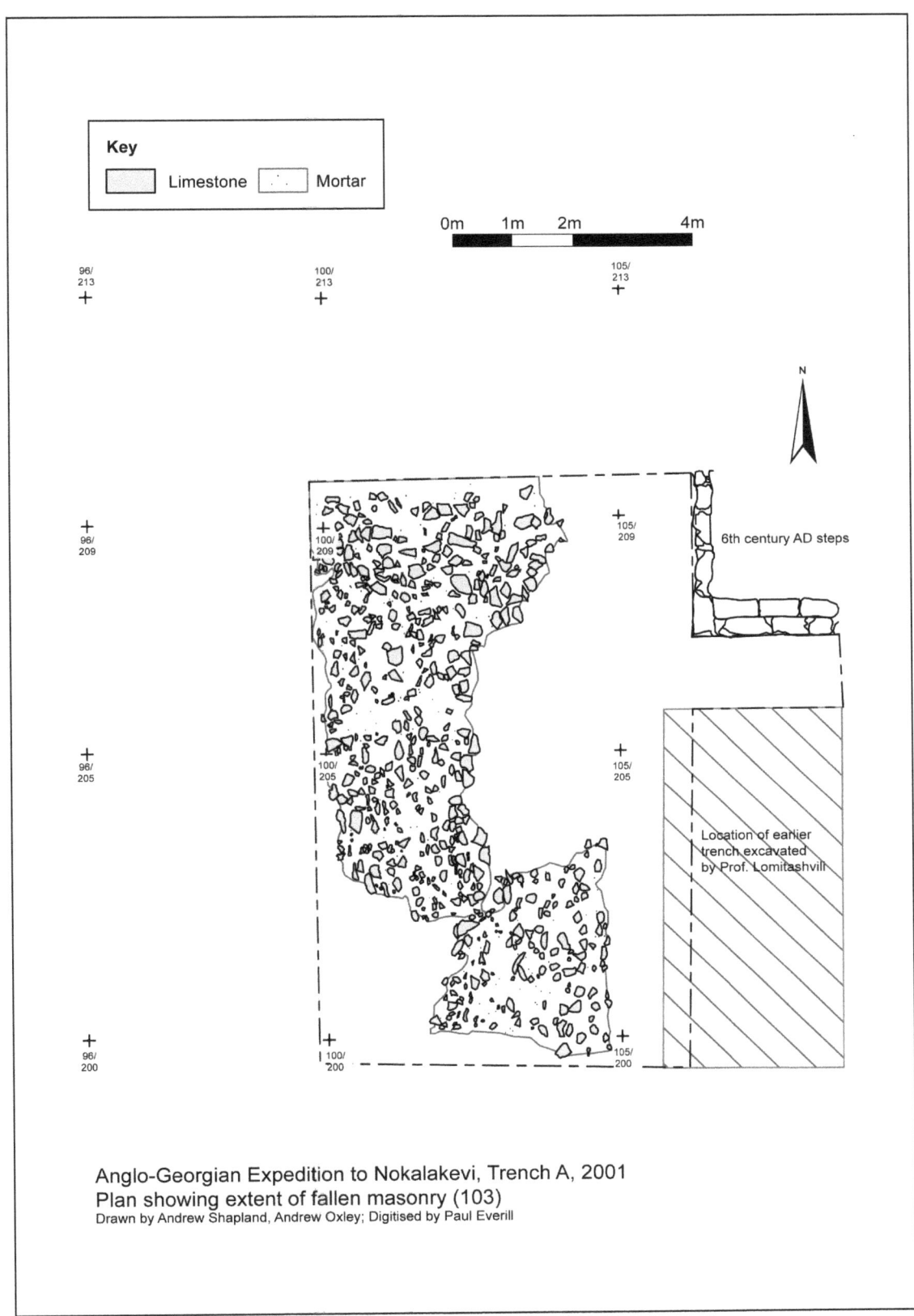

Key

Limestone Mortar

0m   1m   2m   4m

96/
213

100/
213

105/
213

96/
209

100/
209

105/
209

6th century AD steps

96/
205

100/
205

105/
205

Location of earlier
trench excavated
by Prof. Lomitashvill

96/
200

100/
200

105/
200

Anglo-Georgian Expedition to Nokalakevi, Trench A, 2001
Plan showing extent of fallen masonry (103)
Drawn by Andrew Shapland, Andrew Oxley; Digitised by Paul Everill

Figure 4.3: Trench A, 2001

steps adjacent to the trench, which are constructed from large limestone blocks in the same style as the 6th century AD refortifications. The lower foundations of these steps rested upon the mortared material discovered in the 1995 test trench, suggesting that the latter represented the foundation of an earlier phase of fortifications, perhaps relating to the 4th or 5th century walls. The steps abutted the earliest of these.

2002 Season

Excavation of Trench A resumed on the 21st of August 2002 with the removal of plastic sheeting and overburden laid down at the end of the 2001 season to protect the underlying archaeology. Due to the decision to reduce the area under excavation towards the end of the 2001 season there were two contexts, layers **110** and **108**, that needed to be fully excavated and recorded to bring the whole trench back into phase. The removal of layer **108** revealed layer **124**, a localised deposit of medium to large limestone rubble and mortar fragments located in the south-eastern corner of Trench A, which was interpreted as being derived from Wall **119**.

Underlying **124** was an extensive deposit of dark greyish brown sandy silt (**125**) with infrequent inclusions of charcoal, moderate amounts of river stones and frequent small to medium sized pebbles. Layer **125** covered the entire area and was very finds rich, producing 59kg of potsherds and 118.5kg of ceramic building materials (tegula, imbrex and tile), plus animal bone. This layer was interpreted as a levelling deposit imported from nearby to build up the ground surface in preparation for building work, specifically that of the steps.

Deposit **126** was sealed by layer **125** and was interpreted as a construction layer with a large quantity of limestone rubble and mortar that probably relates to the restructuring of the fortifications in the area. To the north of layer **126** were two layers, **127** and **128**, that were associated with the steps and may have related to the construction thereof.

Towards the south of the trench the removal of **126** revealed a cut feature (**129**) that was clearly a continuation of a slot cut into the foundation (**138**) revealed in 1995. This provided evidence that the layers at this level of the sequence were in existence contemporaneously with the slot cutting episode and that the foundation had been reduced prior to this.

2003 Season

Work recommenced on 18th August 2003. Layer **136** had been revealed at the end of the 2002 season, and was the first to be excavated in 2003. It was a dark greyish brown, clayey silt which contained frequent small grains of white grit and small to medium sized charcoal flecks.

Throughout the layer were found to be small, medium and large fragments of angular limestone, some of which showed clear evidence of burning. A large number of tegula and imbrex fragments were also recorded. Pottery fragments were mixed and moderately abraded. This layer was inconsistent in terms of coverage and depth: in some places it was thick and in others was missing entirely, presumably in response to the underlying local topography. This was further complicated by frequent areas of compaction caused by the impact of falling masonry higher up in the sequence. It was interpreted as a levelling layer, deposited ahead of construction of the first phase of fortifications in the 4th century AD.

Excavation of layer **136** revealed three human inhumations, skeletons **138**, **139** and **144**. Perhaps most interestingly, it soon transpired that these were from the Hellenistic period and this represents one of the curiosities seen in the archaeological deposits at Nokalakevi since 2001. For some reason there appears to be an almost complete absence of stratified layers in either trench from the time between the end of the Hellenistic period and the early Byzantine period. While its absence in both Trench A and Trench B may be a result of a number of factors, not least the abandonment of Nokalakevi's 'lower town' or the entire site in this period, there remains the peculiarity of Hellenistic period layers interfacing directly with early Byzantine deposits in Trench A. One interpretation is that the area around the fortifications was reduced prior to construction, in which case it would be unlikely that **136** was then used to build it back up, unless the deposits that had been removed were not considered suitable for building upon. Another interpretation is that soil formation and colluvial movement was minimal in this period, but given that it represents 400-600 years one could reasonably expect to find substantial 'dark earth', abandonment deposits.

Returning to the inhumations, skeleton **138** was a crouched burial of a small child laid on its left side and aligned north-south. The lower body was flexed at the knees and showed particularly poor preservation: no trace was found of the lower vertebrae, pelvis, right femur, right tibia and fibula, or either feet. The remaining bones were fragmentary. To the east of the skull was a well-preserved, handled jug in a fine red fabric. Between the skull and the jug was a copper alloy bracelet of Hellenistic style. Intermingled with the upper body were 24 small beads, three of which were in situ as a string, the rest scattered through the grave fill and recovered through excavation and sieving. Within the skull fragments, a partially degraded copper alloy ring was recovered and beneath the skull two further copper alloy rings in good condition were retrieved. The bracelet type and grave goods suggest a late Hellenistic date for this inhumation. This would be in keeping with previous finds from the 1973-1998 expedition, which indicated a substantial Hellenistic period necropolis extending from east of the 6th century AD walls to the area immediately east of Trench B, and therefore including Trench A.

In contrast, the second burial (**139**), found to the south of **138**, was aligned east-west with the skull to the east. The skeleton was laid supine with both arms flexed at the elbow to cross the pelvis. Bone preservation was fair though fragmentary, particularly the skull which was both crushed and disturbed. This individual appears to have also been immature with unfused epiphyses. There were no obvious grave goods recovered although a folded lead tablet was recovered from near the left knee, which may have been a shroud clasp.

As layer **136** was removed it became apparent that there was a similar but darker deposit to the south of the area in the locale of burial **139**. This was excavated separately as layer **145**, consisting of a mid to dark greyish brown sandy silt with occasional flecks of charcoal and burnt earth. The material within **145** was largely sterile and appeared to have accumulated in situ with material brought in through natural agents such as colluvial movement.

The excavation of layer **145** revealed burial **148**, also aligned east-west (with the head at the east) and laid out supine with lower arms flexed across the abdomen in the same manner as **139**. The bone was poorly preserved and showed signs of crushing, the skull having suffered particularly in this respect. This burial had a complete spindle whorl (Small Find NOK03/A 46) placed over the

sternum in such a way as to suggest that it may have been hung around the neck on a piece of thread. Recovered from the approximate position of the left ear was a copper alloy ring. The spatial relationship between **148** and **139** and the apparent similarities of rite suggested contemporary or near contemporary interment.

A further burial (**144**) was found to the north of the others. It was in a very bad condition and appears to have been a neonate or young baby, flexed at the knees and lying on its left side, aligned east-west with the skull to west. Poor bone preservation, crushed and disturbed skull and a very truncated grave cut (**146**) suggests, as in the others, damage inflicted in antiquity. This may support the hypothesis of a deliberate reduction and levelling of the area in the vicinity of the early Byzantine walls, and consequently the removal of stratified deposits relating to the centuries immediately prior to the construction of the walls.

Removal of these burials allowed the excavation of layer **137** – a mid-reddish brown sandy silt with occasional light patches of burnt clay and frequent fragments of charcoal. However, the discovery of a further two crouched burials brought a halt to the excavation of **137** shortly after the initial cleaning had been carried out. Burial **151** was located towards the centre of the trench and consisted of

*Figure 4.4: Crouched burial **154** with grave goods excavated in 2003*

a crouched inhumation aligned north-northeast to south-southwest. The body had been laid out on the left side with legs flexed at the knee and arms bent towards chest with hands resting under head in 'sleeping' pose. Although considerable degradation and disturbance had affected the preservation of the skeleton, initial examination of the bones suggested the remains represented those of a child. At the foot of the skeleton two fragmentary but mostly complete pottery vessels were excavated. Further grave goods were recovered from the body consisting of a copper alloy bracelet of Hellenistic style (Small Find NOK03/A 47) found on the right arm; a flat copper alloy ring (Small Find NOK03/A 48) found within the lower jaw; and a copper alloy ring (Small Find NOK03/A 49) found within the fill (**149**). Within the area of the head and neck the scattered remnants of a necklace were recovered consisting of 44 beads (Small Find NOK03/A 50). These were primarily of blue paste, but also represented were biconical and circular clear glass beads with gold foil lined centres, and yellow, black and clear glass beads.

Burial **154** (Figure 4.4) contained a crouched inhumation laid out on its left side on an east – west alignment with the head to the west. The legs were flexed at the knee with the heels drawn towards the pelvis. Both arms were flexed at the elbow, the left hand resting under the chin and the right lower arm across the stomach. At the feet were found two lugged pots and, by the head, a fine ceramic vessel of the Hellenistic period. The body had been furnished with a fine selection of grave goods. On the left arm were a pair of copper alloy bracelets (Small Find NOK03/A 51 and 52), and on the right arm one copper alloy bracelet (Small Find NOK03/A 53) and one made of iron (Small Find NOK03/A 54). From the area of the head were recovered two probable earrings (Small Find NOK03/A 55 and 56) and a possible nose ring (Small Find NOK03/A 57). These pieces of jewellery were augmented by the recovery of 373 small blue paste beads and 80 other beads of a huge range of materials, shape and dimensions. It was unclear whether these represented one or more necklaces due to the dislocation of the beads following degradation of the thread. Many of the beads were found during excavation, however a large number were also retrieved by wet-sieving the grave fill excavated from the head and neck area of the body.

2004 Season

Trench A was reopened on the 24th July 2004. The decision had been taken at the end of the 2003 season, having discovered Hellenistic burials directly underlying early Byzantine deposits, that a larger area of excavation was needed in order to establish the extent of the cemetery and its further stratigraphic relationships. The primary aim this season was, therefore, to increase the area of Trench A to 13.5m north-south and 10m east-west, giving a total area of 135m² – a substantial increase on the previous size of 60m² (excluding the now redundant area of the 1995 trench). This was determined by the limitations of existing

fence lines to the west and north of the trench, and the need to also include room for future spoil heaps. At this stage a previously unknown electricity cable was revealed in the southwest corner of the trench, which precluded the establishment of a right-angled corner to the extension. This cable was finally disconnected and removed in 2010, and Trench A could then be made rectangular. Because previous contexts had been fully recorded, and sections drawn, the intention was that layers encountered by the workmen during this season could be quickly recorded and related to the existing section drawings and plans. Throughout this season the original area of Trench A was protected under last year's covering of plastic and backfill. A mechanical excavator was used to move the large spoil heaps that had accumulated over the previous three years. A team of approximately 12 local workmen were then employed to remove spits of approximately 0.3m in depth, under archaeological supervision.

The upper layers included evidence of the repair and reconstruction of the fortification walls in the Soviet period, overlying a deposit containing further sections of fallen masonry. As in the original excavations, the first occupation layer encountered (**108**) produced a large quantity of archaeological material. Finds included a high density of pottery, CBM and animal bones of domesticated livestock. This layer also contained some interesting small finds. These included arrow heads, a knife and dagger blade, fibula brooch, bronze buckle, hairpin, loom weights, bases of wine glasses and a broken glass perfume bottle.

Underlying **108** was layer **125** which in turn overlay **136**. Layer **125** was the last to be removed in this season of excavation and, like layer **108**, **125** contained a high density of ceramic fragments and animal bones. Small finds included an iron spearhead, copper alloy needle, a residual flint blade and a glass fragment, which was decorated with blue spots. Also within **125** were two thin lenses of mortar, still visible in the south facing trench edge, relating to phases of construction of the fortification walls.

In the western area of the trench extension, removal of **125** revealed a layer composed of dark earth and small rounded stones, which accounted for 50% of its volume. This layer could be a continuation of layer **132** – which also lies directly above layer **136** – and is either a metalled surface or stones left over from the wall construction. Fine, rounded river stones are used in the mortar of the wall and this could account for their presence in this layer. Within this layer there also seemed to be a truncated burial, the feet and upper skull of which were exposed. Directly above **136** in the northern part of the trench extension was a thin green sandy-silt deposit, **158**, which was the final layer to be exposed this season. This appears to consist of cess material and may indicate either a period of intense human occupation, some kind of light industrial activity or animal stabling.

2005 Season

The 2005 season began on the 1st August. In this year, the focus was placed on bringing the extension into phase with the original area of Trench A stratigraphy and tying it in with the 2003 sequence. As excavations ensued, a clearer understanding of the activity in the area was helped by the find of three east-west orientated inhumations (**160,163** and **168**) in the south-western area of the extension. Skeleton **168** was lying in a lateral position, orientated northwest-southwest. The arms were flexed so that the hands were situated under the chin. About 0.5m to the north was Skeleton **160**. This burial was orientated northwest-southeast, with the head to the northwest. Lying in a prone position, the left arm was slightly flexed so the hand lay on the pelvis, and the right arm was flexed so that the hand lay under the skull. Immediately to the north, about 0.4m away, was Skeleton **163**, which was orientated east-west, with the head in the west facing south. This individual had been laid out in a supine position, with the left arm flexed so that the hand was over the chest. The right arm was flexed up to the head, with the hand situated under the skull. All three skeletons were assessed in the field as adult males, and the general impression was that they had been buried quickly without the attention to detail one might expect from a typical Christian burial. Their location – cut into the earliest Byzantine deposits present in Trench A – and apparently hurried burial, might suggest an association with the battles of the 6th century AD.

2006 Season

Work on the extension of Trench A resumed on the 31st July, with the original trench area remaining covered for much of the season while the new area was brought into phase (Figure 4.5). Excavation proper began at the southern end of the extension. Almost immediately a feature (**203**) was found through cleaning directly below the north facing bulk; although unexcavated at that time, it was later revealed through the normal course of excavation to comprise flat, rounded, closely placed river stones, each approximately 0.40m in diameter covering an area of around 1m sq. This was initially interpreted as a path, or more elaborately a road, but because the baulk section precluded the potential expanse of the feature it was left to later seasons to reveal more of this surface (see 2010, below). It became apparent later in the excavation season that the feature was surrounded by a number of negative features including possible postholes and a linear feature, looking much like a gully or beam slot. This indicated that the placement of stones was more functional as a hard standing if a structure was placed over or near it.

At a distance of 2.6m north of the southwest corner, a burnt beam was found within layer **170**. This was a limestone rubble layer found in the previous season and covers an area extending 2m east from the west baulk and north by around 7.5m. It was interpreted as left over

mason's material relating to a phase of construction or maintenance of the fortification walls.

At the northern extent of the trench, two hearths were found. Their location next to the baulk made it impossible to determine their extent and consequently to some degree, their function. It was not clear whether the hearths were contained within a structure or not, however, it was noted that a higher percentage of late Roman pottery and glass fragments were recovered from this area within context **171** suggesting either occupation or manufacturing activity.

Lying beneath layer **171** was layer **173**, a largely sterile dark brown-grey silty clay, possibly representing an abandonment deposit. As **173** was excavated, it revealed a line of limestone blocks (**187**) running east-west for 6m with a 1m return to the north at its western end. The dimensions of the stones ranged from 0.7m to 1.5m in diameter. At this stage it was decided to re-open a 2.5m x 2.5m sondage into the northwest corner of the original trench area in order to determine whether **187** was a continuation of angular limestone blocks found in 2003. Not only was a direct continuation of the structure observed, it indicated that the two contexts (**174** and **137**) were contemporary and overlying **187** which was determined as dating from the Hellenistic period

In terms of burials, two were excavated this season. One, **185,** was a child burial, however, skeleton **183** warrants discussion here as it was the first to be found contained within a food storage vessel known as a dergi. The partial remains of a pre-adolescent child lay on half of the vessel, and had been interred on top of the foundations of the Hellenistic period structure. Although pot burials are not unusual in this region, this was the first dergi burial. A similar burial in Nokalakevi was found outside (east of) the fortification walls in which a cut amphora contained a human skeleton. There is no sign that this particular dergi was deliberately cut in half for a funerary purpose as the break is irregular despite the few missing pieces.

2007 Season

Work began on Monday 6th August. The line of stones that had been exposed towards the centre of the trench at the end of the 2006 field season was demonstrated to be part of a building, and other wall lines were exposed during the 2007 season (Figure 4.6). These buildings appeared, judging from the pottery recovered from the deposits sealing them, to belong to the Hellenistic period and are thus roughly contemporary with the building exposed in Trench B in 2005, which provided some indication of the method of construction. They all appear to be represented archaeologically by a line of large unbonded limestone or trench-laid rubble, which would have provided a solid, waterproof base for a clay and timber building. Upon this foundation was laid a beam, which supported the upright posts within which wattle was woven to provide the framework to which daub was applied. The absence

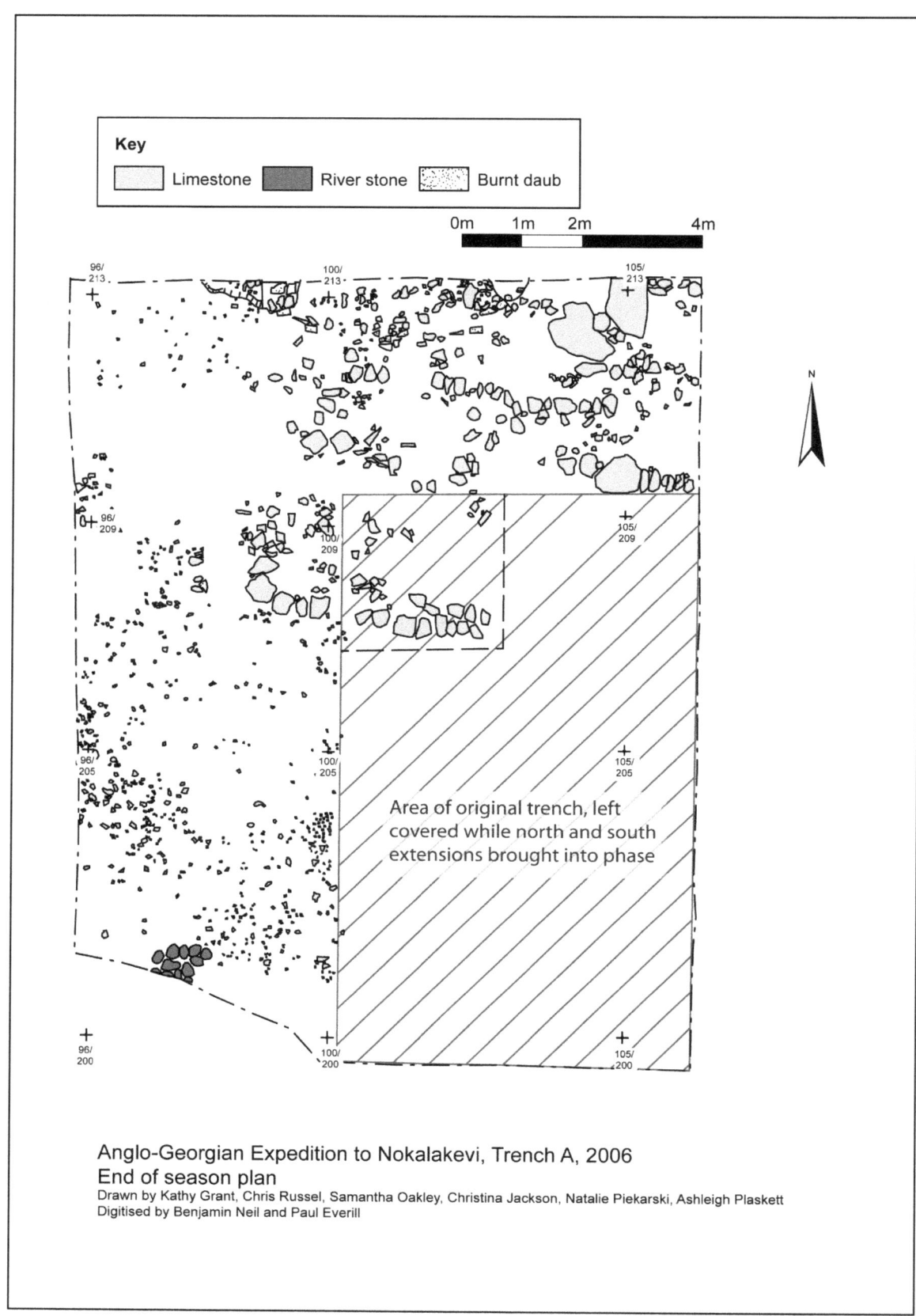

Key

Limestone   River stone   Burnt daub

0m   1m   2m   4m

Area of original trench, left covered while north and south extensions brought into phase

Anglo-Georgian Expedition to Nokalakevi, Trench A, 2006
End of season plan
Drawn by Kathy Grant, Chris Russel, Samantha Oakley, Christina Jackson, Natalie Piekarski, Ashleigh Plaskett
Digitised by Benjamin Neil and Paul Everill

Figure 4.5: Trench A, 2006

of roof tiles from the archaeological record might support the idea that the roofing material consisted of wooden shingles or thatch.

Structure registers and sheets were added to the expedition recording system. This meant that the buildings or phases of building could be given structure numbers, so that the various elements of each could be grouped within the expedition recording system. **Structure 1** consisted of the masonry (**187**) and layer **211**. At the northern end of the return to the north of **187** was a large, possible post-pit (**219**), which may once have held a door post for the entrance to the building. Layer **211** was initially thought to be an abandonment deposit within the walls, which post-dated the use of the building and possibly sealed further structural elements. However further investigation revealed that this deposit pre-dated the use of the building.

Structure 2 consisted of masonry **212** and layer **213**. The former was another line of unbonded limestone boulders running for 4.5m east-west, before a return to the south which extended for 1m. The east-west element was almost parallel to the east-west element of **Structure 1**, and was located 2m to the south of it. Layer **213,** as with **211**, was initially thought to be an abandonment deposit, sealing additional features relating to the structure, but upon investigation was revealed to underlie **212**.

Layer **213** did, however, seal part of **Structure 3**, making this the oldest building or phase of building exposed during the 2007 season. **Structure 3** was rather enigmatic, and was also sealed by a substantial deposit of burnt material, including daub – layer **216** – which lay between **Structure 1** and **Structure 2**. **Structure 3** was roughly square, defined by masonry foundation **230**. It was approximately 2.5m square, with the suggestion that there may have been an entrance at the northwest corner. It lay underneath **Structure 2**, and about half a metre south of **Structure 1**. It appears to have respected the same orientation as the other buildings.

Layer **216**, consisting as it did of large quantities of burnt material, provided a fascinating opportunity to gain an insight into the early settlement of Nokalakevi. A wide range of carbonised seeds were retrieved from this context through the sieving and flotation of soil samples. More detail is provided in the table in Chapter 8, but the samples processed in 2007 produced a wide range of carbonised seeds, including wild and domesticated grape (*vitis vinifera*, *vitis sylvestris*), wheat (*triticum sp.),* pea (*pisum sativum*), rowan (*sorbus sp.*) and black walnut (*junglans regia*) (Bokeria pers comm). The presence of this material in the layer sealing **Structure 3** might indicate that it functioned as a food store.

It was thought possible that the three structures represented a series of rooms in one building and/

Figure 4.6: Trench A during the 2007 season, looking west

or phases of construction within such. An alternative interpretation is that these foundations represent three separate buildings. The square **Structure 3** was thought initially to indicate a small ritual building related to the Hellenistic necropolis, however without associated finds supporting this hypothesis it remains conjectural. In fact, at this stage the indications were that these buildings most likely pre-date the necropolis, and further excavation of inhumations continued to support this interpretation. Consequently the evidence suggests that an early Hellenistic period settlement was partially or completely abandoned in favour of another nearby location. The collapsed buildings, presumably with surviving wall stubs indicating their location above ground, then appear to have provided the setting for a necropolis, within which a number of burials appear to have been laid directly alongside the surviving wall stubs or their stone foundations. It might even be the case that the levelling of the area that appears to have taken place in the Byzantine period, was undertaken in order to remove the undulating ground surface that may well have formed over the remnants of these buildings. It seems possible that enough physical remains survived that its then inhabitants named it 'The Old City' – Archaeopolis to the Byzantines.

Eight burials were excavated in 2007 and, unusually, all except one represented infant and juvenile remains. Three had been placed into coffins made of amphora bodies. Skeleton **190** was a neonate. It was aligned east-west with the head in the west and lay, in a flexed position, on its left side facing north. The new-born had been laid into an amphorae coffin. Skeleton **193** was a juvenile, of about five years old. Like **190** it was east-west aligned with the head in the west. In complete disarticulation and poor preservation, the skeletal elements were highly fragmented, however from its position it was seen to be lying on its left side facing north, possibly flexed at the pelvis and knee. Skeleton **221** was an east-west aligned juvenile interred within an amphora. Despite being fragmentary the individual had apparently been laid on its right side, flexed at the pelvis and knees, facing north. Both the skull and the neck of the amphora were at the east of the grave.

Burials that were highly disarticulated, and in some cases of indeterminate orientation, included skeleton **196**, a probable perinatal individual represented predominantly by cranial fragments plus some fragments of rib, scapula, humerus and clavicle. A sub-circular hole was observed in a cranial fragment. A blue glass bead (Small Find NOK07/A 6) was found in the grave fill (**195**). Of similar poor preservation was skeleton **206**, another newborn, of which enough survived to observe that it was east-west aligned with the head in the east. The surviving skeletal elements of **206** were highly fragmented and placed within an amphora. Skeleton **209**, a juvenile of up to two years old, was aligned east-west with the head in the west, but the disordered disarticulation of much of the burial meant that the position could not be accurately ascertained.

The only cremation was juvenile skeleton **199**. An east west aligned cremation with the head in the east, it was completely disarticulated with a high degree of fragmentation. Finds associated with this individual included a ceramic vessel found in the east of the grave. A copper alloy 'snake' bracelet (Small Find NOK07/A 6) was intimately associated with the skeleton, possibly around the lower arm.

The only adult burial excavated in 2007 was east-west aligned skeleton **227**. This individual was buried lying on its right side, with the head in the east facing north. The arms were flexed at the elbow, with the right hand over the chest and the left on the abdomen. The legs were flexed at the knees. This was a relatively richly furnished burial, having two copper alloy bracelets (Small Finds NOK07/A 21 and 22) on its right arm, a number of glass and stone necklace beads (Small Finds NOK07/A 12, 20, 24, 25 and 28), an earring (Small Find NOK07/A 23) and a ring (Small Find NOK07/A 27). There were also two small ceramic vessels (Small Finds NOK07/A 18 and 19) to the left side of the head.

2008 Season

Work recommenced on Monday 9th July with the reopening of Trench A for the season's excavation. This season was characterised by the continued revealing, excavation and recording of contexts relating to the Hellenistic structures (Figure 4.7).

In terms of new structural elements, **244** was revealed as a short, probable east-west wall comprising of seven unbonded, undressed, limestone blocks (averaging 400x100x70mm) which extended for approximately 1.5m. One very large limestone block (560x750x330mm) was located at the western end of **244**. The eastern extent of this wall continued under the baulk/steps. A second wall, **245**, also consisted of seven unbonded limestone blocks, extending for 1.5m on an east-west alignment, continuing into the baulk.

Between the two, context **234** was a rubble layer, comprising very frequent angular and sub-angular limestone within a matrix of dark greyish brown fine clay silt. This context seemed discreet and may represent the foundation layer for a path, yard or floor surface, perhaps even part of an eastern entrance to **Structure 1**. A few animal bones as well as a large piece of pot with rim and handle were uncovered within this deposit. No daub is present within this context which clearly distinguished it from the overlying layer (**235**), which included a notable quantity of pottery and burnt daub.

Foundation **242** was also revealed for the first time this year. This wall consisted of sub-angular limestone boulders (averaging 160x200x50mm) arranged in an L-shape with the longer arm on an east-west alignment and the shorter arm on a north-south alignment. The wall segment was located north of **187**.

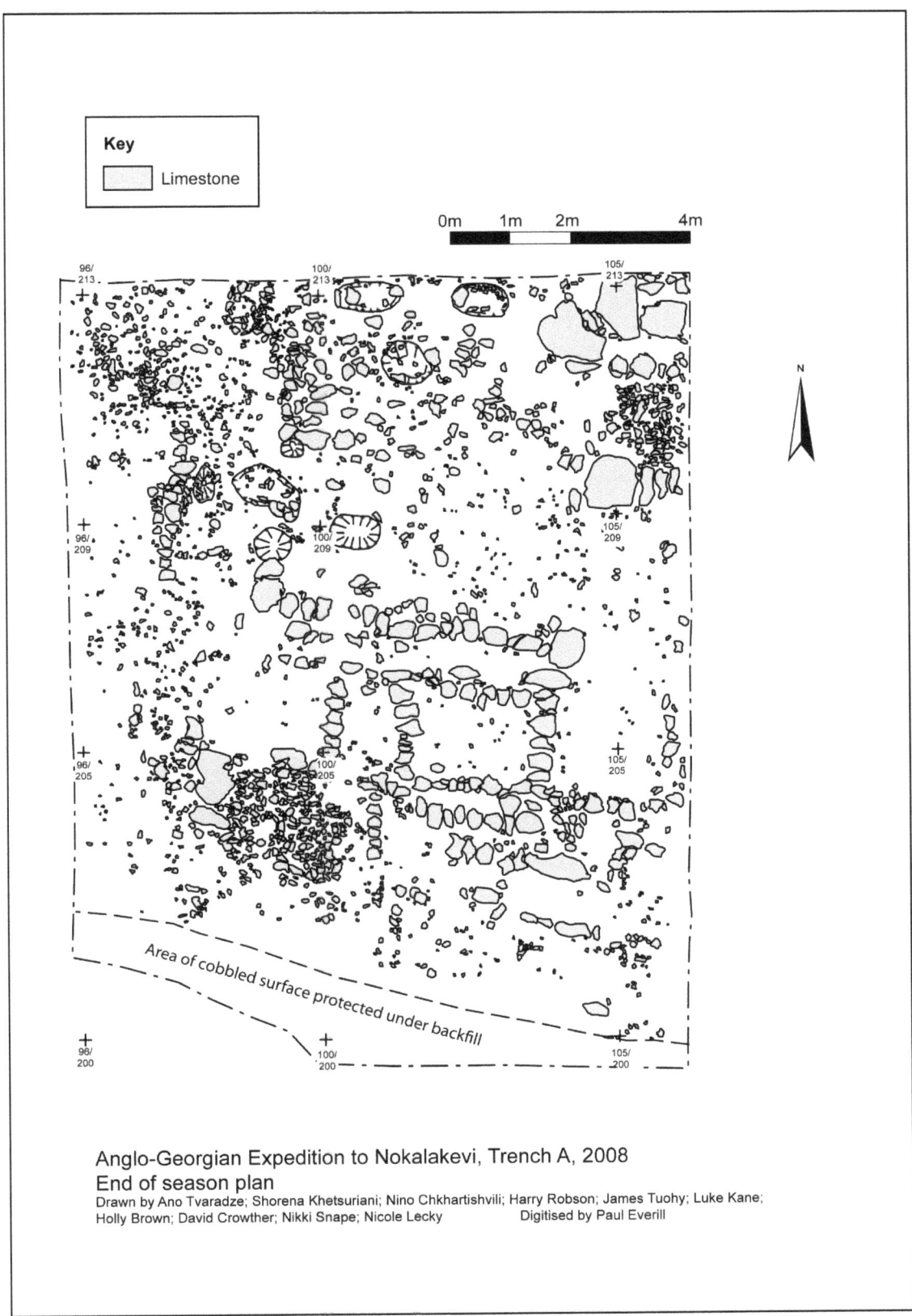

Key

Limestone

0m   1m   2m   4m

N

96/213   100/213   105/213

96/209   100/209   105/209

96/205   100/205   105/205

96/200   100/200   105/200

Area of cobbled surface protected under backfill

Anglo-Georgian Expedition to Nokalakevi, Trench A, 2008
End of season plan
Drawn by Ano Tvaradze; Shorena Khetsuriani; Nino Chkhartishvili; Harry Robson; James Tuohy; Luke Kane;
Holly Brown; David Crowther; Nikki Snape; Nicole Lecky   Digitised by Paul Everill

Figure 4.7: Trench A, 2008

Also revealed was **243**, a small wall orientated north-south consisting of unbonded, angular limestone blocks (averaging 190x250x70mm). One larger block was present at the northern end (230x470x50mm). This wall segment has no returning arms and may therefore constitute a screen, or dividing wall.

Three Hellenistic period burials were also excavated in 2008. Of particular note was skeleton **237,** which was aligned east-west with the head at the west, just north of possible posthole **219.** It was a young child, of around four years old. The skeletal elements were highly fragmented, friable and disturbed. Also worth noting was the cremation of an adult male (**241**), which was found with an associated pottery vessel. Fragments of a possible copper alloy bracelet were also recovered from within this burial.

Cut **251** represented an inhumation grave located along the northern baulk with a river stone capping the grave and a stone at the western end of the grave (by the feet). Contained within this grave was skeleton **253**; a young child (around 5 years old) buried in a flexed position with the head at the east and the feet at the west. A copper bracelet (Small Find NOK08/A 10) was found around the left ankle, two copper earrings (Small Find NOK08/A 11) and a turquoise and blue beaded necklace (Small Find NOK08/A 9) were collected from around the skull. A broken ceramic vessel was found at the foot of the grave.

2009 Season

Work began on Monday 5th July with the reopening of Trench A for the season's excavation. The majority of excavation this year was concentrated on the northern half of the trench to bring it into phase, given that it remained a little higher than the southern half. Excavation of the thick layers **217** and **235**, first uncovered in 2007 and 2008 respectively, continued. Several small finds were recovered from layer **235** including: three copper alloy pin fragments (Small Find NOK09/A 2-4), two worked flint tools (Small Find NOK09/A 5 and 17), a flint arrow-head (Small Find NOK09/A 20), and a loom weight/spindle (Small Find NOK09/A 19). The removal of stones that appeared out of phase also helped clarify the wall lines that had been revealed previously. The difficulty in establishing proper phasing was largely a result of the gross similarity in layers which had, it appeared, been formed largely through a series of colluvial episodes between periods of occupation. With the exception of possible yard surfaces, no clearly definable floor layers survived in the record – perhaps an indication of raised timber floors supported on the stone sills that did survive. Whatever the cause, the end result has been a series of layers with often poorly defined interfaces, which has required a degree of caution in their excavation. Consequently, isolated stones that were unrelated to the structures only became evident when the removal of spits revealed that obviously structural stones continued into the surrounding layer. In

contrast, non-structural stones clearly sat within the layer being excavated and were removed. This process helped to define the real extent and form of the structures.

In terms of noteworthy burials, skeleton **255** was aligned east-west and located in the northern part of the trench immediately south of wall segment **242**. It was of an adult female aged approximately 36 to 43 years old. The individual's head was located at the east while the feet were at the west. The skeleton was in a flexed position on the left side with the head tilted back and facing southeast. Soil samples were taken from the fill, from various areas around the skeleton and from the vicinity of associated small finds for palynological and palaeobotanical analysis. Several small finds/grave goods were also present within the grave, including a pottery vessel (Small Find NOK09/A 9) next to the skull, several coloured glass beads (Small Find NOK09/A 8) from around the neck area, two copper alloy earrings (Small Find NOK09/A 16), two copper alloy bracelets (Small Find NOK09/A 12 and 13). It is also likely that the almost complete pot vessel (Small Find NOK08/A 4) found last season was placed into the western end of this grave.

Of particular note was grave cut **262**, located a little south of **255**, which contained human skeleton **261** and a partially articulated animal skeleton **263**. The inhumation burial (**261**) represented the remains of an adult male individual about 26 to 35 years old with the head located at the east. The skeleton was found in a semi-supine position (back and arms flat to the base of the grave) with the legs flexed at the pelvis and the knee towards the midline. The right arm was extended alongside the right part of the trunk and the left arm was flexed with the hand lying over the right humerus. A sub-complete carcass of a chicken (**263**) was located in the northeast corner of this grave cut, and represented the first, and to date only, animal burial found associated with a human inhumation in Nokalakevi. The implication is that the practice was perhaps rare, but that this individual had been provided with a sacrificial meal. Measurements taken on the humerus, tibiotarsus and tarsometatarsus suggest that it was from a small breed of domestic fowl (see Chapter Ten).

Several grave goods were also found associated with **261**, including a ceramic vessel (Small Find NOK09/A 14), several blue paste beads (Small Find NOK09/A 7) from around the neck area and next to the left humerus, two copper alloy earrings (Small Find NOK09/A 15) and two copper alloy bracelets (Small Find NOK09/A 10).

Soil samples were taken from the fill (**260**) and from various areas around the skeleton (**261**) and were analysed by E. Kvavadze. The sample taken from the region of the forehead produced residues of human hair and textile fibres that probably represent the remains of a shroud or head covering. These fibres were predominantly of grey and yellow flax, with a smaller number of cotton fibres that had been dyed black. A single sheep hair was found.

Microscopic cells of tree wood were thought to represent evidence for some kind of wooden construction, perhaps a coffin. Plant pollen was dominated by pine and cereals, including wheat, but evidence was also found of hazel, alder, lime, nettle and hoary plantain (Kvavadze pers comm).

Microscopic remains of a large number of grass plants were also found, which was interpreted by Kvavadze as evidence for the burial being laid onto, or covered by, a layer of grass. The sample taken from the region of the eyes of skeleton **261** produced similar evidence for tree wood, flax and cotton, but with the additional discovery of yellow wool fibres and evidence of ticks. In addition to the plant pollen described above, evidence was also found of beech, spruce, fir, oak, chestnut, hornbeam and celery.

A third sample, taken from around the neck vertebrae of skeleton **261**, produced evidence of bird feathers/ down. This was interpreted by Kvavadze as the remains of a down pillow which had been placed under the head – though of course archaeological evidence might suggest that this came from the chicken buried alongside **261**. There was further evidence of flax and cotton fibres, and ticks or mites. Tree pollen included, in addition to those described above, caucasian wingnut and caucasian elm. Grains of domesticated grape vine and walnut were also found. Grass pollen was dominated by what Kvavadze (pers

comm) refers to as yard and garden weeds, including knot grass, chicory, fragrant wormwood and hoary plantain. There was also evidence of emmer wheat and two-rowed barley.

2010 Season

Work began on Monday 19th July. The replacement and rerouting of an electrical cable over the preceding winter made it possible to extend the south-western corner of Trench A, and to finally make the trench rectangular (Figures 4.8 and 4.9).

The removal of the south-western corner of the trench exposed a larger area of the cobbled surface **203**, first exposed and recorded in 2006. This was shown to extend beyond the south-western corner of the site. A deposit of yellowy brown, compacted silty, sandy-clay **282** was shown to overlie this surface within the newly exposed south-eastern corner, also filling a large void within the stone surface itself. The compacted nature of **282** suggested it to be an accumulative deposit related to a road or yard surface.

Following the removal of the previously recorded structural elements, the cleaning of the underlying deposits across Trench A allowed a reassessment of the deposits that had been numbered but unrecorded in previous seasons.

Figure 4.8: Trench A at the start of the 2010 season, looking west

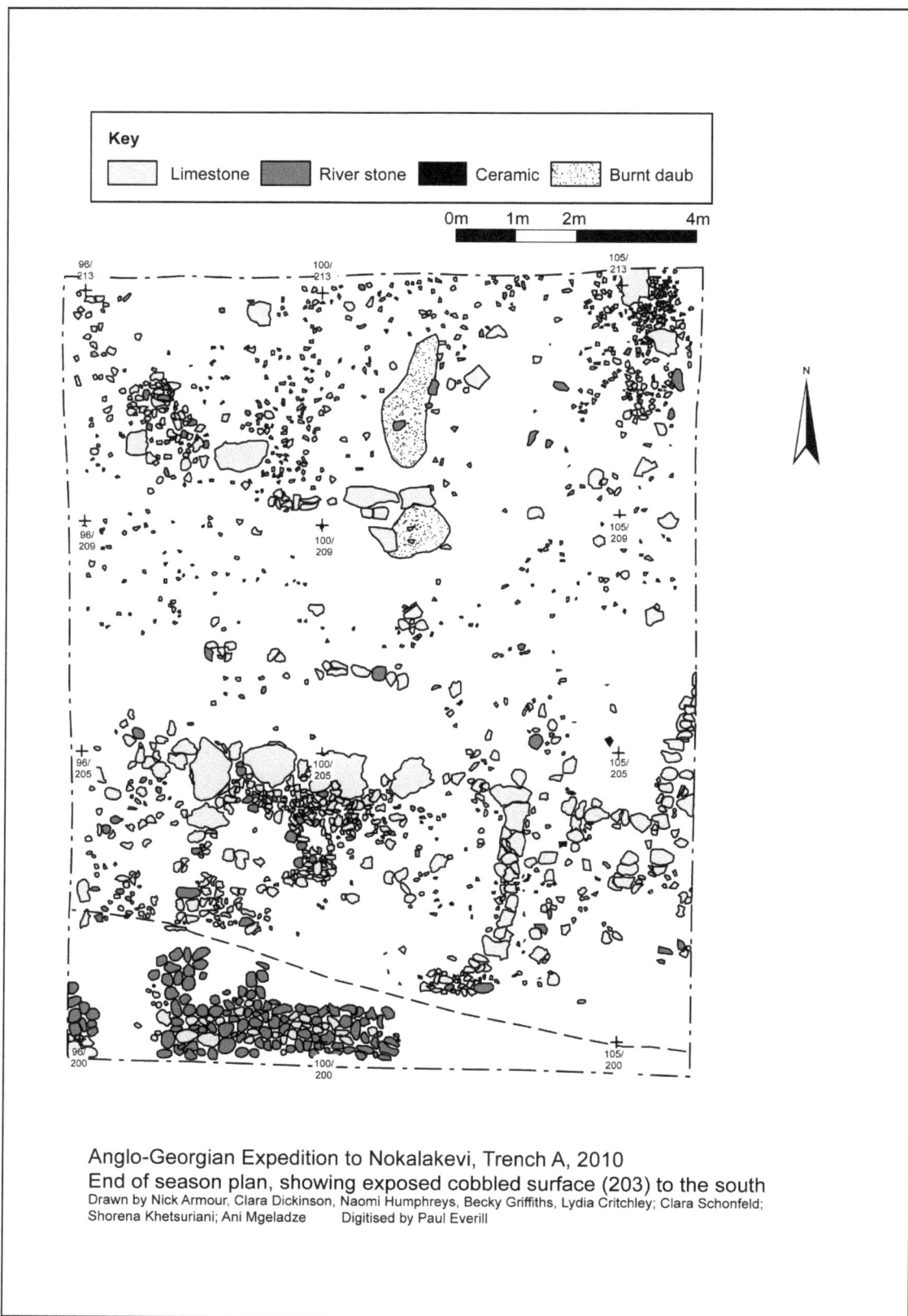

Anglo-Georgian Expedition to Nokalakevi, Trench A, 2010
End of season plan, showing exposed cobbled surface (203) to the south
Drawn by Nick Armour, Clara Dickinson, Naomi Humphreys, Becky Griffiths, Lydia Critchley; Clara Schonfeld;
Shorena Khetsuriani; Ani Mgeladze   Digitised by Paul Everill

Figure 4.9: Trench A, 2010

Similarities between layers **213,** within the southern half of Trench A, and **217,** within the far west of the area, led to them being agglomerated into a single stratigraphic unit, **268**. Layer **235** (within the far north of the site and stratigraphically overlying layer **217**) and layer **268** were shown to be sufficiently distinct from these deposits to remain as a separate contextual block.

Examination of **235** (a mid grey, moderately compacted clay silt, located within the northern area of Trench A, which was first identified during 2008 and partially excavated in 2009) demonstrated it to be a thin veneer of material, a maximum of 20mm in thickness. It overlay **268** and the northern end of **217**, and represented the very base of the thicker deposit excavated in previous seasons. **235** was completely removed during the 2010 excavation.

Following the removal of deposit **235**, the full extent of underlying deposit **268**, itself an amalgamation of several previously numbered deposits (see above) could be seen.

268 was a materially rich colluvial silty-clay which extended across the entirety of the site. High quantities of largely unabraded ceramics, as well as animal bone that demonstrated rodent and root damage, were recovered from the deposit. This suggested that it represented an accumulative occupation horizon. By the end of the 2010 excavation season, small patches of **268** were still present within the centre, east and southeast of the excavated area, highlighting the irregularities of the underlying deposits.

The complete removal of **235** and **268** exposed the full extent of **232** – an underlying deposit containing small angular limestone fragments – identified during earlier seasons and initially thought to extend across the whole western side of the trench. A dense and discrete deposit of larger limestone and riverstone rubble towards the southwest of the trench was subsequently assigned its own context number, **281**. Masonry **280** appeared to be partially covered by the rubble deposit **281** and represented a newly identified structure. It was comprised of four large, apparently unworked boulders aligned east-west with a suggestion of a north-south return at the western end. The eastern end was comprised of a narrower, north-south aligned wall of smaller, roughly-shaped stones (not fully revealed in 2010). A second structure was partially exposed, which comprised an east-west aligned wall with a north-south aligned return that extended beyond the eastern limit of excavation. Because their full extent and nature was not revealed in 2010, these walls were not numbered this season.

Also revealed by the removal of **268** was a small cluster of four irregular stones creating a shallow void, **275,** which was believed to represent packing at the base of a posthole. No cut through **268** was identified, although **275** is likely to be contemporary with posthole **219** to the north, the base of which also corresponded with the lower horizon of **268**.

The reduction of **268** within the north-eastern corner of Trench A exposed a deposit of rubble (**272**), the coarse components of which varied in size from large unworked limestone blocks to small angular stones, within a matrix of silty clay. The base of **272** contained the fragmented remains of a ceramic zoomorphic figurine, although it was not clear at the time of excavation whether this was *in situ*, residual or intrusive.

Underlying **268** within the northern and central part of Trench A was the upper horizon of a context that appeared to represent an occupational layer. Within this, so far unnumbered deposit, were patches of orangey brown heat affected clay (**273** and **274)** likely associated with occupation. These were not excavated but demonstrate the base of the **268/ 235** colluvial episodes.

Two burials were identified, excavated and recorded during the 2010 season. A third, **265**, was re-exposed and removed, having been fully recorded in 2009. The first newly identified burial, **271,** was located immediately east of the southern end of wall **242**. Skeleton **271** was an incomplete, largely disarticulated, neonate. The fill (**270**) contained two copper alloy bracelets (Small Finds NOK10/A 1 and 3). This burial as well as surrounding fill was block lifted for off-site excavation.

A second burial, **278**, was identified within a sub-circular cut, **279**, truncating the apex of the rubble layer **232**, and located immediately to the west of wall **242**. A burial vessel consisting of the base of a large dergi/ pithos, with a second base as a lid, **277**, was contained in this cut. Within the vessel was an incomplete, partially disarticulated juvenile, **278**. A fragmented and incomplete skull was contained within the base of the vessel, overlain by broken long-bones, and a complete set of ribs, adjacent to a fragmented pelvis and vertebrae. A high concentration of incomplete and fragmentary bones was located throughout the burial with a notable absence of smaller bones such as tarsals. A copper alloy bracelet and earring as well as beads likely associated with a necklace were within the grave fill, **276**, immediately on top of the burial (Small Finds NOK10/A 9, 10 and 13) and an unidentified ferrous object (possibly a nail) was recovered from the very base of the ceramic vessel (Small Find NOK10/A 12).

The removal of the colluvium further emphasised the discrepancy between the underlying physical topography, which is becoming more apparent, and that created by many centuries of occupational and colluvial deposition.

The two burials excavated during the 2010 season were stratigraphically contemporary with those excavated during 2009. The similarity of the fills of the graves to the surrounding deposits made the top of the grave cuts impossible to determine, and consequently graves were often only located when the burials at the bottom were revealed. However, like a number of other Hellenistic period burials excavated in Trench A since 2003, **271** and **278** had been placed in graves that respected the alignment

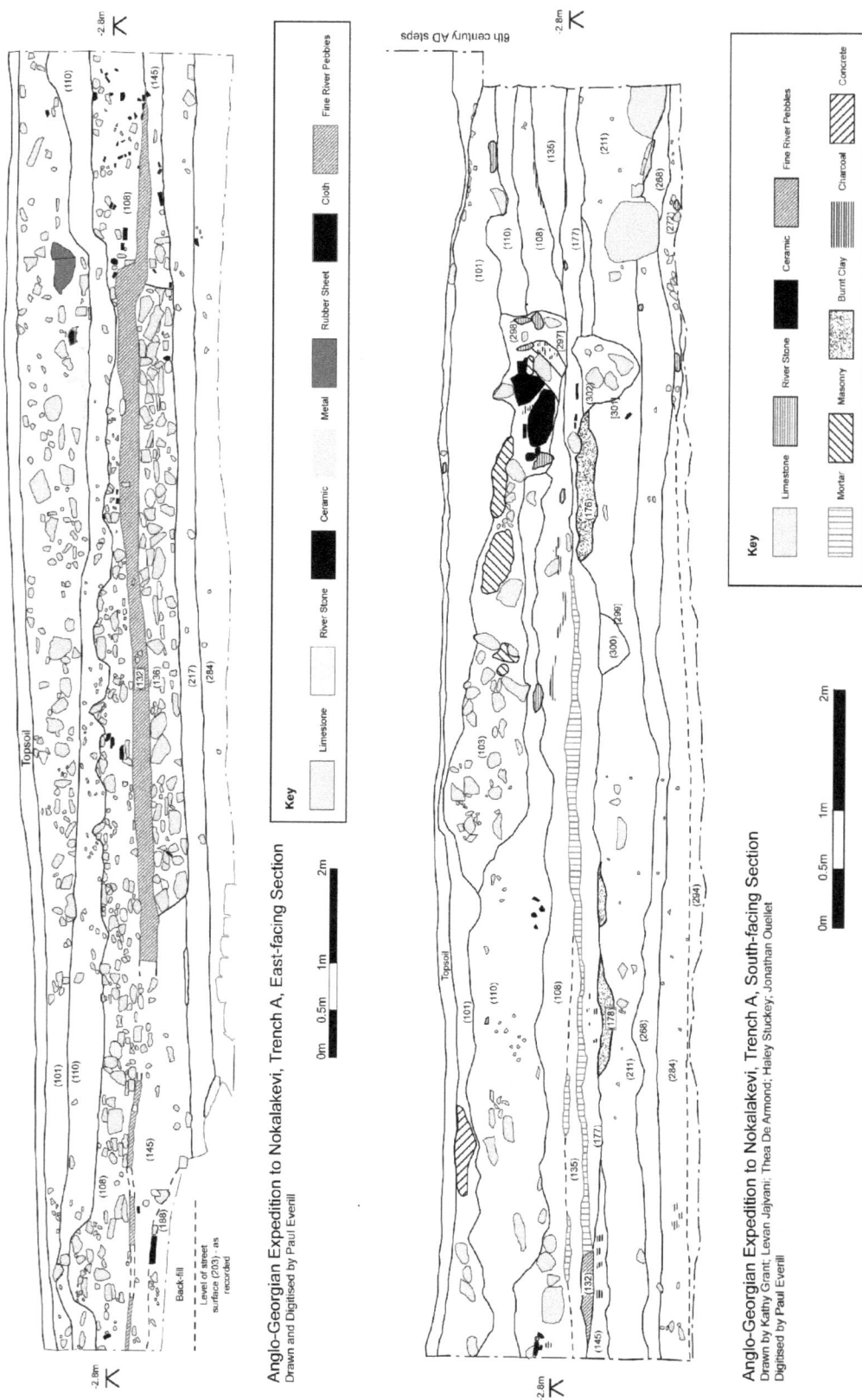

Figure 4.10: Trench A, section drawings

of the, probably by then ruinous, Hellenistic structures removed during the 2010 season: in this case wall **242**. The 2010 burials, that of a child and a neonate both with grave goods of copper alloy jewellery, offer insights into the population demographics of nearby settlement when considered alongside the existing evidence from adult, sub-adult, child and infant burials found since 2003. The incomplete and disarticulated nature of both the burials from 2010 suggests an extended post-mortem period before the inhumation took place; this is particularly true of dergi burial **278**.

Conclusion

Ten years of excavation have revealed a complex stratified sequence at Nokalakevi (Figure 4.10), which adds to the understanding of the site developed through the excavations which took place from 1973-1998. The methodology employed in Trench A allowed previously undiscovered details of this sequence to be identified, both through stratigraphic analysis and the work of a great variety of other specialists that contributed to this process, as outlined elsewhere in this volume. It hardly needs stating that work has continued in Trench A while this publication has been in preparation, and excavation and analysis of material continue to add to our understanding of the development, occupation and abandonment of the site. However, within the period with which this publication is concerned – the 2001-10 seasons – it is fair to characterise the phases evident as follows. The 2001 season (and 2004 season during the extension of the trench) encountered modern overburden, containing very mixed deposits including finds from the Hellenistic period through to the 20th century. Directly underlying these deposits were large sections of masonry that had fallen from the fortification walls sealing the underlying deposits, testament to the long-term degradation of the standing Byzantine remains once they had ceased to be maintained. Underneath the masonry, deposits relating to various phases of wall construction from the 4th to the 6th centuries AD were revealed, along with associated occupation. Somewhat surprisingly, though probably providing evidence of ground clearance at the time of the Laz/ early Byzantine fortification of the site, Hellenistic period (4th-2nd centuries BC) burials were revealed directly underlying the earliest of these deposits. These burials included flexed inhumations with associated jewellery, cremations and inhumations within amphorae and cooking vessels. Evidence suggests that the Hellenistic period was a time of great change at Nokalakevi, with structures dating to that time stratigraphically underlying the burials though physically very close. This may indicate a shift in the focus of the settlement in those centuries and absolute dating techniques may, in the future, further clarify the temporal relationship between these phases, as further excavations elsewhere at the site shed more light on settlement foci. Towards the end of the period of excavation being discussed here, Early Antique period deposits (6th-4th centuries BC) were being revealed, along

with material that seems to predate even that. All of this is testament to the longevity of settlement at Nokalakevi, and the value of further analysis.

Bibliography

Armour, N. and Colvin, I. 2004. *Nokalakevi Expedition Interim Report 2001-2003 Seasons*. Unpublished AGEN report.

Everill, P. 2007. *NOK 07/A Interim Excavation Report*. Unpublished AGEN report.

Everill, P. and Ginns, A. 2005. *Anglo-Georgian Expedition to Nokalakevi: Trench A 2004*. Unpublished AGEN report.

Everill, P., Slater, A., James, L. and Colvin, I. 2011. *Anglo-Georgian Expedition to Nokalakevi: Interim report on excavations in 2010*. Unpublished AGEN report.

Grant, K. and Everill, P. 2009. *Anglo-Georgian Expedition to Nokalakevi: Interim report on excavations July 2008*. Unpublished AGEN report.

Grant, K., Russel, C. and Everill, P. 2010. *Anglo-Georgian Expedition to Nokalakevi: Interim report on excavations July 2009*. Unpublished AGEN report.

Lomitashvili, D., Lordkipanidze, B., Zamtaradze, M., Kebuladze, N., Kapanadze, T., Colvin, I., Everill, P. Neil, B., Ginns, A., and Connolly. D. 2005. Anglo-Georgian Expedition to Nokalakevi: Report on the International Archaeological Expedition to Nokalakevi 2004. Unpublished report (in Georgian)

Lomitashvili, D., Lordkipanidze, B., Zamtaradze, M. Kebuladze, N., Kapanadze, T., Colvin, I., Everill, P., Neil, B., Armour, N., and Murghulia, N. 2006. Anglo-Georgian Expedition to Nokalakevi; Report on the International Archaeological Expedition to Nokalakevi 2005. Unpublished report (in Georgian)

Lomitashvili, D., Lordkipanidze, B., Colvin, I., Neil, B., Kebuladze, N., Murghulia, N., and Zamtaradze, M. 2007. Anglo-Georgian Expedition to Nokalakevi; Report on the International Archaeological Expedition to Nokalakevi 2006. Unpublished report (in Georgian)

Lomitashvili, D., Tvalchrelidze, Z., Kebuladze, N., Murghulia, N., Bokeria, M., Kvavadze, E., Colvin, I., Everill, P., Timby, J., and Neil, B. 2010. Report on the Field Work in 2007 by the Georgian-British Nokalakevi Archaeological Expedition. *DZIEBANI Journal of Georgian archaeology.* №19: 51-57 (in Georgian)

Lomitashvili, D., Tvalchrelidze, Z., Kebuladze, N., Murghulia, N., Bokeria, M., Kvavadze, E, Colvin, I., Everill, P., Timby, J., and Neil, B. 2011. Report on the Field Work in 2008-2009 by the Georgian-British Nokalakevi Archaeological

Expedition. *DZIEBANI Journal of Georgian archaeology*. №20: 140-153 (in Georgian)

Lomitashvili, D., Tvalchrelidze, Z., Kebuladze, N., Murghulia, N., Tvaradze, A., Bokeria, M., Kvavadze, E., Colvin, I., Everill, P., Timby, J., and Neil, B. Forthcoming. Report on the Field Work in 2010 by the Georgian-British Nokalakevi Archaeological Expedition. *DZIEBANI Journal of Georgian archaeology*. №21 (in Georgian)

Neil, B. *2006. Area A Field Report*. Unpublished AGEN report.

CHAPTER FIVE

AGEN Trench B Results: 2002-2010

By Paul Everill, Davit Lomitashvili, Ana Tvaradze, Benjamin Neil, Laura James and Chris Russel

Introduction

Trench B was first opened on the 21st August 2002 and originally measured 7.5m x 7.5m. It was extended to its current size of 7.5m east-west x 20m north-south in 2003. Its southwest corner is located at 268973.14 E/ 4693271.18 N (WGS84 UTM Zone 38N). The trench is orientated fractionally off a true north-south alignment, with the northeast corner located at 268978.69 E/ 4693292.64 N. It is situated 30 metres to the north east of the Forty Martyrs Church, which was first constructed in the 6th century AD and still serves as the parish church for the village of Nokalakevi. Elements of the ecclesiastical boundary wall survive above ground to the south and west of the trench, along with a small square building with arches and a vaulted ceiling ten metres to the south. This would historically have served as an entrance to the precinct, and is used as a makeshift bell tower by the current church authorities. Trench B is located on the northern edge of the 'lower town' of historic Nokalakevi, where flatter ground gives way to the steep hillside to the north (Figure 5.1).

It was decided to open a 7.5m by 7.5m area at this location, partly to further expose a north-south wall that extended northwards from the 'bell tower', and partly because of the results revealed in an adjacent trench excavated in 1997/8 by the S. Janashia Museum expedition to Nokalakevi. This trench was located to the east of the current Trench B and produced, from its lower layers, examples of double-headed ceramic zoomorphic figurines dated to the 8th to 7th centuries B.C. It was hoped that Trench B would provide further clarification of the internal structures in the vicinity of the ecclesiastical complex and also of the deposits associated with the earlier ritual figurines.

Annual reports were produced which discuss the progress in detail (Everill 2003; Everill 2005a; Everill 2005b; Everill et al 2011; Grant et al 2010; Lomitashvili et al 2005, 2006, 2007, 2010, 2011, and Forthcoming;), however, the trench can currently be divided into two principal zones of interest:

1. a predominantly Christian cemetery first established in the early Byzantine period (about the 5th/6th century AD), revealed in the southwest corner of the trench. This has produced 35 burials in excavations from 2002-2010, with two further partial burials revealed beyond the crude wall which defines the cemetery zone. This wall measures between 0.8m and 0.92m wide, with a

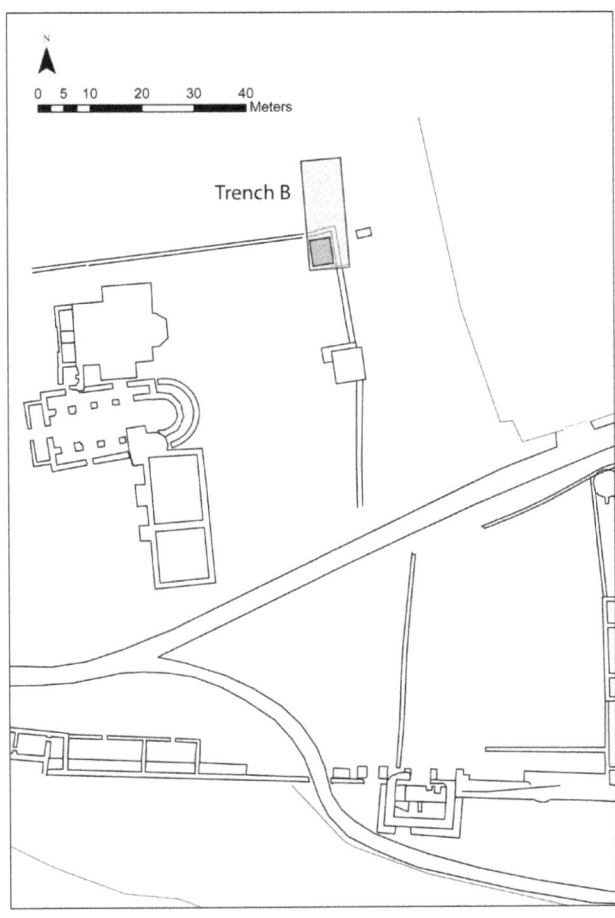

Figure 5.1 Location of Trench B by Forty Martyrs Church, showing 2009 excavation area within the cemetery walls

maximum surviving height of 1m. It was constructed from a mixture of riverstone; large, natural limestone boulders; and small, dressed limestone blocks, possibly robbed from the first two phases of fortification wall (4th – 5th century AD). It also includes one large, dressed limestone block, presumably robbed from the final, early Byzantine (6th century AD) phase of fortifications, as a cornerstone at the outside northeast corner. This indicates that the cemetery wall must certainly post-date the mid-6th century, though it is not known precisely when the fortifications ceased to be maintained. The requirement to preserve the wall precluded the archaeological assessment of underlying layers, but it seems likely that it was constructed no earlier than the 17th century, possibly replacing an earlier boundary.

2. a Hellenistic period clay and timber structure and associated deposits located towards the north of the trench

The contexts excavated will be discussed further below. Trench B was extensively excavated from 2002 to 2005, with a decision taken to focus on Trench A from 2006. The cemetery zone of Trench B was returned to in 2009, and the entire trench was once again reopened in 2010.

Thirty seven human burials have been excavated in Trench B, of which all bar two were within the 5m² area of the northeast corner of the cemetery exposed in the southwest of the trench. The intercutting nature of many of the burials, combined with associated 5th/6th century AD material culture in some graves, and the apparent survival of coffin timber in one other appear to suggest that the cemetery was in use from the early Byzantine period through to the 20th century, with an hiatus in use from about the 9th to the 17th centuries when Nokalakevi appears to have been all but abandoned. All bar three burials appear to have been laid out in a standard Christian manner. Skeletons **304**, **377** and **392** were supine and orientated north-south (feet to the south) and may represent a socially liminal family group buried at the northeast corner of the cemetery.

Archaeologically, Trench B was sealed by a number of thick layers representing several episodes of colluvial movement. The upper layers contained a very mixed assortment of finds – plastic and metalwork dating from the second half of the 20th century; 19th century pottery and metalwork; Byzantine pottery and glass and Hellenistic pottery. Photographs of the area around the site, taken in the 1960s and 1970s, show the hillside to the north under low shrub, rather than mature trees like today. Schneider recorded the line of the fortification walls and some of his plans show the cemetery walls still clearly above ground at this point. Putting these facts together suggests that the hillside was cleared of vegetation to allow further investigation and this resulted in a substantial quantity of material from the hill being deposited around the area of Trench B in the last 70 years. If the tree-felling was for the benefit of, or resulting from the work of, the first archaeologist to excavate in Nokalakevi, it is ironic that these actions appear to have ultimately led to the burial of the walls and the creation of a new archaeological record.

2002 Season

Trench B was opened on the 21st August 2002. Excavation began with the stripping of turf and topsoil (context **100**) by a team of local workmen under archaeological supervision. It was unclear initially how much material had been deposited through colluvial movement from the hillside to the north. At first it was thought that a quantity of rubble from a collapsed wall higher up the slope was present beneath the topsoil, however in situ mortared blocks of limestone were unearthed after 0.1 to 0.15m of material had been removed during cleaning. Initial

Figure 5.2: Walls 104 and 105 being exposed in 2002, looking west

investigations appeared to indicate remnants of a north-south wall (**104**) but also fragments of an east-west aligned wall (**105**) although initially no relationship between the two could be ascertained. The removal of a light rubble layer with patches of mortar (**101**) to the southwest of the area and a considerably more robust layer of rubble (**102**) to the north of the second wall (**105**) revealed that in fact the two walls did join to form a corner. With the removal of a further rubble layer (**103**) in the east of the area the wall structures were clarified (Figure 5.2). Layer **101** was a mixed deposit measuring approximately 1m thick. It was confined predominantly to the area between the walls and the southern limit of excavation. Considerable quantities of potsherds were recovered dating from the 4th century BC to the 17th century AD with an additional two fragments of transfer-printed stoneware depicting, quite improbably, a 19th century street scene of Horse Guards Parade in London (Everill 2012). Also present within the deposit were animal bones representing the main domesticated species (sheep/goat, pig and cow) and fragments of human radius, pelvis, mandible and ulna.

Layer **102**, north of wall **105**, consisted of similar large limestone blocks, averaging 0.25m x 0.15m x 0.1m in size. It measured 0.6m thick but contained a higher density of rubble than either layers **101** or **103**. The soil matrix within this layer was dark and humic and it appeared that the rubble represented the partial collapse of wall **105**, but also quite probably the process of larger limestone rubble accumulating against the northern face of **105** as a result of colluvial action. As with layer **101** there was a large quantity of pottery, animal bone and ceramic building material (CBM) from many different periods as one would expect to find in layers formed in this manner.

Layer **103** on the other hand was the slightest of the three rubble layers. The limestone blocks averaged 0.15m x 0.1m x 0.05m and the rubble was denser towards the south of the trench where the slope began to break onto a more level area. It was situated to the east of the north-south wall **104** and colluvial movement, combined with partial collapse of this wall, would seem to account for this pattern of deposition. Also found within this layer was a substantial fragment of a human femur and distal humerus, presumably from a disturbed burial further up the slope.

The construction of walls **104** and **105** was uncoursed with predominantly unfaced limestone blocks, large rounded river cobbles and robbed earlier masonry laid in mortar (Figure 5.3). The joining between the two walls was partially accomplished by use of a large, faced, limestone block, measuring 0.65m x 0.8m x 0.5m that had clearly been salvaged from the 6th century fortifications and re-used as a cornerstone. A similar provenance was also suspected for some of the larger pieces of limestone rubble within the walls, although the presence of river cobbles suggests that other local materials were being utilised. Construction appears to have been directly onto the contemporary ground surface with little or

no foundation. This is a strong factor in explaining the subsequent bowing and lean in wall **105** created by the pressure of colluvial materials on its northern face.

Within the enclosure created by walls **104** and **105** excavation continued beyond the rubble layer **101**. In the small area of Trench B outside the walls work was suspended after the removal of layers **102** and **103** had revealed layer **106** – a dark brown clay-silt with approximately 20% inclusions of fine to moderate limestone fragments. This was, in part, due to safety concerns of over-exposing the wall which had clearly already been weakened in places, but also because the small area would become increasingly difficult to work in. Now that work was concentrated within the walls the removal of layer **101** revealed what appeared to be a buried topsoil (**303**) and only a matter of centimetres from that interface were found the first indications of human inhumations in the north-west corner of the enclosed area. The first bones (**108**) were an assortment of long bones arranged roughly east-west and were nearly dismissed as a disturbed burial when the articulated skeleton of a child (**111**) was found close by. Continued careful excavation revealed that there were two articulated adult skeletons underneath, one (**114**) cutting the other (**117**). It seems likely, following osteological analysis, that the bones that make up **108** are in fact disturbed elements of **117** which were afterwards reburied on top of **114**. All were orientated east-west and there were no grave goods by which to date the burials. It seems most likely that the burials were not exactly contemporary, but that only a short period of time elapsed between them. It is also very tempting to view these remains as representing a family group with a male and female in their early twenties joined later by a child. The stratigraphy is somewhat complicated by the fact that individual cuts were not apparent during excavation. This is due mainly to the gross similarity between the fills and the layer the graves were dug through (**303**). At this stage it was becoming clear that the "buried topsoil" layer (**303**) was in fact a cemetery soil - the result of intercutting graves and the mixing of up-cast with humic material. It was a dark browny-grey, sandy clay with approximately 20% angular and sub-angular limestone fragments (average 50mm x 50mm) and abraded pieces of CBM. It is consequently reasonable to assume that it indicates fairly accurately the extent of the burial area. In the last days of the 2002 season these skeletons were recorded and lifted and as work continued in the southern part of the enclosed area a further human skeleton (**300**) was revealed. It was decided that this skeleton should be covered and protected until we could return in 2003 to excavate it properly.

The dates of the enclosure walls and the burials within them are currently subject to a great deal of debate. Based on the crude form of the walls it is felt that they most likely date to the 17th/18th centuries AD. During this period, more noticeably than before, riverstone was utilised in wall building alongside old Byzantine blocks salvaged from crumbling walls.

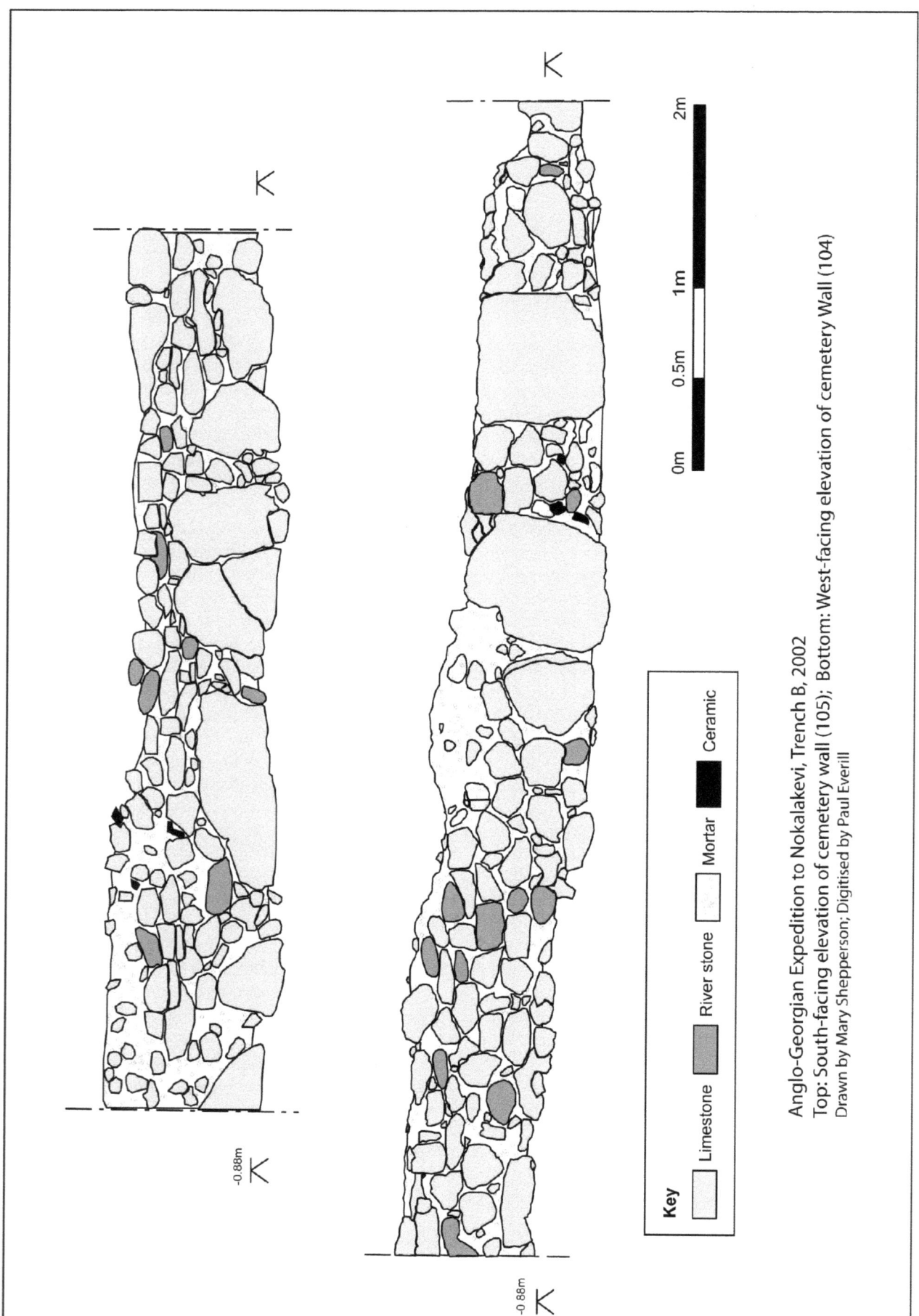

Anglo-Georgian Expedition to Nokalakevi, Trench B, 2002
Top: South-facing elevation of cemetery wall (105); Bottom: West-facing elevation of cemetery Wall (104)
Drawn by Mary Shepperson; Digitised by Paul Everill

Key
Limestone
River stone
Mortar
Ceramic

Figure 5.3 Elevations of the cemetery walls revealed in Trench B

2003 Season

Work began on Monday 25th August after the plastic sheeting and moderate backfill laid down at the end of the 2002 season had been removed. It had been decided to extend Trench B so that the stratigraphy outside the walls could be examined in order to determine if there was any evidence of terracing, structures, or further burials further up the slope. An extra 12.5m was measured out northwards making the total size of the trench 7.5m x 20m. It was felt that layers **100**, **101**, **102** and **103** represented reasonably modern (certainly post-medieval) colluvial movement and, as such were not archaeologically significant. These layers were removed by workmen under archaeological supervision. This topsoil/ overburden layer produced a large quantity of pottery and CBM from Hellenistic wares to modern glazed ceramics, as well as a disturbed burial of a large, robust male aged 25-30 found by workmen to the north, represented only by disarticulated leg, foot, pelvis and skull fragments.

At a depth of approximately 1m, in the north of the trench, the rubble came down onto **326**. This layer is a mid-brown, silty clay with a high percentage of degraded daub and charcoal within its matrix, including a large burnt beam measuring approximately 1m x 0.20m. Excavation of this layer was not possible during the 2003 season as it was only in the last few days that the workmen achieved this depth, but there was a strong indication of the close proximity of timber framed building(s). Approximately 7m south of the northern edge of Trench B, layer **326** appeared to be overlain by **106** which continued to the south.

Archaeological work this year was almost entirely limited to the excavation of nine further burials and the gradual excavation of cemetery soil **303**. The nine burials included **300** which had been left covered since last year and was found to be very badly truncated, presumably by other grave cuts. Also of interest was **316**, a male aged 35-40, which was found 0.1m below the grave of skeleton **117** and may well represent an addition to the hypothetical family group. There were three very interesting aspects of the burials excavated this year which warrant highlighting.

1) By the ankle of skeleton **304** was found a small, but finely executed gold artefact with a blue enamel background and two lines of ancient Greek lettering outlined in gold with white enamel inside (Figure 5.4). There is some damage to the lettering, but the top line appears to read: *damaged letter (possibly delta or lambda), ligatured omicron, upsilon, chi, two damaged letters*. Bottom line: *mu, alpha, mu, omicron, nu, omicron, nu.* A possible, though partial, reading of this lettering would therefore be: *"-oux-- mamonon".* The object was semi-circular and approximately 40mm x 20mm x 3mm, with a plain reverse side. The lack of fixings for jewellery suggests it was perhaps part of the decoration of a larger object. It is unclear, particularly from its location at the ankle, whether it is deliberate deposition within the grave

Figure 5.4: Gold and enamel object found in 2003

or an accidental loss and part of the mixed deposits of **303**. For caution it was recorded as being from layer **303**. On stylistic grounds (notably the form of the mu) it was dated to the 6th century by T. Kaukhchishvili. It is also interesting to note that skeleton **304**, a male in his fifties with a possible perimortem blade trauma to the maxillo-facial region of the skull, was the first north-south burial found in Trench B. A north-south orientated female adult (**392**) and neonate (**377**) were revealed close by in 2005 (see below). The most likely explanation for the north-south orientation of these adults and their location in the far northeast corner of the cemetery is that they were of a liminal status. If they belonged to a non-Christian faith, the fact that their arms were crossed over the abdomen might perhaps be explained by their burial by a Christian community unfamiliar with the details of their burial practice.

2) Skeletons **322** and **323**, a female and male respectively, were buried east-west with the head in the west. The former had been placed directly on top of the latter, with the head slightly to one side. They are not the only pair as **319**, a young child, was buried with **325**, an adult female, but they are interesting for two reasons. Firstly a copper alloy buckle, with an iron tang, provisionally dated to the 6th-10th centuries AD was found associated with **322**. This buckle was of a type associated with the Khazars, a semi-nomadic Turkic people who established a major empire in the Western Steppe and, despite adopting Judaism in the 8th century, remained an ally of the Byzantine world against the Persians and the Arabs**.** Skeleton **323** appeared to have suffered a perimortem blade trauma to the proximal right femur, which could certainly have been the cause of death. It is tempting to infer from this that both **322** and **323** were killed in the same incident during that period.

3) Skeleton **307**, a female aged 40-50 and possibly suffering with leprosy, was buried in a coffin. Traces of the wood survived in places, including a piece of the lid over the pelvis, and larger sections of the sides and base. Given the limited survival of archaeological wood in the ground at Nokalakevi, it seems likely that this burial is considerably later than others excavated this year, possibly dating to the 19th century.

2004 Season

The season began on Wednesday 21ˢᵗ July. Within the southern part of the walled enclosure it was clear that the cemetery soil **303** was still present and with it the possibility of further burials. In the north of the cemetery a brown layer (**340**), containing a large quantity of burnt daub and clay was revealed. This layer appeared to be very similar to layer **326**, north of the walls, which at the time led to it being interpreted as an early Byzantine occupation layer covering the entire trench and containing evidence of timber buildings. However, this hypothesis was proved incorrect through excavation in 2005.

Layer **326** initially appeared to be present only in the far northwest corner of the trench following the removal of **106** which continued to the east and south of it. Layer **106** was thought at this time to represent a continuation of the cemetery soil beyond the walls, indicating that they represented a later formalisation of the burial ground. This hypothesis also was subsequently proved incorrect, and only two, very partial and disturbed burials have been excavated beyond the cemetery walls. Instead the colluvial nature of **106** was apparently demonstrated by mixed finds from it, including a small gold earring with serpent heads which was dated to the Hellenistic period (Small Find NOK04/B 4). Having trowelled the whole trench it seemed that there was a line of lighter coloured material about 1m wide running directly north of the north-south wall **104**. Further investigation at the time was inconclusive, but it should be noted that in 2012 a fine rubble-filled ditch or palaeochannel [**458**] was observed in the south-facing trench edge. This feature had apparently been missed in plan, on account of it cutting colluvial rubble, but its rubbly fills contained Hellenistic and earlier pottery, and it was apparently backfilled in that area prior to the construction of the Hellenistic building (see 2005, below). It appears that the projected line of the feature seen in section in 2012 would have been close to the colour change observed in 2004, which was perhaps therefore a result of differential drying/ draining of the soil, or the remnants of a bank. This may also account for the apparent relationship with the north-south wall **104**, as the cemetery might quite conceivably have utilised an earlier boundary, later formalised with the construction of wall.

Removing layer **106** to the northeast of the trench exposed more of **326** including further structural elements within it. Four metres east of the burnt beam found in 2003, an area of clean and very compact, dark brown clay with large limestone blocks underneath was revealed. This provided further indication of a well-built timber structure which at this stage was assumed to date to no earlier than the early Byzantine period lying, as it did, directly underneath the substantial colluvial deposits.

To the south of the exposed occupation layer (**326**), removal of the colluvial soil (**106**) revealed a similar, probably colluvial deposit, layer **339**. The removal of this layer revealed the brown occupation layer (**326**) underlying it. The underlying topography was now seen to be much steeper than had previously been thought.

As well as the two disturbed burials beyond the cemetery, nine more were excavated within the walled enclosure during the 2004 season. Many were truncated, demonstrating that the cemetery had been in use for an extended period. On a number of occasions excavations revealed a truncated burial with the disturbed elements reburied, disarticulated but orientated east west, on top of the more recent burial.

Two burials in particular provided special interest. Skeleton **328** was a partially articulated juvenile with a crude copper ring (Small Find NOK04/B 3) consisting of one piece of copper alloy overlapping itself. The ring was still *in situ* on a finger of the right hand. It seems possible that this was an adult-sized ring that was modified to fit a smaller, adolescent finger.

Skeleton **362** (found to the southern edge of the trench) was also particularly interesting, not least because it was clearly one of the earlier burials and as such the fill was noticeably different from the ubiquitous cemetery soil (**303**), which had until now made positive identification of the grave cuts virtually impossible. Not only was this a nearly complete, articulated adult burial with a clearly defined grave cut, but it also had a complete, lugged Byzantine pot (about 0.2m maximum diameter at its shoulder) beyond the skull in the western edge of the grave. This represented an interesting depositional practice with an apparently early Christian burial in this area.

2005 Season

The 2005 season began on the 1ˢᵗ August and following an initial trowelling two key areas of focus were identified: the structural elements of the clay and timber building discovered at the north of the trench in 2004; and the continued excavation of any further human remains from inside the cemetery (Figure 5.5). Work in the initial stages of the season revealed a number of important pieces of information. These in turn forced a rethink of interpretations developed at the end of the 2004 season.

Firstly, it soon became clear that the layer of burnt daub and clay (**326**), north of the cemetery, had not yet been fully exposed. Instead there remained a layer of quite fine limestone rubble, possibly colluvial material, over a large area in the north of the trench. This rubble was assigned the number **379**. Colluvial deposits **106** and **339** had been removed in 2004 and in reinterpreting their relationship it was now felt that these soils were broadly similar, with **379** almost certainly representing the denser elements within this broader colluvial deposit overlying the demolition layer **326**.

Secondly, at the far north of the trench it became clear that the two or three large limestone blocks that had

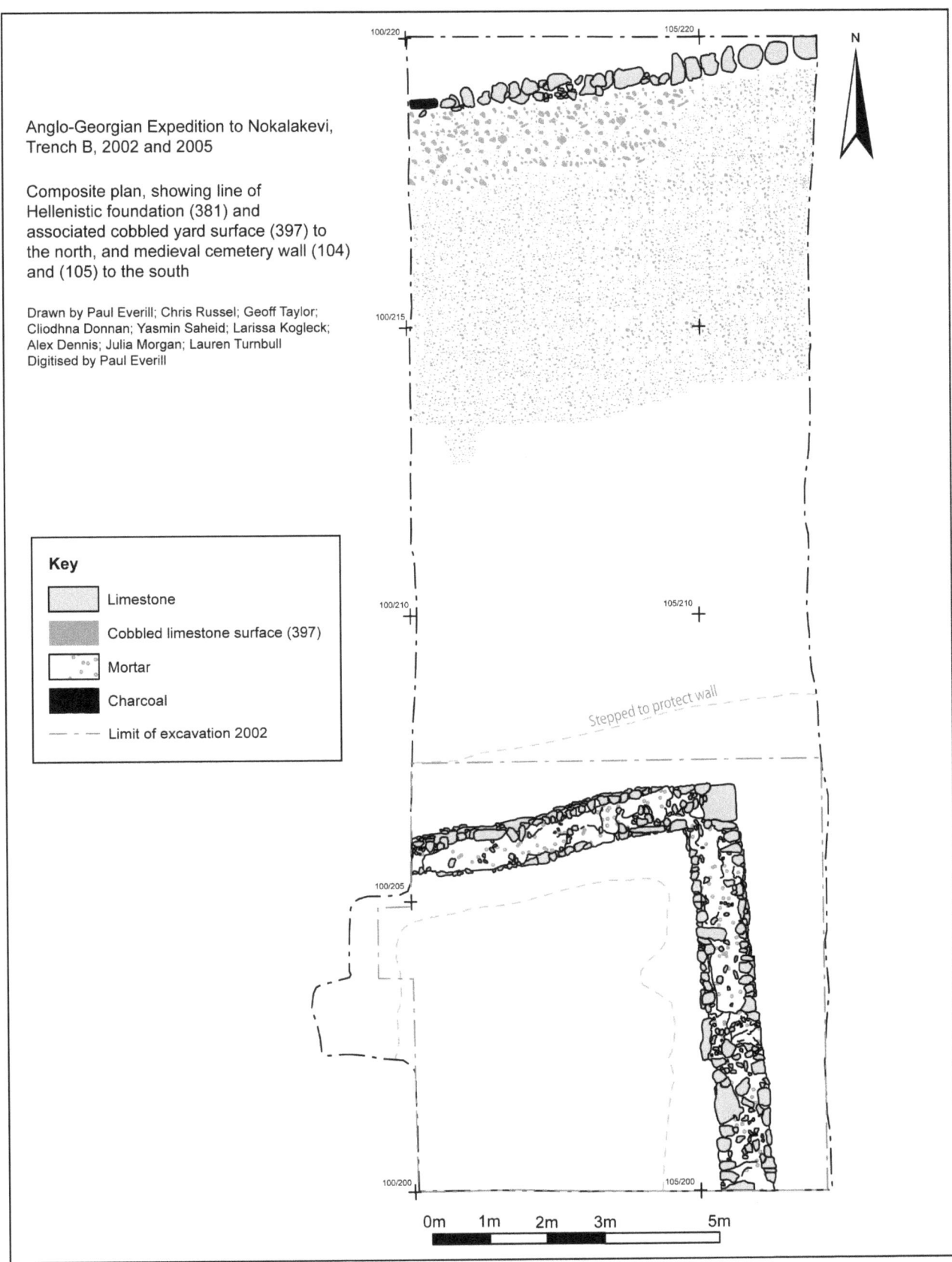

Anglo-Georgian Expedition to Nokalakevi, Trench B, 2002 and 2005

Composite plan, showing line of Hellenistic foundation (381) and associated cobbled yard surface (397) to the north, and medieval cemetery wall (104) and (105) to the south

Drawn by Paul Everill; Chris Russel; Geoff Taylor; Cliodhna Donnan; Yasmin Saheid; Larissa Kogleck; Alex Dennis; Julia Morgan; Lauren Turnbull
Digitised by Paul Everill

Key

- Limestone
- Cobbled limestone surface (397)
- Mortar
- Charcoal
- — ∙ — Limit of excavation 2002

Stepped to protect wall

0m 1m 2m 3m 5m

Figure 5.5: Trench B, 2005

been exposed in 2004 were actually merely part of a line of stones (**381**) that ran the complete width of the trench. This line linked the burnt beam at the west of the trench (which had first been exposed by workmen during the trench extension in 2003) with an area of dark reddish brown clay at the north-east. Removing **379**, a layer of rubbly colluvium, the layer of burnt clay and daub (**326**) was shown to cover much of the north of the trench. It became clear that this represented the final collapse of this building, with sections of daub wall still fairly coherent and containing the impressions of wattle and burnt remains of wooden posts. This was the case particularly toward the west of the trench and signs of heat-scorching on some of the stones that formed the base of the walls suggested that the destructive fire had its seat in this area. This was also close to the charcoal beam that was found lying *in situ* on top of the stone foundation (**381**).

The method of construction can be inferred from the small area of the building exposed, and is consistent with the evidence of analogous buildings revealed from 2006 onwards in Trench A. It involved the laying of an unbonded line of large limestone blocks as a foundation, or sill, onto which was placed a wooden beam or beams. Upright posts measuring approximately 0.1m in diameter, such as the ones found as charcoal, or as impressions in pieces of daub, were fixed to this horizontal beam. A wattle and daub wall was constructed on this framework. There was no archaeological evidence for the roofing material, which is most likely to have been wooden shingles or thatch. The areas of very clean, compact red clay (**380**) north of the foundation (**381**) are almost certainly surviving elements of a 'beaten earth' floor common in this kind of structure though not, it should be noted, observed in any of the Trench A structures. To the south of the building, a large area of crude cobbling (**397**) was revealed. This is clearly some kind of surface. It is not metalled enough to be a road, nor is it confined in any way, but merely peters out away from the building. It appears instead to be a yard surface and there is an indication of a step up to the wall, where a dump of domestic rubbish (**388**), predominantly pottery, was found. This may indicate the presence of a doorway close by.

As was stated above, the initial interpretation of this structure, being the first significant archaeological feature revealed underneath colluvial deposits at the north of the trench, was that it might be early Byzantine. However, during removal of the demolition/ collapse layer (**326**) such a large quantity of Hellenistic period pottery was recovered from immediately above the yard surface (**397**), including several large and unabraded sherds, that the building had to be reinterpreted.

Four further human burials were excavated within the cemetery, and one more exposed (**395**). Two of these were another north-south burial (**392**), which was a very well preserved adult female, and a north-south neonate (**377**) to the east of the adult. The latter was situated directly up against the cemetery wall. It had been so badly exposed

and disturbed by soil erosion from under the wall over the previous year that the placement of the burial could not be planned, and the bone was simply retrieved. As has been noted above, **392** and **377** were in close proximity to an older male (**304**), which was also orientated north-south and situated just to the west of the female.

After the 2005 season there was a hiatus in excavation within Trench B, with resources and staffing being focused on Trench A from 2006 to 2008.

2009 Season

The cemetery area of Trench B was reopened by a small team in 2009 with work beginning on Monday 5th July. The removal of the daub rich layer **340**, first revealed in 2004, exposed rubble layer **413** which appeared to represent colluvial material underlying the cemetery as no further burials were detected in this area. Where it was exposed, layer **413** appeared to be relatively homogenous in nature. Of the five skeletons excavated during the 2009 season only **411** appeared to be of an adult. All were aligned east-west and supine. Skeletons **403** and **406**, similarly aged juveniles, appeared to have been buried side by side. It is interesting to note that there were items of jewellery associated with two of the burials (**406** and **408**) suggesting that they may have been buried with these items. Skeleton **406** was found to have a copper alloy earring (Small Find NOK09/B 3) to the left side of the skull, and with skeleton **408** a copper alloy earring, or pendant, (Small Find NOK09/B 5) was found in close proximity to the ribcage.

2010 Season

Work began on Monday 19th July. The cemetery enclosure had accumulated a lot of silt and vegetation since the 2009 season, which had seen substantial rainfall. Furthermore the northern part of the trench, beyond the cemetery wall, had not been actively excavated since 2005 and consequently was dominated by vegetation and a large quantity of silt and colluvial material.

In the north of the trench, layer **397** – a crudely metalled surface consisting of highly compacted small cobbles and stones within a greyish brown matrix – was first exposed in 2005 and was interpreted as a yard surface associated with the Hellenistic period building to the immediate north of the layer. The structure of the building will not be excavated until it can be fully exposed in the future, but the recording and removal of **397** this year revealed the full extent of the underlying layers **425** and **423**. Layer **425** consisted of large limestone rubble within a light greyish brown silty clay. Given its location immediately adjacent to the Hellenistic wall (**381**) it was interpreted as a structural 'make-up' deposit which may have provided support for an external walkway/ surface attached to the southern aspect of the building. Layer **423** was a 0.2m thick colluvial deposit consisting of a dark greyish brown silty clay with frequent limestone inclusions and chalk flecks.

The removal of **425** and **423** revealed two very similar layers – **422** and **429**. Layer **422**, towards the north of the trench, consisted of large angular cobbles within a matrix of silty clay. It contained frequent inclusions of charcoal and burnt clay/ daub. Further south, towards the cemetery wall, was found **429**. Initially this layer seemed identical to **422**, and was therefore not assigned its own number until both deposits had dried and a colour difference became apparent: **422** was mid to light greyish brown, whereas **429** was mid brownish grey. There appeared to be a clear demarcation between the two deposits that runs east-west across the trench. Neither layer was fully excavated in 2010 (Figure 5.6).

The demarcation between contexts **422** and **429**, aligned roughly east-west across the trench and apparently following a contour, may indicate underlying topography.

Three further burials were excavated during the 2010 season, all from areas in the cemetery in which colluvial material (**413**) had not yet been exposed. All of the inhumations had been disturbed by cemetery activity to some extent, with **415** being the most disturbed. Items of jewellery were found associated with skeleton **427**. A copper bracelet was found around the right wrist and three beads were found near the right clavicle and thoracic vertebrae. Part of a bronze earring was recovered

from the grave fill. These burials brought the total from this area to 35 between 2002 and 2010 (Figure 5.7). The removal of further cemetery deposits continued to reveal the underlying colluvial layer **413** and by the end of the 2010 season, though it was not known at the time, all bar one of the burials from this corner of the cemetery had been exposed.

Conclusion

As previously outlined in the conclusion to Chapter 4 the excavation of Trench B, like Trench A, has contributed to our understanding of the site, and continues to be excavated as this volume is prepared. By 2010, however, the trench could be characterised as representing two complex stratified sequences, both sealed by a series of significant colluvial events (Figure 5.8). The south of the trench, the original location of Trench B, produced evidence for a predominantly Christian cemetery first established in the early Byzantine period (about the 5th/6th century AD). This area produced 35 burials in excavations from 2002-2010, with two further partial burials revealed beyond the crude wall which defines the cemetery zone. It seems likely that this wall was constructed no earlier than the 17th century, possibly replacing an earlier boundary. The intercutting nature of many of the burials, combined with 5th/6th century AD artefacts in some graves and the apparent survival of coffin timber in one other, appear to suggest that the cemetery was in use from the early Byzantine period through to the early 20th century,

Figure 5.6: Trench B at the end of the 2010 season

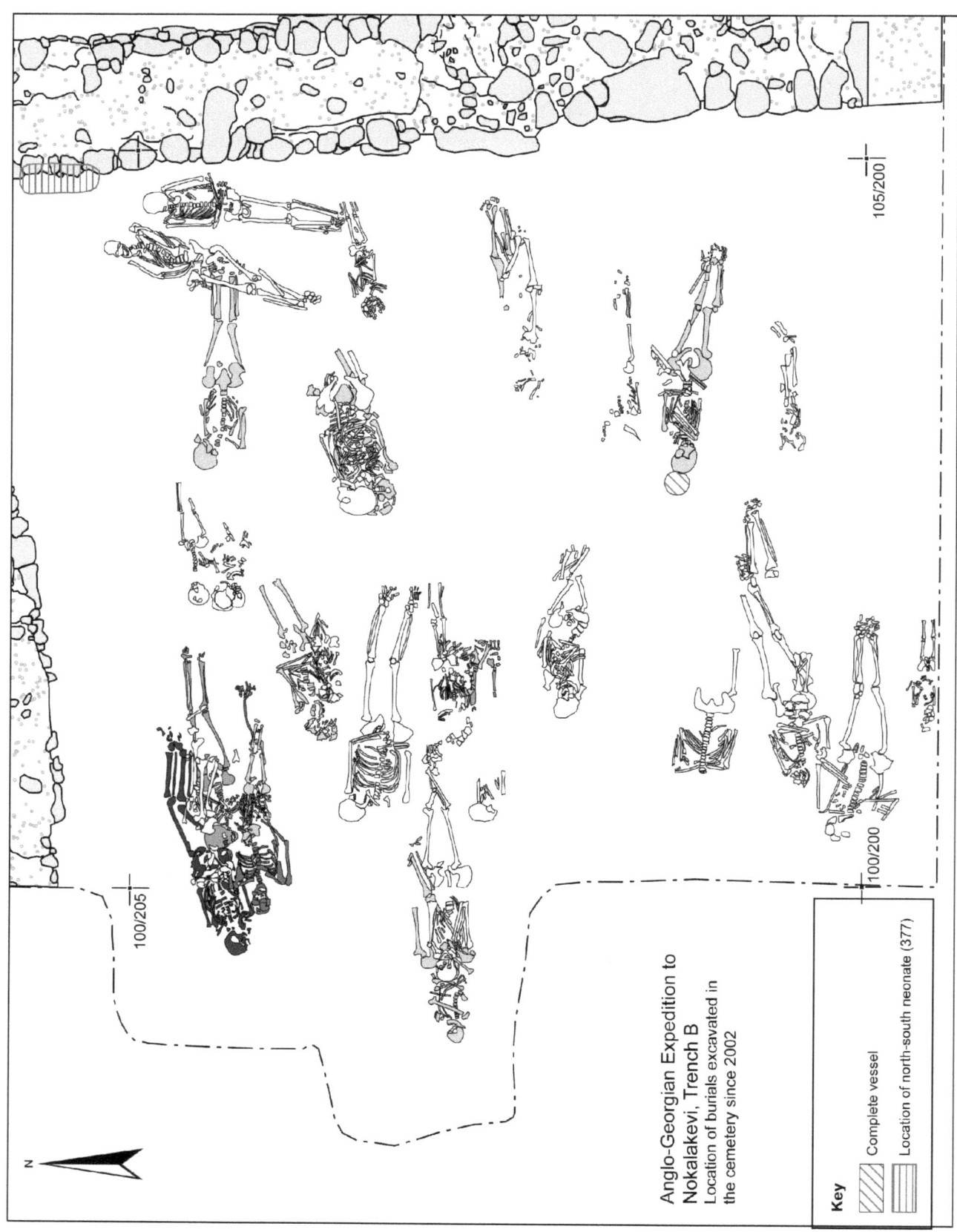

Anglo-Georgian Expedition to
Nokalakevi, Trench B
Location of burials excavated in
the cemetery since 2002

Key

Complete vessel

Location of north-south neonate (377)

Figure 5.7: Burials from the south of Trench B (Grid coordinates are site grid, in metres)

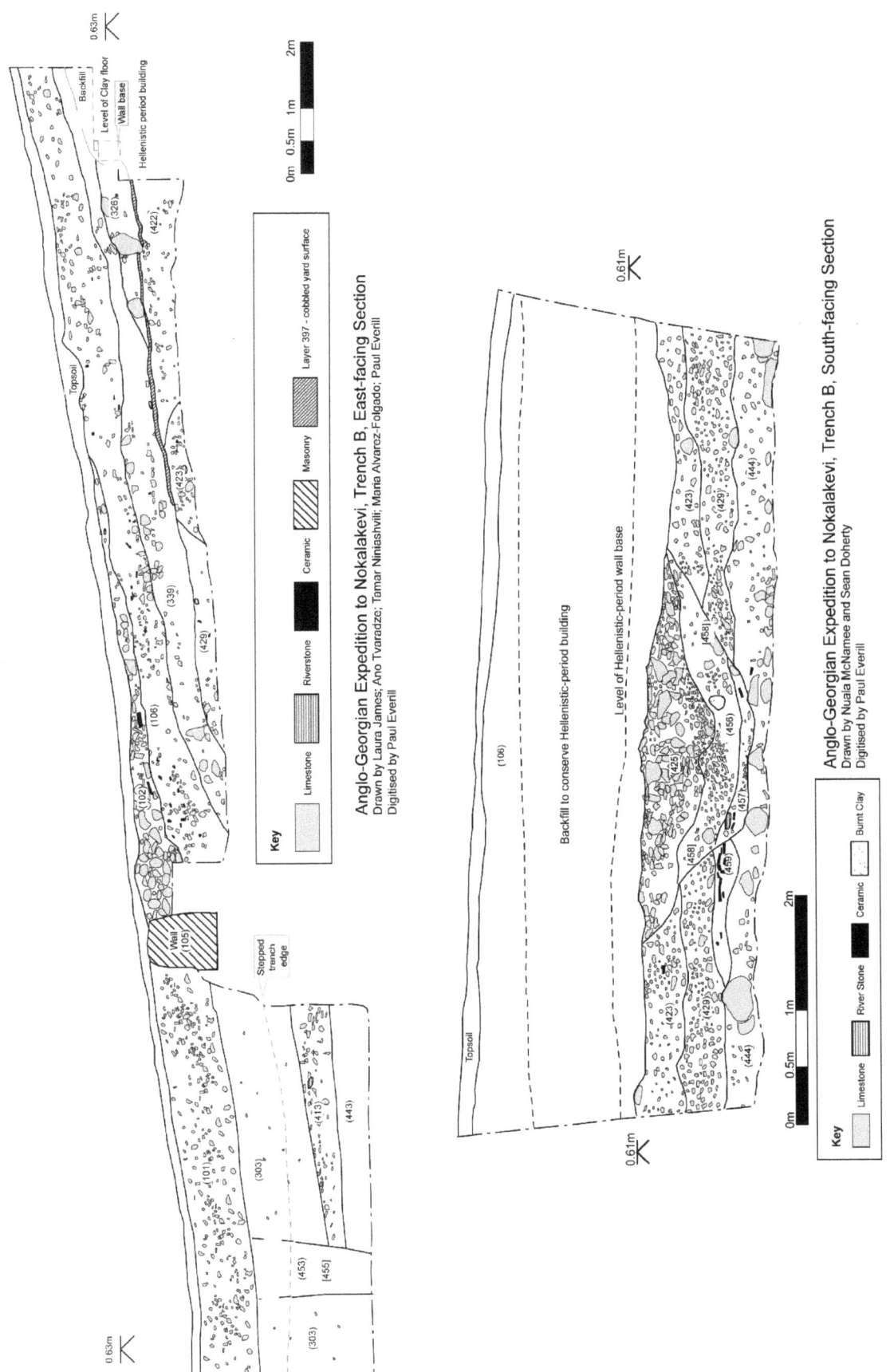

Figure 5.8 Trench B, section drawings

with a possible hiatus between the 9th and 17th centuries. At the north of the trench, and somewhat surprisingly, a significant series of colluvial deposits sealed a Hellenistic clay and timber structure and associated deposits. This underscores the oddity of the apparent absence of layers from the first three centuries AD at the site, and perhaps also indicates that settlement in the early Byzantine period was not as dense as might have been expected. However, a series of absolute dates for the sequence will allow for more detail to be applied in future analyses.

Bibliography

Everill, P. 2003. *Anglo Georgian Expedition to Nokalakevi: Trench B: 2002-2003*. Unpublished AGEN report.

Everill, P. 2005a. *Anglo Georgian Expedition to Nokalakevi: Trench B: 2004*. Unpublished AGEN report.

Everill, P. 2005b. *Anglo Georgian Expedition to Nokalakevi: Trench B: 2005*. Unpublished AGEN report.

Everill, P. 2012. Excavating a memory: the British in Georgia. *Anatolian Studies* 62: 153-162

Everill, P., Slater, A., James, L. and Colvin, I. 2011a. *Anglo-Georgian Expedition to Nokalakevi: Interim report on excavations in 2010*. Unpublished AGEN report.

Grant, K., Russel, C. and Everill, P. 2010. *Anglo-Georgian Expedition to Nokalakevi: Interim report on excavations July 2009*. Unpublished AGEN report.

Lomitashvili, D., Lordkipanidze, B., Zamtaradze, M., Kebuladze, N., Kapanadze, T., Colvin, I., Everill, P. Neil, B., Ginns, A., and Connolly. D. 2005. Anglo-Georgian Expedition to Nokalakevi: Report on the International Archaeological Expedition to Nokalakevi 2004. Unpublished report (in Georgian)

Lomitashvili, D., Lordkipanidze, B., Zamtaradze, M. Kebuladze, N., Kapanadze, T., Colvin, I., Everill, P., Neil, B., Armour, N., and Murghulia, N. 2006. Anglo-Georgian Expedition to Nokalakevi; Report on the International Archaeological Expedition to Nokalakevi 2005. Unpublished report (in Georgian)

Lomitashvili, D., Lordkipanidze, B., Colvin, I., Neil, B., Kebuladze, N., Murghulia, N., and Zamtaradze, M. 2007. Anglo-Georgian Expedition to Nokalakevi; Report on the International Archaeological Expedition to Nokalakevi 2006. Unpublished report (in Georgian)

Lomitashvili, D., Tvalchrelidze, Z., Kebuladze, N., Murghulia, N., Bokeria, M., Kvavadze, E., Colvin, I., Everill, P., Timby, J., and Neil, B. 2010. Report on the Field Work in 2007 by the Georgian-British Nokalakevi Archaeological Expedition. *DZIEBANI Journal of Georgian archaeology*. №19: 51-57 (in Georgian)

Lomitashvili, D., Tvalchrelidze, Z., Kebuladze, N., Murghulia, N., Bokeria, M., Kvavadze, E, Colvin, I., Everill, P., Timby, J., and Neil, B. 2011. Report on the Field Work in 2008-2009 by the Georgian-British Nokalakevi Archaeological Expedition. *DZIEBANI Journal of Georgian archaeology*. №20: 140-153 (in Georgian)

Lomitashvili, D., Tvalchrelidze, Z., Kebuladze, N., Murghulia, N., Tvaradze, A., Bokeria, M., Kvavadze, E., Colvin, I., Everill, P., Timby, J., and Neil, B. Forthcoming. Report on the Field Work in 2010 by the Georgian-British Nokalakevi Archaeological Expedition. *DZIEBANI Journal of Georgian archaeology*. №21 (in Georgian)

CHAPTER SIX

Interim report on the pottery from the 2001-2010 excavations

By Jane Timby, Davit Lomitashvili and Rob Ixer

Introduction

Pottery is one the largest single categories of find to come from the ongoing Anglo-Georgian excavations at Nokalakevi and as such offers a range of possibilities for the interpretation of the site and for developing pottery studies in Western Georgia. Nokalakevi is one of a small number of sites to be excavated by a joint Anglo-Georgian team (cf Vickers and Kakhidze (2004)) introducing new methodologies in terms of site excavation and recording as well as learning from and developing local expertise. In terms of pottery it is perhaps the only site to date in Georgia where there has been an attempt to produce a quantified form and fabric record of the whole assemblage.

Work on the current trenches started in 2001 and it has been fortunate that the Georgian Head of the Anglo-Georgian Expedition, Professor Davit Lomitashvili, is, amongst many other things, a pottery expert. His thesis was focussed on the pottery from Western Georgia and thus his knowledge of local forms and chronology is unrivalled (Lomitashvili 2003). It is this knowledge that has underpinned the establishment of a chronology for the site and is based on the recognition of specific forms and the development of typological sequences based on stratigraphic associations both from this site and the religious complex at Vani (see below). At the time of writing the site chronology can be divided into three basic phases: Byzantine (c 4th-6th century AD); Hellenistic period (c 3rd-1st centuries BC) and early Antique (c 6th-4th centuries BC). Residual material from the 8th-7th centuries BC is featuring in the upper levels hinting at earlier occupation and odd finds of worked flint, stone and a distinctive handmade pottery suggest a phase of earlier prehistoric is likely on the site.

The excavation trenches, whilst not large in area, are complex in that there is a very high level of residuality present. This is a consequence not only of the general topography of the location at the base of a slope where deposits of colluvium have developed, but through on-going soil disturbances through various building works (see Chapters Two, Four and Five). Soil has been constantly moved through the digging of the defensive Byzantine wall, road construction near the entranceway, construction of buildings, digging of pits and postholes and the use of the area as a cemetery. This high level of residuality is reflected both in the intermixing of pottery from different periods but also a higher fragmentation rate.

Georgian pottery from all archaeological periods is virtually unknown outside the country. In part this is due to a general lack of detailed publication in accessible literature; it is also a consequence of the political history of the country and the structure of the education system. Archaeology is a relatively new academic discipline and one that even in Western countries has only developed extensively in the past 40 years or so. The author was invited to participate in the excavations in 2007 with the aim to introduce a systematic recording of the pottery assemblage, and to teach the students participating in the excavation how to process, record and draw pottery. There are clearly constraints in working on foreign assemblages both in terms of time and continuity. For reasons of security and further work the finds assemblages from each season's excavation are removed from the site and taken to the Georgian National Museum in Tbilisi. Before this happens the assemblages are scrutinised and a preliminary sort undertaken by the Georgian staff whereby featured or interesting sherds or groups are taken back to Tbilisi but other material is left at the local museum at Nokalakevi. For this reason between 2007 and 2010 the pottery has been rapidly sorted, quantified and recorded on site during the excavation season (see methodology below) (Timby 2007; 2008; 2009; 2010). The pottery recording work has also been carried out alongside a programme of restoration work undertaken by Dr Nino Kebuladze (see Chapter Seven). The assemblages from each season are scanned for joining sherds and when sufficient of these have been recovered the sherds are glued back together and conservation work undertaken to recreate the original vessel forms.

Potential of pottery studies

Perhaps one of the most important roles of pottery for the archaeologist is to provide a date for a particular horizon or feature on a site. This is however by no means the only use of pottery and there are a wide range of other areas it can inform on, for example: trade and distribution; function; social and economic status; settlement organisation; aspects of manufacture and ceramic technology; ritual activity; cultural expression; and the nature of archaeological deposits and site formation processes. The level to which these individual areas of study can be taken will vary from site to site and is reliant on many factors, not least size of assemblage; method of excavation and level of recording; type and complexity of site; level of expertise and time.

Chronology. Pottery itself is not inherently datable but relies upon a detailed study of the development of forms and fabrics through time, looking at the association of these types and creating sequences. These are generally dated by other means, for example, an historical event, inscriptions or coins or through the application of scientific dating techniques. Association with more datable fine wares is also a valuable tool for dating more local domestic wares. The importation of Greek fine wares provides a particularly useful datable horizon for several sites in Georgia, particularly the Greek settlements on the coastal plain.

Trade and distribution. Some pots are made and used locally; others are traded away from their production sites. The latter are often more specialised vessels such as fine table wares, or containers for other products, for example amphorae or large jars used for wine, oil or other comestibles. Vessels may be transferred from their source areas for a number of different reasons. These could include economic commercial transactions; political or diplomatic gifts; as personal possessions or souvenirs; or through military supply systems. In order to identify distributions of traded pots some insight has to be gained into the likely sources of individual pots. This is often done through the study of the fabrics and in particular the inclusions in the fabric. At the most basic level this can be done through macroscopic observation aided by the use of a binocular microscope. More sophisticated analyses can be undertaken using petrological or chemical analysis. Clays with a more distinctive mineralogical component are much easier to single out compared to those from areas of more sedimentary geology which tend to lack any distinctive inclusions. Likely source areas can be identified based on the mineralogy. Other attributes useful for identifying non-local products include vessel form, decoration or surface treatment and manufacturing technique.

The establishment of a distribution for a specific pottery type depends on the study of material from several sites. Also the likely mechanism by which pottery gets moved around needs to be considered, for example coastal or riverine transport, pack horses, army supply chains and the location of local markets.

Function. Identifying a likely function for a pot can be difficult unless there are clues such as sooting patterns on cooking vessels or lamps, internal residues of food or other material (for example, mortar, pigments, metal slag) or the vessel has a very distinctive shape which shows is to be designed for a specific purpose, for example pouring liquids. A pot designed for one purpose could have been subsequently used for another, for example, the use of an amphora as a burial vessel or as a water container. Some uses, particularly those of a more ritual or religious nature

dictated by cultural beliefs, cannot be ascertained. In some cases the choice of a particular temper might reflect the intended use of a pot be it for cooking where it needs to be able to withstand thermal shock or a vessel that allows slow evaporation through the walls to help cool the contained liquid. Most vessels appear to be designed for the transport, storage, processing and consumption of food and liquids. On this basis assemblages can be divided into six likely functional categories: (a) fine wares such as cups/ mugs, goblets, small bowls, platters and other drinking vessels used as tableware, entertaining or for display; (b) coarse-wares used for cooking and food processing (jars, bowls, dishes, sieves, lids, mortaria, luteria); (c) liquid carrying and dispensing vessels (flagon, spouted jars, jugs); (d) storage vessels (dolia, pithoi); (e) transport containers (amphora, sealable jars) and (f) specialised vessels such as lamps.

Vessel function can be studied using a combination of the fabric, form and size of the vessels, presence of residues and sometimes the context in which the vessel(s) were found.

Aspects of manufacture and ceramic technology. Details of manufacturing technology can be reconstructed by recording details of fabric, form, manufacturing techniques such as handmade, wheel-made, wheel-finished, slab built, or coil built. The application of handles, spouts can also be observed as well as the use of decorative motifs and / or surface treatments such as burnishing, wiping, or the application of a slip.

Social, cultural and economic status. Pottery as a reflection of social status or group identity is rarely studied in great detail although there is potential to create a profile for different sites in terms of the quantities of traded wares, fine wares, and range of vessel types, locations of recovery and patterns of use. The proportions of decorated versus undecorated wares and the nature of the designs used may also play a role in identifying cultural links. Sites with a higher proportion of fine or traded specialist wares or a more diverse range of wares are generally regarded as being of higher status.

Settlement organisation. A study of the distribution of different fabrics and forms across a site may inform about different activities or processes carried on in different areas of that site.

Nature of archaeological deposits and site formation processes. Understanding how and why the pottery gets deposited where it is found is a complex area of study. It is important to be able to recognise redeposited or residual material in order to achieve an accurate assessment of the date of a context. Some level of interpretation may be achieved by looking at the fragmentation rate of the sherds, the degree of abrasion of the edges and surfaces, and the general composition of the group. Cross-joining of sherds across contexts can also be useful in terms of site interpretation. Negative features such as pits and ditches tend to contain better preserved material compared to, for example, a road surface or other surface layer.

Methodology

In order to address some of the potential uses of pottery outlined above it is necessary to create a coherent, systematic record of the assemblage. From 2007 to 2010 the author studied the pottery assemblage, and its stratigraphic situation, over a two-week period during each summer excavation season. Due to logistical and financial constraints no attempt has yet been made to recreate a similar record for the 2001-2006 material, although in theory it is possible to revisit selected components of the assemblage, for example, the amphorae. This gives an insight into the range of vessels present but not the relative proportions. The recording work has been carried out with the assistance of the students, and the whole process has been very much a learning curve for all involved.

The pottery from each recorded context has been sorted into fabric groups based on the nature of the constituents of the clays taking into account the types of inclusions, their size and frequency. Fabric codes were used to designate different fabrics. An alpha-numeric system has been used where letters have been used to indicate the major inclusion(s) present followed by a unique Arabic number, thus LI= limestone; CA = calcite; SA = sand etc. PY (pyroxene) has been temporarily used to designate black sand (volcanic fabrics) until the precise geology of these can be determined microscopically. A common name is sometimes used to define certain fabrics, for example Sinopean mortaria, Colchian amphorae etc. Attributes relevant to the definition of a fabric include colour, firing, hardness, feel and texture, and inclusions. In addition to their identification the inclusions are defined by their frequency, shape and size. Frequency (after Shvetsov, as described in Terry and Chillinger [1955]) is defined by rare (less than 3%), sparse (5-7%), moderate (10-15%), common (20-25%), very common (30-40%) and abundant (40-50%). Size ranges commonly used are very fine (up to 0.1mm); fine (0.1-0.25mm), medium (0.25-0.5mm), coarse (0.5-1.0mm) and very coarse (larger than 1.00mm). Once sorted into fabric groups and assigned a code, the sherds from each context were counted and weighed and the details filled in on a pottery-recording sheet. Rim sherds were separated out and measured for diameter and the percentage of rim present (estimated vessel equivalent) using a chart. The rims were coded to basic form, for example, jar/ cooking pot (dergi), pithoi, lamp, with sub-divisions for more specific details of rim shape. This area of work constantly requires modification and updating as a greater understanding the repertoire of vessels is gained particularly when dealing with small fragments. To assist in this process most of the defined types were drawn and identified through consultation with Professor Davit Lomitashvili. Other diagnostic pieces such as handles, bases, spouts etc were noted on the recording form along with any decoration or surface treatment. Ultimately the goal is to define a form type series.

The data from the pottery recording sheets was entered into an MS Excel spreadsheet. A quantified summary of this can be found in Table 1.

Typology and chronology

The principles of typological classification

The typological classification of the pottery and other finds from Nokalakevi was the subject of a doctoral thesis (Lomitashvili 1990; 2003). In studying the finds a similar model was adopted to that used at Vani (Lortkipanidze *et al.* 1981) with a few adjustments to take in to account local variations specific to Nokalakevi. The ceramic typology was based on the form of the vessels which is determined by its functional purpose. Obviously functional division is subjective, because specific vessels could be used for a different purpose as well as the conventional one. For example, in the establishment of ceramic forms, the size of the vessel will determine whether a form is a wine storage jar (*kvevri*) or a large clay pitcher (*dergi*) which shared a similar form to wine storage jars.

The ceramic material was divided into the following groups:

a) Agricultural vessels and objects connected with the procurement, processing and storage of food: *kvevri / pithoi*; amphorae; spouted bowls (*luteria*); spindle-whorls; fishing-net weights and lamps.
b) Cooking wares: pots [*kotnebi*]; cooking pots [*kvabebi*]; earthenware bread-baking dishes [*ketsebi*] and lids [*khupebi*].
c) Table vessels for the serving and consumption of food and drink: plates; bowls [*jamebi*]; pitchers (without a handle) [*dokebi*]; jugs (pot-bellied, broad-lipped with a handle) [*kheladebi*]
d) Building ceramics: brick, tile; ceramic pipes.
e) Ritual or cult items; communion bread stamps; incense burners.
f) Transport vessels used for the movement of wine, oil and other consumables: amphorae.

The 2001-2010 excavations have produced a useful stratigraphic sequence of pottery from the two excavated trenches (Trenches A and B) that demonstrate the development of ceramic styles through time. The sequence is not clear cut as both areas investigated have been used as burial grounds; thus the soil has been continuously disturbed and redeposited. Added to this is the proximity of Trench A to the defensive walls, the construction of which must have caused further disturbance to nearby deposits and the location of both trenches at the base of a steep slope which is likely to have bought down colluvial deposits containing mixed finds from upslope. However, from comparison with other known and independently dated sequences from sites with datable Greek imports – such as the religious centre at Vani and coastal settlements such as Pichvnari – certain vessel forms and techniques of decoration can be identified as characteristic of different chronological periods.

At present the excavated sequence at Nokalakevi can be divided into four main chronological periods. At the time of writing the pre-Antique/ early Iron Age levels (8th-7th century BC) are being excavated and the pottery and ceramic objects from these levels will be reported on in a future publication. These levels are succeeded by the Early Antique phase of activity dating to the 6th-4th centuries BC, which in turn are followed by the local equivalent of the Hellenistic period (the beginning of the 3rd century B.C – 1st century B.C.). There then appears to either be a complete hiatus in the stratigraphic sequence for the Roman period in the trenches investigated, perhaps because the levels relating to this period have been removed completely by subsequent building works (see Chapters Four and Five). As the pottery from the upper levels has not been analysed it is difficult to know at present whether there is residual Roman material in the upper horizons. The latest levels excavated belong to the Late Roman /early Byzantine period (4th-6th centuries A.D.).

Early Antique Period (6th- 4th centuries B.C.)

The pottery in use in this period is mainly of local or regional manufacture reflecting a well-developed phase of Colchian workmanship (see Figure 6.1). The assemblage can be divided into the following categories: traded goods (economic); household wares for domestic purposes, (storage, food preparation, cooking); table or serving vessels; decorative or display vessels; those designed for ritual use and other vessels of uncertain purpose.

From at least the mid-6th century BC there was Greek colonisation around the Black Sea. As a consequence Greek amphora from Chios, Thasos, Mende, Lesbos and other sources, and fine wares (Attic ware) are well represented on these coastal sites (cf Kacharava 1997). Nokalakevi, situated well inland, did not appear to have extensive access to these traded items but there are a few poorly preserved sherds of probable Greek amphorae (Fig. 6.1) and a few fragments of black-slip Greek fine-wares probably imported via these coastal settlements such as Pichvnari (Tsetskhladze 1999). The household assemblages mainly comprise pithoi (Fig. 6.1. 6-9), strainers, lamps and lids. Cooking vessels include pans and jars (Fig. 6.1. 10, 16) some of which are sooted through use. Amongst the table wares are drinking vessels (handled mugs), pedestalled goblets (Fig. 6.1. 12-15) decorated drinking mugs (Fig. 6.1 17-18), basins and jugs (Fig. 6.1. 2-5, 19). Copies of imports rarely occur, such as the double-handled bowl (Fig. 6.1. 11). Jugs with hollow handles/ spouts (pipe handles) (Fig. 6.1. 22-3) also feature. Many vessels, particularly the table wares and some perhaps used for display are decorated with a variety of motifs and incised decorative schemes (Fig. 6.1. 24). Possibly ritual vessels are represented by vessels with zoomorphic handles (Fig. 6.1. 5, 20-1) and perhaps the pithos with the incised design (Fig. 6.1. 25). The earlier Antique vessels are predominantly fired at relatively low temperatures in a reducing atmosphere resulting in dark grey, black or brown coloured wares. There is a quite high incidence of decoration employed largely using impressed or incised techniques.

Pithoi with identical comb-impressed decoration dating to the 5th-4th centuries BC have been published from Gonio-Apsaros along with hollow-handled vessels and jugs with zoomorphic handled (Mamuladze and Khlavashi 2009, Taf 5 and Taf 12).

Catalogue of illustrated figures

Figure 6.1 (nos 1-26) Early Antique (6th-4th centuries BC)

1. Amphora with oval section handles. Oxidised, very micaceous fabric. Possibly a Thasian amphora made on the Greek island of Thasos in the late 6th to early 5th centuries. Context (235).
2. Handled jug with a squared rim. The handle is decorated with three applied pellets with indented centres, probably both decorative and functional as a thumb-stop. The body is decorated with bands of impressed comb crosses. Fabric: (LI1). Layer (234).
3. Handled jug. The top of the handle has four applied pellets. Fabric LI1. Layer (217).
4. Handled conical-mouthed jug with an expanded rim. Row of five clay pellets at top of handle. Fabric: LI1. Context (216).
5. Handled conical-mouthed jug. Two applied pellets at the top of the handle and piercing down the centre. Fabric: Fabric: LI1. Context: Trench B (106).
6. Pithos with a thickened rim. The rim is decorated with an impressed combed-lattice with random piercings. Fabric LI1. Layer (235).
7. Pithos with a decorated collar rim internally beaded. The exterior rim face is decorated with combed wavy line. There are also random circular stabs, presumably to assist drying before firing to prevent spalling. Fabric LI1. Layer (234).
8. Pithos with a triangular rim similar to Vani type 1A dated to the 5th century BC. Similar vessels have been found at Gonio-Apsaros (Mamuladze and Khalvashi 2002, Taf v, 4-5). Decorated on the outer face by two lines of coarse rouletting. Fabric LI1. Layer (235).
9. Wide-mouthed jar/ pithos with a folded-over rim. Fabric: LI3. Context (239).
10. Flared rim jar decorated with an incised wavy line. Fabric LI1. Layer (217).
11. Double handled bowl possibly copying a fine ware import. Fabric: LI3. Context (232).
12. Handled goblet with a slightly asymmetrical pedestalled base. Fabric: LI4. Context (268).
13. Goblet decorated with incised wavy lines. Fabric: LI4. Context (268).

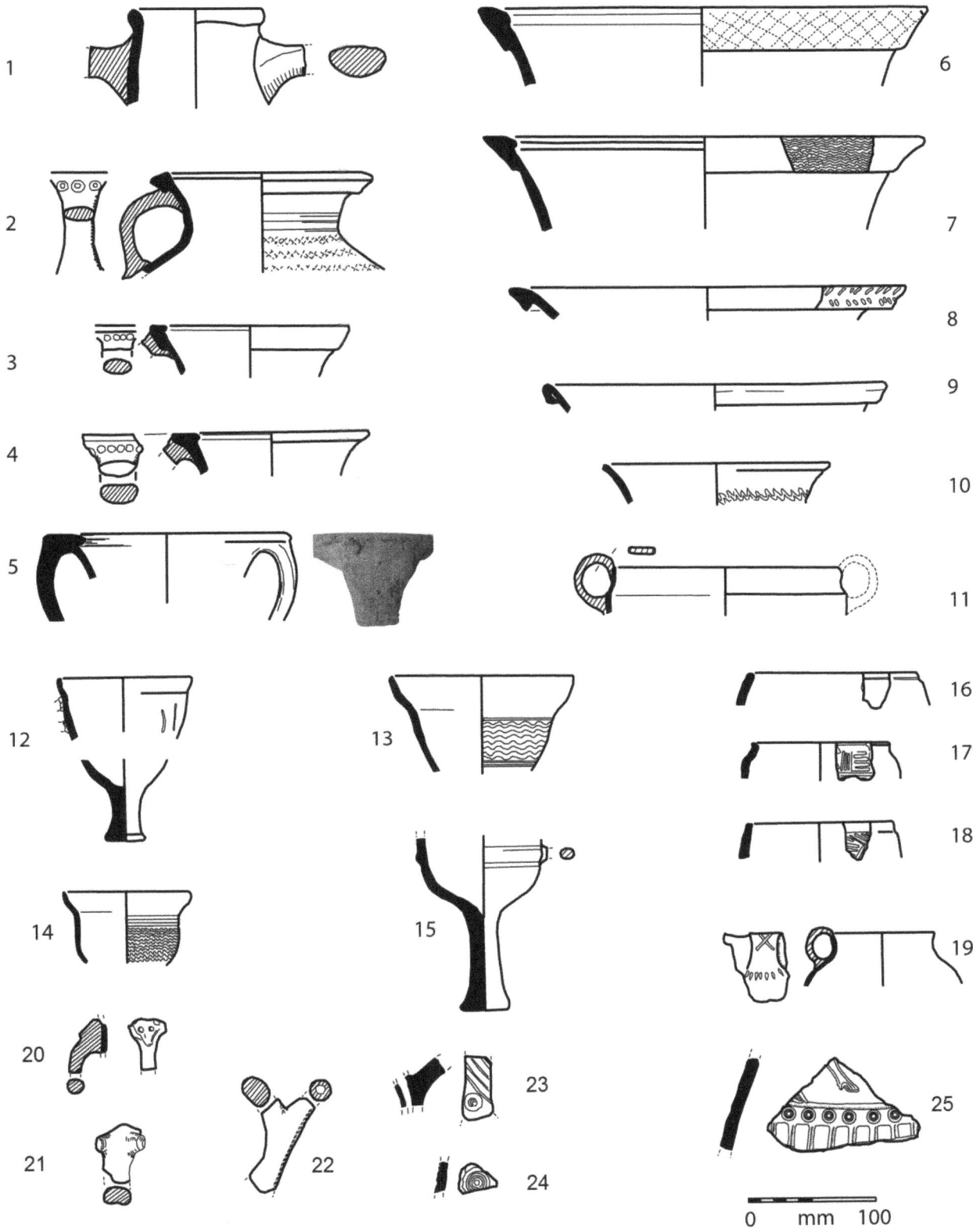

Figure 6.1: Examples of Early Antique (6th-4th centuries BC) ceramic from Nokalakevi

14. Cup/ goblet with a hemispherical body and concave rim. Decorated with combed wavy lines. Fabric LI1. Sherds from contexts (235) and (236).

15. Cup with a hemispherical body and concave rim. Decorated with combed wavy lines. Fabric LI1. Sherds from contexts (235) and (236).

16. Handmade, simple rim, jar. Fabric: LI3. Context (235).

17. Handmade jar/ drinking vessel decorated with tooled lines in a geometric-style design. Fabric: LI3. Context (235).

18. Handmade jar/ drinking vessel decorated with tooled multi-directional groups of lines. Fabric: CA1. Context (235).

59

19. Jar with a single wide strap handle decorated with a cross on the upper visible surface and radiating stabs on the lower edge. The rim is decorated with incised lines on the upper face. Fabric: LI3. Context (232).

20. Handle decorated with an animal head. Fabric: LI1. Context 174.

21. Handle originally decorated with two 'horns' since broken. Fabric: LI1. Context 174.

22. Fragment of a handled spout (colloquially known as a pipe-handle). Fabric LI1. Layer (235). This form appears at Nokolakevi around the 7th to 6th centuries BC.

23. Fragment of a handled spout. Diagonal incised lines on the handle. Fabric LI3. Layer (217).

24. Small bodysherd decorated with raised concentric rings. Black sandy fabric ?MU1. Layer (235). Residual. Typical of 8th-6th century BC.

25. Bodysherd from a large vessel, probably a pithos, decorated with depressed rectangular impressions above which is a line of ring-and-dot impressions. The zone above this shows the two front lower legs of a hoofed animal incised into the clay. Fabric: GR3. Context (235). The vessel may belong to the same tradition as a pithos from Pichvnari decorated with an incised image of a cock (Kakhidze and Vashakidze 2010, 465, grave 181), and may even date to the Pre-Antique period (8th-7th centuries BC).

Hellenistic period (3rd - 1st centuries B.C.)

Although the Hellenistic period at Nokalakevi is essentially a continuation of the Early Antique period, there are important changes in the pottery styles perhaps reflecting changes in fashion and taste or contact with other cultural styles (see Figures 6.2 and 6.3). It may also reflect other changes in terms of food preparation or the availability of different food stuffs. The number of imports increases suggesting the importance of Colchian society at this time. Increased trading suggests improved economic status and the opening of trade routes into the interior. Braund (2010) discusses some of the commodities which may have been traded in exchange for Mediterranean wares. Amongst the recognisable amphorae are examples from Rhodes (Fig. 6.2. 29-30) and a few black gloss fine table wares (Fig. 6.2. 36-7). The imported fine wares were clearly being copied more locally in the Pontic region and several examples of such vessels also occur at Nokalakevi (Fig. 6.2. 32-5).

Amongst the regional imports at this time are Colchian amphorae possibly made locally and further along the Black Sea coast (Fig. 6.2. 26-8) and Sinopean amphora (Fig, 6.2. 31). The Colchian amphorae are thought to mainly contain wine and to have been in production from around the mid-4th century BC through to the 1st century AD (Tsetskhladze and Vnukov 1992, 360; Vnukov 2010). The early oval-bodied amphorae resemble their Sinopean counterparts and there are different typological variants in terms of size and capacity (Gamkrelidze 2009). The typology of the examples found in the Hellenistic period levels correspond to variant B in the provisional typology proposed by Tsetskhladze and Vnukov dating from the end of the 3rd to the end of the 1st century. In particular the rim forms resemble those from the Chaika city-site in the northwest of the Crimean Peninsula, dated to the 2nd-1st centuries BC. Another feature illustrated by the Nokalakevi examples is a slightly swollen neck, also thought to be a development in the 2nd-1st centuries BC (op. cit, 368). The three Nokalakevi vessels were re-used as burial containers. Kilns have been discovered in Colchis near the village of Gvandra (Abkhazia) dating from the 3rd century and there are similar kilns near Sukhumi and a site south-west of Gulripshi (Gamkrelidze 2009).

Some of the Colchian vessels found in the Early Antique levels do not continue into the Hellenistic period, in particular zoomorphic-handled jugs and various drinking vessels. In their place stylistically new forms appear, for example: jugs with different rim shapes (Fig. 6.3. 49), handled mugs (Fig. 6.3. 50) and *luteria* (large spouted basins) (Fig. 6.3. 51). Another new vessel type found at this time but yet to be recognised at Nokalakevi is a flask with a rounded, flattened body (cf Vickers and Kakhidze 2004, fig. 48.1; fig. 61.1-3). Concomitant with the introduction of new vessel styles is a change in decoration. More utilitarian forms such as storage and cooking jars (Fig. 6.3. 39-40, 54) and pithoi (Fig. 6.3. 43-5) continue to feature but in slightly different styles. Other forms encountered include shallow open lamps often with internal sooting (Fig. 6.3. 41-2), perforated vessels perhaps used in cheese-making (Fig. 6.3. 47-8) and shallow bowls or dishes (Fig. 6.3. 52-5).

The variations in vessel style are accompanied by changes in the clays used; their preparation and the firing. In the Hellenistic period the reduced vessels characteristic of the Early Antique period are increasingly replaced by oxidised wares suggesting a greater level of sophistication in terms of the firing technology where the levels of oxygen in the kilns can be controlled more efficiently. This may reflect a transition from essentially bonfire or clamp kilns to a more permanent kiln structures. The clays also become more refined with finer tempering material. This improvement probably allowed a greater output of wares and perhaps reflects an increased market and higher population levels at this time.

Catalogue of illustrated vessels

Figure 6.2 (nos 27-38) Hellenistic period (3rd-1st centuries BC)

26. Colchian amphora. Complete apart from basal knob. Double finger depressions at base of handles. A trident symbol on the neck inscribed before firing. The vessel has been deliberately holed just below the handle. Burial 191, context (189).

27. Colchian amphora. Single finger depression at the base of each handle. Upside-down 'anchor' symbol on neck and three parallel lines under handle loop inscribed before firing. Burial 222, context (220).

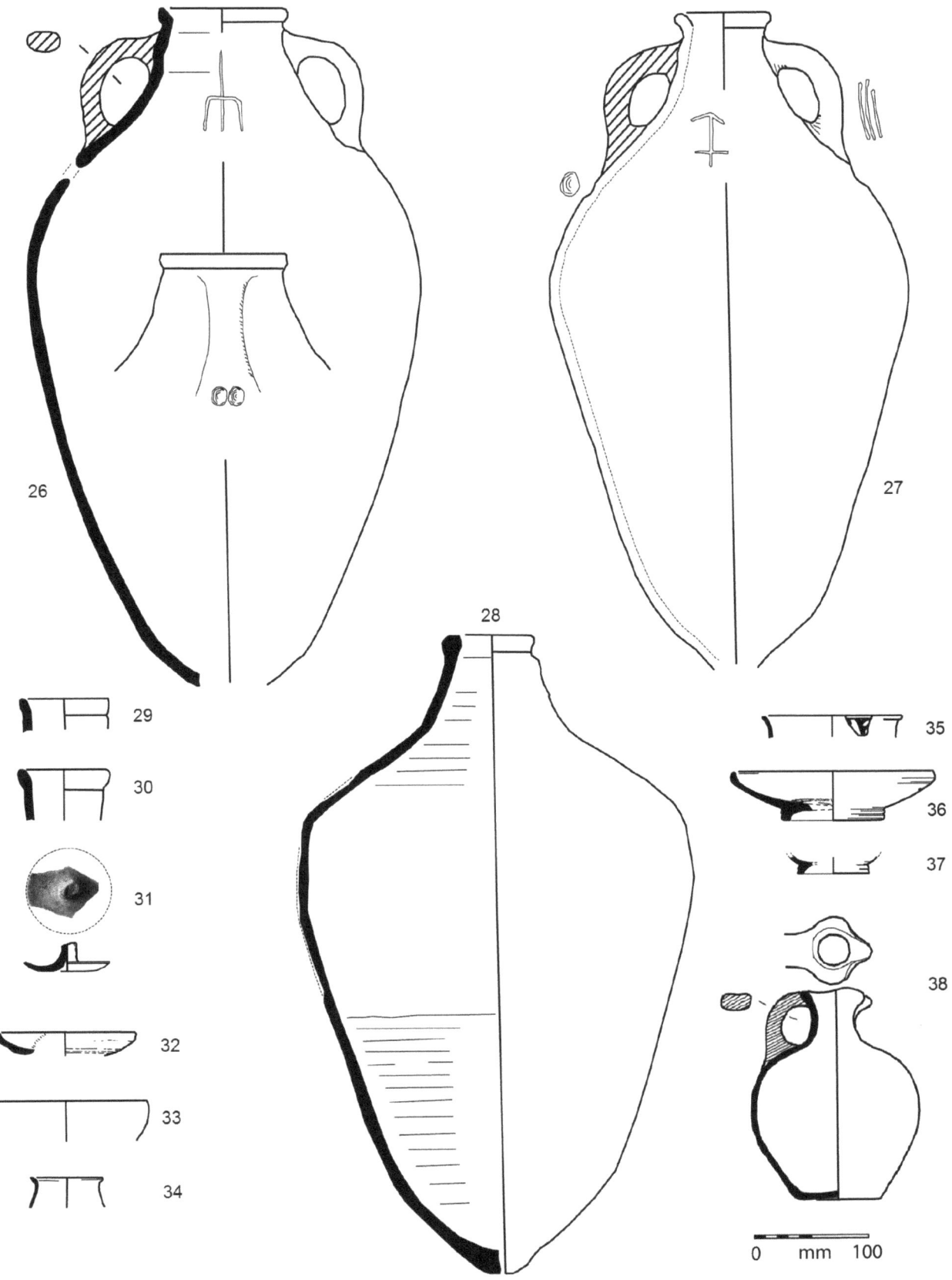

Figure 6.2: Examples of Hellenistic period (3rd – 1st centuries BC) ceramic from Nokalakevi

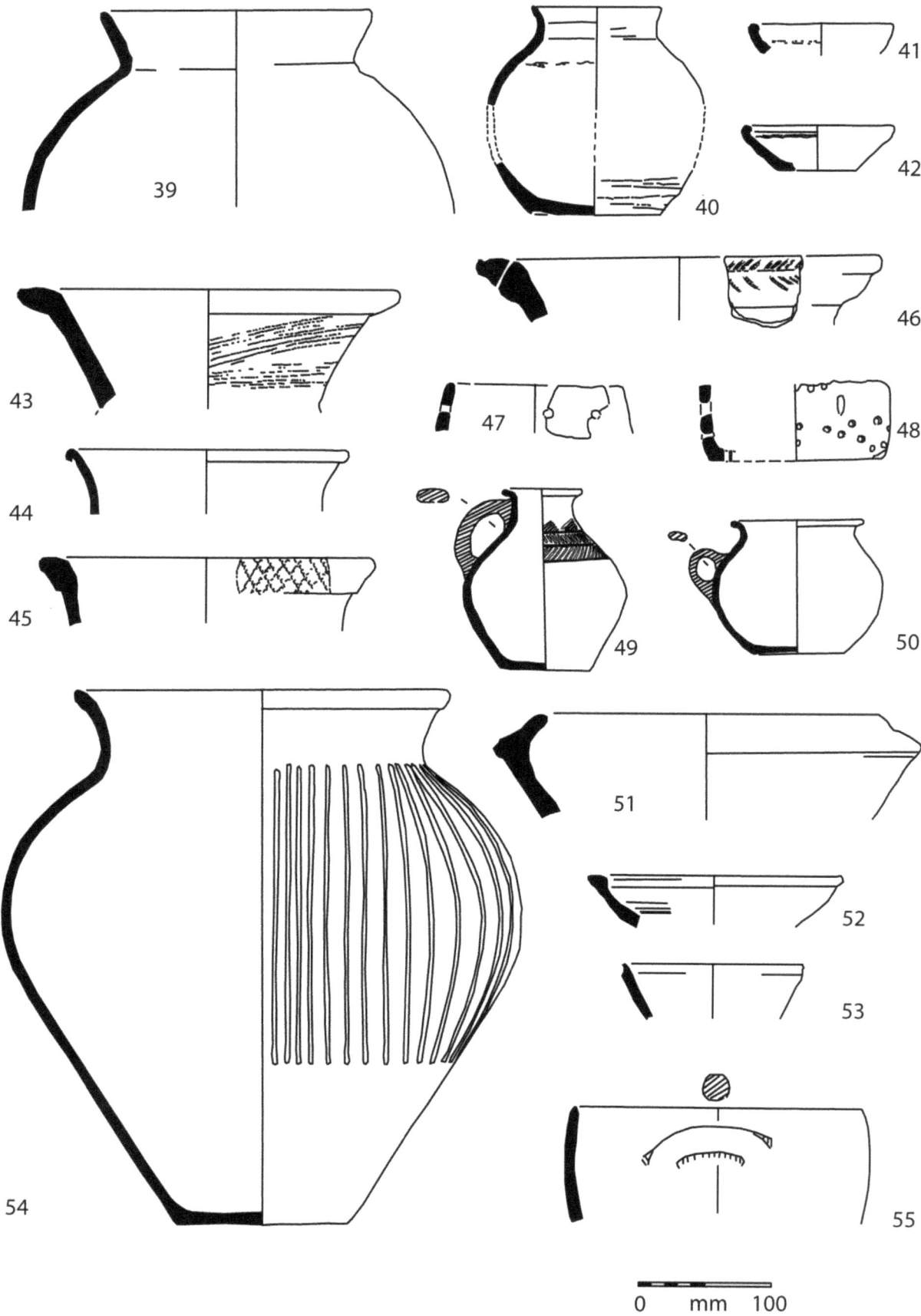

Figure 6.3: Examples of Hellenistic period (3rd – 1st centuries BC) ceramic from Nokalakevi

28. Colchian amphora. Badly spalled through burning. Handles lost. Evidence internally that the vessel was made in two halves. Feature 207, context (205).

29. Amphora. ?Rhodian. Layer (217).

30. Amphora rim. Oxidised. ?Rhodian. Context (226).

31. Operculum from an amphora ?Sinopean. Context (108).

32. Shallow dish decorated in the interior with a rouletted ring. Brownish-black worn slip on a pale buff fabric with a pinkish core. Pontic copy of imported fine ware. Context (217).

33. Curved-wall dish with smoothed surfaces. Fabric: LI3. Context (259).

34. Fine ware beaker with a red slip. ?Pontic copy of imported fine ware. Fabric: FW2. Context 137/174.

35. Fine ware vessel with a black slip on the interior surface and part of the exterior. Pontic copy of imported fine ware. Context 137.

36. Curved-wall dish in Greek black gloss ware decorated on the interior with a detached unframed palmette, probably one of four stamps surrounded by a rouletted wreath. A hole has been drilled through the upper wall after firing. Trench B, context (106). See also Fig 6.4

37. Base of a black-slipped fine ware dish. Trench B, context (106).

38. Complete (reconstructed) pinch-mouthed, handled flagon. Oxidised. Fabric LIPY. Layer (235), SF 4.

Figure 6.3 (nos 39-55) Hellenistic period (3rd-1st centuries BC)

39. Large storage jar with a sharply everted, flaring rim with a slightly uneven top. Oxidised. Fabric: LI2. Context (235).

40. Upper and lower parts of a handmade simple, everted rim, jar. Fabric GR2. Layer (217).

41. Small open lamp, sooted on the interior. Fabric: LI3. Context (259).

42. Small lamp. Sooted on the interior just below the rim and on the exterior of the rim. Fabric LI1. Layer (217).

43. Large, conical mouthed pithos with a finely combed exterior surface. Fabric: GR1. Context (217).

44. Slightly hooked rim jar/ pithos, burnished on the interior. Fabric: LI3. Context (258).

45. Thickened rim pithos decorated with impressed comb latticing on the exterior of the rim. Fabric: LI1. Context (259).

46. Heavy rim large jar or pithoi (dergi/pithoi). The rim is perforated probably to facilitate drying during manufacture. Impressed decoration on rim. Fabric: LI1. Context (137).

47. Handmade vessel with perforations ? cheese-press. Fabric: LI1. Context (235). Possibly residual Early Antique.

48. Handmade, perforated vessel, ?cheese press. Fabric: GR1. Context (235). Possibly residual Early Antique.

49. Complete, handmade, handled jug. Slightly asymmetrical about the central axis. Burnt. Quite crudely incised decoration. Fabric ?GR2. Grave [253] fill (252).

50. Complete, globular, handled beaker. Fabric GR2. Cremation burial (246).

51. Luterium. Fabric FE2. Layer (235).

Figure 6.4: A curved-wall dish in Greek black gloss with palmette stamp and rouletted wreath (See Fig 6.2. 36)

52. Curved-wall dish with a triangular rim (jame). Oxidised exterior, grey interior. Fabric: LI1. Context 137.

53. Small dish (jame). Fabric: LIPY. Context 137.

54. Large wide-mouthed storage jar (dergi) decorated with vertical spaced burnished lines. Fabric: GR2. Burial 279 (277) with joining sherds from (232).

55. Curved-wall bowl with a horizontal handle placed over top of No. 54 as a lid. Fabric: GR2. Burial 279 (277).

Late Roman/ Early Byzantine period (4th-6th centuries A.D.)

From the end of the 3rd century A.D. the relative stability seen in the preceding late Antique period dissolved and the Kingdom of Lazika (Egrisi) saw many changes with various invasions, incursions and periods of cultural assimilation. In the 3rd century there was a marked military deployment along the frontier regions of the Roman Empire and concomitant with this would have been an extensive military supply system in operation to supply the troops. In the 5th and 6th centuries AD Roman garrisons previously stationed along the Black Sea coast moved inland and Persian forces became active in Lazika (Braund 1994, 268).

From the second quarter of the 4th century, the emergence of Christianity as the prime religion of Colchis resulted in a change in burial practice. This was both in terms of body position, from the crouched bodies associated with the Hellenistic period to supine burials, and a reduction in grave goods which was a feature of the earlier burials.

For the first time the ceramic assemblage sees a number of imported amphorae of types typically associated with the Roman military supply system (see Figure 6.5). Types of note include examples of Late Roman amphora (LRA) type 1 (Peacock and Williams 1986, class 44; Opait 2004, 8-10) (Fig. 6.5. 66); LRA 2 ibid. class 43) from the Argolid; LRA 3 (ibid. class 45; Zeest 95); LRA 5 from Palestine (ibid. class 46) (Fig. 6.5. 60) and large cylindrical amphora from North Africa (ibid. class 35). A visual survey would suggest that the late amphorae assemblage is dominated by the LRA 1 amphorae, a type which evolved through the 4th-7th centuries which was produced in the Roman provinces of *Cilicia* and Cyprus although there may be other as yet unknown sources. The principal content was probably wine. These along with the other imported amphorae are all types typically associated with the Late Roman military supply system in the 5th-6th centuries and would have largely carried wine and olive oil and perhaps other comestibles. Alongside these amphorae are later Colchian types (Fig. 6.5. 56-9) for which a source at Nokalakevi has been proposed (Lomitashvili and Colvin 2010). A number of other types are also present but yet to be studied and identified (e.g. Fig. 6.5. 61-5, 67). Alongside these are a small number of fine red-slipped wares which are also probable imports to the site (Fig. 6.5. 70-2).

Such constant turmoil would have also seen profound changes in the economy which would be reflected in the ceramic record. At Nokalakevi building material appears in quantity for the first time reflecting urban development. Two kilns have been found within the city, still visible today, suggesting a level of self-sufficiency in terms of ceramic production. Bricks, tiles and water pipes were probably manufactured within the city walls to meet local demand. A change of emphasis of the economic base in the early Feudal period to one focused around agriculture and production would have created a change in the ceramic record with the introduction of new forms to perform new functions. Certain vessels such as locally-made storage jars and pithoi continue to feature (Fig.6.5. 68-9) but it seems that ceramic drinking vessels were exchanged for glass vessels. Other ceramic items which appear at this time are portable ovens with flat bases and a central hole (Fig.6.5. 73)

Catalogue of illustrated vessels

Figure 6.5 (nos 56-73) Late Roman / Byzantine (4th-6th century AD)
56. Colchian amphora. Fabric: GR4. Partially burnt. Context (267).
57. Colchian amphora. Fabric: fine GR1. Context (267).
58. Colchian amphora. Fabric: GR4. Context (267).
59. Several sherds from a small torpedo-shaped Colchian amphora. Irregular scored grooves on the body. Light yellow-brown exterior with a darker orange-brown interior and interior core margin. The coarse textured fabric contains a scatter of larger dark red-brown inclusions (?iron), 2-3 mm in size and a scatter of black volcanic sand and other inclusions. Context (267).
60. Late Roman amphora (LRA5). Oxidised sandy textured fabric. (Context 267).
61. Pithos. Fabric: GR1.Context (267).

62. Rolled rim amphora. Oxidised, micaceous fabric. Context (267).
Figure 6.5 Examples of Late Roman / Early Byzantine (4th-6th century AD) ceramic from Nokalakevi
63. Small amphora. Fabric: Oxidised with limestone inclusions. Context (267).
64. Amphora ridged below the rim. Cream coloured, smooth textured, fabric containing a fine scatter of volcanic black sand and occasional red iron. Context (267).
65. Amphora with a slight internal lid seating. Oxidised fabric with limestone. Context (267).
66. Amphora (LRA 1). Context (104).
67. Handled flagon or small amphora. Fine, oxidised ware with some limestone and mica. Fabric: OXIDF. Context (267).
68. Heavy out-turned rim with a narrow neck from a large pithos, Fabric: GR1. Context (267).
69. Storage jar (*dergi*). Fabric: GR1. Context (108).
70. Basesherd from a red-slipped fine ware open form with rouletted decoration. Fine, oxidised, fabric with a matt orange-red slip. Context (267).
71. Basesherd from an imported red-slipped fine ware open form with rouletted decoration. Fine, oxidised, fabric with a matt orange-red slip. Context (267).
72. Fine red-slipped ware. Import. Context (267).
73. Orange-red-slipped ware dish showing possible brush marks (?). Import. Context (125). The form is broadly comparable to some imitation African red-slip wares from Jordan thought to be of Palestinian origin (Hayes 1972, fig. 93.2) probably dating to the later 4th century.
74. Flat base of a portable oven with a central hole approximately 70 mm diameter. Fabric: GR1. Context (267).

Fabrics by Jane Timby incorporating petrographical reports by Rob Ixer

Introduction

The pottery assemblage largely comprises coarse wares accompanied by a few fine wares and amphorae. On-site macroscopic analysis of the pottery between 2007-2010 has identified eleven basic groups: 1: calcareous wares including various limestone-tempered types; 2: calcite-tempered ware; 3: sandy wares; 4: mixed grits containing quartz sand, limestone and various other rock fragments; 5: flint-tempered; 6: iron rich; 7: micaceous ware; 8: mudstone; 9: feldspar-based; 10: amphorae and 11: non-local fine or specialist wares (see above). Definition of wares is on-going and new fabrics or variants are being added each season.

Initial impressions might suggest that the assemblage mainly comprises wares of local origin with few imported or traded wares. The entire amphorae component of the recorded assemblage accounts for just 2.5% of the assemblage by count (excluding the burial vessels) and the fine wares present barely registered at 0.2%. A small

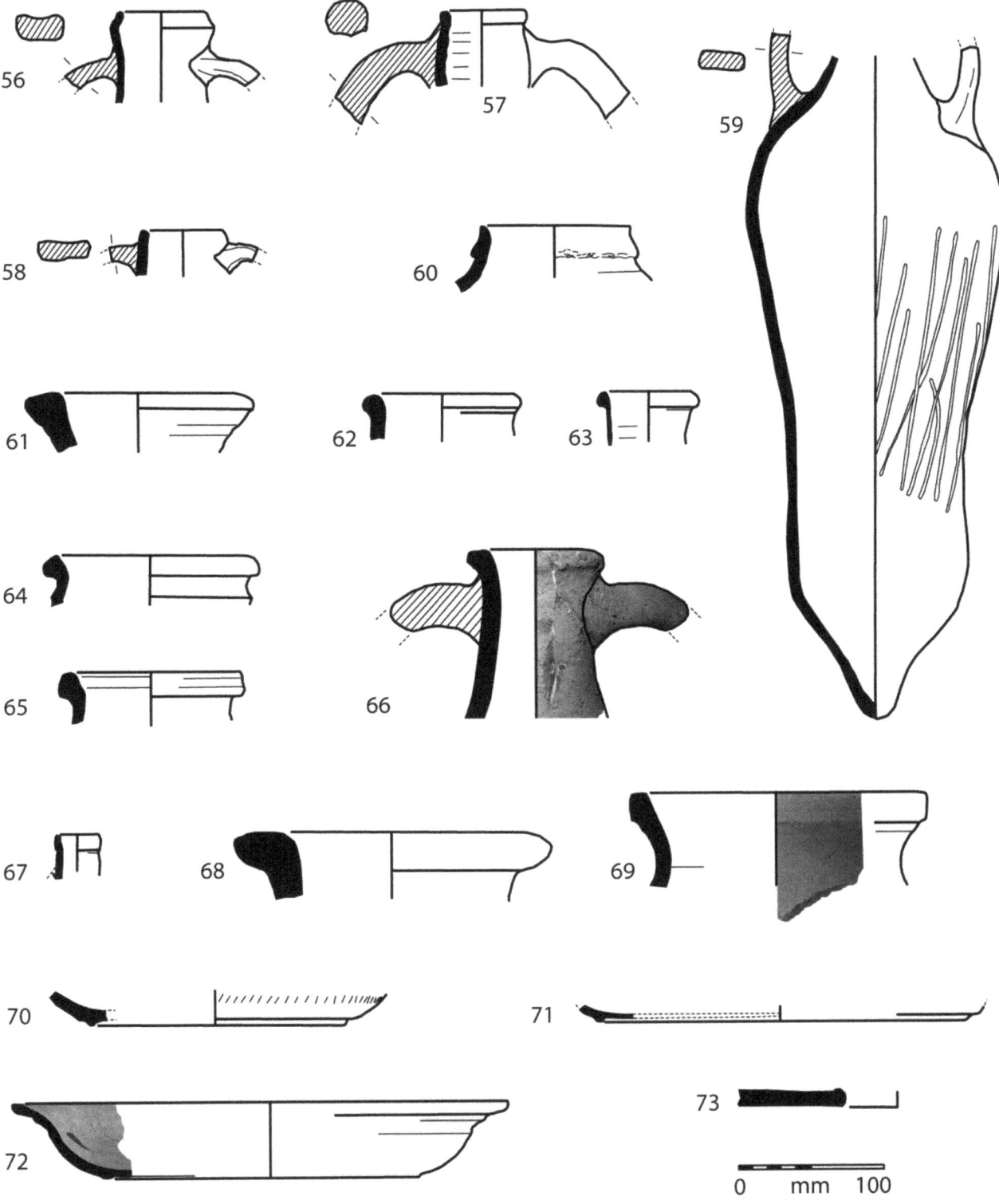

Figure 6.5 Examples of Late Roman / Early Byzantine (4th-6th century AD) ceramic from Nokalakevi

number of other imports can also be recognised but not provenance, one exception being a Sinopean *luterium*.

The petrology of the material is quite interesting and would repay further work to determine whether all the constituents founds in the different fabrics are locally available. There is clearly quite a diverse geology with both sedimentary (calcareous) rocks and volcanic source material, sometimes occurring together, sometimes separately. This would involve a fairly extensive field study. The local river cuts through limestone bedrock but there are a large number of large pebbles of diverse geological origins on the river beaches brought down from the upper reaches during flood.

The commonest fabric by far is a buff, mainly oxidised, limestone-tempered ware (fabric LI1), which accounted for over half the assemblage recorded, 53% by count. This was used to make a variety of jars, pithoi and shallow bowls. Four other limestone fabrics were defined which collectively account for a further 20.8% of the assemblage. Calcite-tempered fabrics account for 1.3% of the group and included both wheel-made and handmade vessels. The mixed-grit group contained various inclusions both of sedimentary (limestone, flint) and volcanic origin and accounts for 9.9% of the assemblage. Sandy wares account for 5.3% and micaceous wares for 0.1%. A feldspar fabric with pyroxene and other inclusions accounts for 3.8% whilst a distinctive ware with predominantly feldspar and ferruginous pellets (fabric FDFE) accounts for less than 1%.

Description of main fabrics

Group 1: calcareous wares

This group currently includes various limestone-tempered types and calcite-tempered ware. To date eight limestone-tempered variants (LI1-8) and one limestone and ferruginous fabric (LIFE) have been defined. Fabrics LI2-5, LI7-8 broadly date to the 'Hellenistic' period; fabric LI6 only found in Trench B is possibly earlier prehistoric. The distinction between the various fabrics is largely based on the size and frequency of the limestone inclusions and the technology of the vessels. The most common by far is fabric LI1 which is undoubtedly of local manufacture and used to make a range of mainly closed forms such as jars and pithoi. Thin-section analysis of a representative sample of fabric LI1 was undertaken by Dr Rob Ixer who provided the following petrographic report:

FABRIC LI1: a fine-grained (micritic) limestone-tempered pot

Macroscopic description

The surfaces and cut surface have all fired to a uniform, medium reddish-orange colour. Non-plastics comprise about 5 – 10% of the surface area, they are rounded to sub-angular, evenly distributed and show a tight size range with most being a coarse sand size, 0.3 to 0.5mm in diameter. The clasts are polylithic with pale 'quartz' and dark grains; dark pyroxene, micrite, muscovite are rare. Voids within the pot are infilled with later fine-grained carbonate. The surfaces are gritty to the touch.

Thin section

A very clean clay has been evenly tempered with sub-rounded to sub-angular pale green pyroxene; fine-grained micrite/chert and rounded, red mudclasts that are 0.5 to 1mm in diameter. Large non-plastics are sparsely distributed.

Microscopic description

Petrographically the pot has a dark, clean clay with a little, fine-grained quartz accompanied by trace amounts of

Figure 6.6. Details of limestone fabric LI1 (surface view).

monominerallic amphibole and very zoned plagioclase. The non-plastics show a bimodal size distribution with fine-grained quartz in the clay and larger rock fragments; this suggests that the pot has been tempered.

The main non-plastic component is micrite (calcite mud), some with calcispheres and some with foraminifera/gastropod fossils. A single bivalve shell and rare sparite clasts accompany the micrite clasts. Fine-grained chert clasts, some of which are limonite-stained, very in size and are the only other rock-type of significance. Igneous rocks are rare and are medium-grained, plagioclase-rich basic rocks.

Manufacture

The bimodal size range of the non-plastics and tight size distribution of the micrite clasts suggests tempering of a clean, or cleaned, clay. The shape of the micrite clasts varies from angular to rounded, perhaps suggesting the use of a micrite sand rather than crushed material.

Group 2: Calcite-tempered wares

These wares are distinguished by having rhombic-shaped calcite crystals as the main tempering agent. Vessels are black, brown or orange in colour and appear to be mainly handmade. In some cases the calcite has leached out leaving a very vesicular, 'corky' fabric, particular on the surfaces.

Group 3: sandy wares

A range of wares with quartz sand in the fabrics accompanied by sparse grains of iron and rare other inclusions such as flint. Variants include a medium grained, sandy textured ware with a slightly rough feel to a finer, smoother variant and one where the quartz grains are distinctly facetted.

Group 4: mixed grit-tempered

This is a large and quite diverse group of wares and frequently used to make large storage vessels with quite a coarse, rough textured fabric. The fabrics tend to contain quartz sand, limestone, feldspar, pyroxenes, calcite, flint and various other rock fragments. As many of the vessels are large pithoi, this and the apparent mixed geology of the fabrics, suggest a likely local source for the clay. Firing colour varies from grey, brown, black to orange.

Group 5: flint-tempered

A rare fabric contained a moderate frequency of angular crushed flint inclusion 1-2mm in size. Handmade.

Group 6: iron-rich

A hard, fired ware characterised by distinct rounded grains of iron up to 3-4mm accompanied by a sparse scatter of other mixed inclusions and other argillaceous fragments.

Group 7: mudstone

Brownish-grey ware containing a common frequency of dark grey rounded to sub-angular argillaceous inclusions up to 1mm in size and finer. These are accompanied by a sparse scatter of similar-sized limestone and very rare flint.

Group 8: micaceous ware.

A minor fabric but extremely distinctive with plates of black (biotite) and white (muscovite) mica visible on the surfaces with flecks up to 1.5mm in size. Generally black in colour and used for wheel-made vessels.

Group 9: Sandy ware with feldspar and other rock inclusions

These wares are quite difficult to identify in the field and there is quite a diversity of sub-types. The group undoubtedly overlaps with the mixed grit category of fabrics. Two sherds were submitted for thin-sectioning to clarify the petrography and Dr Rob Ixer provided the following reports:

Fabric: PY1

Macroscopic description
The surfaces have fired to a light brown colour. The inner surface is smooth but the outer is slightly gritty. Non-plastics comprise about 5% of the surface area hence, are sparse; they are medium/coarse sand size (0.5mm) and comprise white and dark red clasts. The cut surface

Figure 6.7: Details of fabric PY1 (surface view).

shows a pale yellow brown core within a 1mm and 0.2mm wide, light brown, inner and outer rim. Very rare, pale-coloured, rounded clasts are 1 – 2mm in diameter as are dark, poorly bonded clasts. Post-depositional fine-grained carbonate has infilled void spaces.

Thin section
The pot has fired to a give an 11mm thick, dusky yellowish brown core within light brown, 1mm wide rims. The non-plastics are densely concentrated; they are 0.1 – 0.2mm in diameter plus very rare, bigger clasts. Pale brown clasts are 0.2mm in size. Voids are present.

Microscopic
Petrographically the pot has a dark-coloured clay with abundant, fine-grained quartz accompanied by feldspar; the non-plastics have a unimodal size distribution. The non-plastics are polylithic comprising monominerallic grains and rock clasts.

Monominerallic grains include clinopyroxene; unaltered, very zoned plagioclase; plagioclase altering to fine-grained white mica; potassium feldspar including very rare microcline; quartz with patchy extinction and minor amounts of epidote and brown amphibole. Opaque mineral grains are rounded.

Rock fragments are varied. Very fine-grained feldspathic lavas with microphenocrysts of zoned plagioclase, some with trachytic textures suggest they are weathered/altered andesite/basalt. Other clasts comprise quartz-plagioclase, quartz-feldspar, and pyroxene-plagioclase intergrowths. Non-igneous rocks include chert some with brown margins, sandstone/siltstone and phyllite.

Black, limonite-rich areas carry fine-grained quartz. Pale brown areas are unidentified, they are very probably inorganic; some may be brown-stained chert and others look like iron-rich cutan material.

Manufacture
The pot may be tempered with very fine-grained quartz or may be a fired, silty clay.

Fabric : FDFE: feldspar and iron

Macroscopic description
The surfaces have fired to a pale reddish brown colour. Non-plastics comprise about 5% of the surface area; they are rounded and evenly distributed with most being a medium/coarse sand size, 0.3 to 0.5mm in diameter. The

Figure 6.8: Details of fabric FDFE (surface view).

clasts include much 'grog'/limonite/mudclasts. The cut surface shows a 7mm thick, light brown grey core within a 2mm wide, moderate orange pink rim. Rare, large clasts are white or brick red and mainly 0.3 – 0.5 but up to 2.0mm in diameter.

Thin section
The pot has fired to give a 7mm thick, pale yellowish brown core within light brown 3mm wide rims. The non-plastics are densely concentrated; they are 0.2 – 0.3mm in diameter with very rare clasts up to 2mm in size. Most clasts are rounded and are cloudy (micrite) or clear. Limonite-rich areas are 0.5 –1.0mm in diameter.

Microscopic description
Petrographically the pot has a clay with abundant angular to sub-rounded, stained quartz with trace amounts of epidote, muscovite, potassium feldspar including microcline, very zoned plagioclase and altered feldspar. The non-plastics have a unimodal size distribution.

The non-plastics are dominated by monominerallic quartz grains but rock clasts are also present in minor to trace amounts. They include trachytic lava with feldspar laths in an opaque weathered/altered matrix, feldspar or pyroxene microphenocrysts in a glassy matrix, sandstone, quartzite, phyllite chert/rhyolite and spherulitic quartz. Potassium feldspar-plagioclase and feldspar altering to epidote and muscovite clasts occur and may be from more acidic rocks.

Larger rounded micrite clasts that may carry microfossils are more common than sparite clasts. Limonite-rich areas carry quartz inclusions and some look like mud clasts.

Post depositional, fine-grained carbonate forms thin veinlets cross-cutting the pot.

Manufacture
The pot may have been manufactured from a natural clay. If the pot is tempered then it is with a quartz temper.

Group 10: Amphorae
The amphorae include few diagnostic featured pieces from the 2007-2010 assemblage apart from some complete or semi-complete Colchian amphorae (Fig. 2, 27-9) with a distinctive volcanic black sand fabric presumably from the Black Sea coast (see detailed description below). In addition there are some typical Aegean-type fabrics, in particular Rhodian-type amphorae which are probably redeposited from earlier horizons. A considerably larger and more diverse range of amphorae are clearly present from the later, Byzantine levels (see above).

Fabric: Colchian amphora: a polylithic tempered pot with much fine-grained, weathered lava.

Macroscopic description

The natural surfaces and cut surface have all fired to a uniform, medium reddish orange colour. Non-plastics

Figure 6.9: Complete Colchian amphora with detail of fabric.

comprise about 5 – 10% of the surface area, they are rounded to sub-angular, evenly distributed and show a tight size range with most being of a coarse sand size, 0.3 to 0.5mm in diameter. The clasts are polylithic with pale 'quartz' and dark grains; dark pyroxene; micrite and muscovite are rare. Voids within the pot are infilled with post-depositional, fine-grained carbonate. The surfaces are gritty to the touch.

Thin section
Petrographically the pot has a very clean clay with no white mica; the non-plastics have a bimodal size distribution with the larger size temper having a tight size range. The non-plastics are polylithic and include monominerallic grains and rock clasts.

The main non-plastic components are single grains including zoned, clinopyroxene (perhaps titanaugite); unaltered, very zoned plagioclase; plagioclase and potassium feldspar both altering to fine-grained white mica and clays; quartz with abundant fluid inclusions or patchy extinction and minor amounts of zoned, brown amphibole. Opaque mineral grains are rounded.

Rock fragments are varied with igneous rocks being more abundant than sediments / metasediments. Feldspar-pyroxene-brown amphibole; plagioclase-potassium feldspar; quartz-potassium feldspar; quartz-plagioclase; potassium feldspar-pyroxene; plagioclase-amphibole clasts suggest that are from a fine-grained intermediate rock (granodiorite/diorite). Very fine-grained feldspathic lavas with microphenocrysts of pyroxene and plagioclase and some with trachytic textures suggest they are andesite/basalt. Glassy acid lavas including spherulitic

rhyolites/pitchstones are minor in amount and a single quartz-microcline-biotite clast may be a granite. Quartz-epidote, feldspar-epidote and plagioclase-epidote clasts are altered igneous rocks. Non-igneous rocks include sandstone, arkose, chert and phyllite. A single, possible, bone fragment is present.

Manufacture
The bimodal size range and tight size distribution of the larger non-plastics suggests tempering of a naturally clean, or cleaned, clay. The range of lithologies suggests tempering by a natural sand rather than a single crushed rock, although as most single grains and rock fragments are granodiorite/diorite in composition, crushed rock remains a possibility.

Changes through time

Table 6.1 summarises the pottery groups analysed between 2006-2010 by sherd count and weight against the stratigraphic phasing. This appears to demonstrate that some broad trends can be picked out which, potentially, could be refined by looking at the individual fabrics which may be more chronologically sensitive rather than amalgamated groups. The table however, serves to show the potential of creating a fabric seriation. Amphorae are most common in Phases I-III dropping considerably in Phase VIII to disappear. A few sherds are present from Phase XI. The mixed grit group of wares are well–represented throughout perhaps demonstrating a long local tradition of using such fabrics for large storage vessels. The limestone-tempered group appears to show a peak in Phase IX so it is possible that the smaller amounts in the upper phase contain largely residual

Fabric	Phase I-III No %	I-III Wt %	VIII No %	VIII Wt%	IX No%	IX Wt%	X No%	X Wt%	XI No%	XI Wt%
Amphorae	37.1	37.5	12.9	7.3	0.0	0.0	0.0	0.0	1.5	2.3
Mixed grit	34.8	44.9	47.0	75.5	12.2	23.4	24.4	21.7	19.6	34.9
Limestone	17.1	9.6	27.6	12.1	83.7	69.6	68.6	57.7	74.5	57.9
Feldspar and black sand	4.8	3.8	4.3	2.4	0.0	0.0	2.3	6.2	1.2	1.4
Sandy	3.0	1.2	2.6	0.3	0.0	0.0	0.0	0.0	0.3	0.2
Calcite	1.8	1.6	2.6	0.8	0.0	0.0	2.3	1.7	1.0	1.3
Iron-rich	0.7	1.0	3.0	1.5	2.4	4.5	1.2	7.4	0.7	1.0
Mudstone	0.2	0.1	0.0	0.0	0.0	0.0	0.0	0.0	0.0	0.0
Fineware	0.5	0.3	0.0	0.0	0.0	0.0	0.0	0.0	0.3	0.2
Feldspar and iron	0.0	0.0	0.0	0.0	0.0	0.0	0.0	0.0	0.6	0.6
Micaceous	0.0	0.0	0.0	0.0	0.8	0.5	0.0	0.0	0.0	0.0
Miscellaneous	0.0	0.0	0.0	0.0	0.8	2.1	1.2	5.3	0.3	0.2
TOTAL	**100.0**	**100.0**	**100.0**	**100.0**	**100.0**	**100.0**	**100.0**	**100.0**	**100.0**	**100.0**
	1326	38129	232	7872	123	1703	86	1523	4668	85008

Table 6.1: Proportions of the main fabric groups by stratigraphic phase

material. Most of the other fabrics are present in small amounts throughout. The fine and specialist wares like the amphorae show a later and earlier presence perhaps demonstrating more contact with outside trade at these points in time. The Group 8 micaceous wares only appear in Phase IX and the feldspar with iron fabric (Group 9 subtype) appears to be quite an early fabric.

Potential and future work

The assemblage is probably the first from an archaeological site in Georgia to be studied using fabric and form analysis and quantification. The later Byzantine assemblage, on the basis of the amphorae present, demonstrates strong links between Georgia and the west with, in particular, links to Africa, Cicilia, Crimea, and Turkey amongst other places presumably through a military supply system. The earlier amphorae appear to be local Black Sea types with a few Aegean vessels. It is possible that Nokalakevi itself was one of the centres of production for later Colchian amphorae (Lomitashvili and Colvin 2010). Unfortunately the earlier assemblage, with a few exceptions, lacks imported wares which would help provide important chronological reference points. This must be due in part to the inland location of the site well away from the coast where many contemporary sites such as Pichvnari were getting Greek fine wares from the 5th century BC (Braund 1994, 114) but may also reflect the status or function of the settlement at different points in time.

The research potential of the assemblage can be defined at four main levels:

1) *Site level*: analysis of the pottery contributes to the dating of the complex stratigraphy of the site. It informs on site formation processes. Quantified analysis of the fabrics and forms provides information on aspects of economy, social behaviour, function and cultural background.

2) *Local*: looking at the wider picture in the future the assemblage should be compared with other contemporary groups recovered from other sites in the locality. Do the assemblages share the same forms and fabrics? What does it tell us with regard to how Nokalakevi interacted with its hinterland and did this change through time. Can local kilns supplying the site be identified?

3) *Region*: the assemblage can be used to characterize the site and place it in its regional context within the local territory and Western Georgia as a whole. Comparison of the assemblage with other settlements will establish how normal or unusual it is and whether this changes with time.

4) *Black Sea region*: the early Byzantine assemblage has considerable potential to extend our knowledge with regard to the sources of some of the imports which would be of both national and international significance. Whilst some of the imports are well known there are a large number whose provenance can only be general. Liaison with colleagues working in the field may help identify some of this material. It is hoped that this study has demonstrated the immense value of pottery in terms of understanding the chronological, economic and social development of the site at Nokalakevi. Such detailed analysis would not be possible without the application of a rigorous methodology recording the pottery stratigraphically, allowing the opportunity to search for patterns in space and time.

It is hoped that this will provide a platform for future pottery studies both at Nokalakevi and elsewhere in Georgia.

Acknowledgements

I am greatly indebted to Ian Colvin and Paul Everill for inviting me to participate in the excavations at Nokalakevi and to the immense generosity and friendship shown by our Georgian collaborators and hosts. Professor Davit Lomitashvili has demonstrated great patience as I have tried to get to grips with Georgian pottery and has imparted much knowledge from his own researches.

The supervised annual recording and drawing work has been undertaken by a great many students from many countries between 2006 and 2010 and to these individuals I extend my thanks as without them there would be no pottery record. The pottery figures used in this interim have been collated from field drawings made by David Connolly, Ana Tvaradze and the author. Figures 6.1, 6.2, 6.3 and 6.5 have been skilfully digitised by Paul Everill.

Bibliography

Braund, D. 1994. *Georgia in Antiquity. A history of Colchis and Transcaucasian Iberia 550 BC- AD 562*, Oxford

Braund, D. 2010. Amphorae in the eastern Black Sea: contexts of geography and exchange, in in D. Tezgör and N. Inaishvili (eds*) PATABS: production and trade of amphorae in the Black Sea: actes de la table ronde international de Batoumi et Trabazon, 27-29 avril 2007, Varia Anatolica*, 21: 119-25

Gamkrelidze (ed) 2009, *Iberia – Colchis. Researches on the archaeology and history of Georgia in the Classical and early medieval period.* Georgian National Mus pubn No 5

Hayes, J.W. 1972. *Late Roman pottery. A catalogue of Roman fine wares*, The British School of Rome, London

Kacharava, D. 1997. The Graeco-Kolkhian trade connection in the 7th-4th centuries BC, in J.M. Fossey (ed) *Proceedings* of 1st international conference of the archaeology and history of the Black Sea, Amsterdam: 137-45

Kakhidze, A. and Vashakidze, N. 2010. *Pichnvari Vol. 3 1965-2004. Results of the excavations conducted by the N. Berdenenishvili Batumi Research Institute Archaeological expeditions and the joint British-Georgian Pichnvari expedition* (Batumi / Oxford)

Lomitashvili, D. 1990. *Central Egrisi's IV-IVth cc. A.D. Concerning Archaeological Materials of Nokalakevi.* Unpublished dissertation for the degree of candidate in the Faculty of Historical Science, Tbilisi

Lomatashvili, D. 2003. *tsentraluri kolxeti dzv.ts. VIII-ax. ts. VIss: tsikhegoji-arkeopolisi-nokalakevi.* Unpublished Doctor of Historical Sciences Thesis, Tbilisi

Lomitashvili, D. and Colvin, I. 2010. Late Roman- early Byzantine kilns and production from Nokalakevi-Archaeolopolis, in D. Tezgör and N. Inaishvili (eds) *PATABS: production and trade of amphorae in the Black Sea: actes de la table ronde international de Batoumi et Trabazon, 27-29 avril 2007, Varia Anatolica*, 21: 35-8

Lortkipanidze, O., Gigolashvili, E., Kacharava, D., Licheli, V., Pirtskhalava, M. and Chqonia, A. 1981. VI-IVth cc. BC Colchian ceramics from Vani, *Vani, Archaeological Excavations, "Metsniereba"*, Tbilisi, Vol. V: 12-14

Mamuladze, S. and Khalvashi, M. 2002. Archäologische Untersuchungen im Dorf Kolotauri, Kreis Kedi, in Geyer, A. and Mamuladze, S. (ed) *Gonio-Apsaros III*, Logos Tbilisi

Opaiţ, A. 2004. *Local and imported ceramics in the Roman Province of Scythia (4th—6th centuries AD): aspects of economic life in the Province of Syria*. BAR International series 1274. Oxford

Peacock, D.P.S., and Williams, D.F. 1986. *Amphorae and the Roman economy: an introductory guide*. London

Terry, R. and Chillnger, G. 1955. Summary of 'Concerning some additional aids studying sedimentary formations' by Shvetsov, M. S. in *J Sedimentary Petrol* 25: 229-34

Timby, J. 2007. *Nokalakevi, Georgia: Interim Report on the Pottery from the 2007 Season*. Unpublished AGEN report

Timby, J. 2008. *Nokalakevi, Georgia: Interim Report on the Pottery from the 2008 Season*. Unpublished AGEN report

Timby, J. 2009. *Nokalakevi, Georgia: Interim Report on the Pottery from the 2009 Season*. Unpublished AGEN report

Timby, J. 2010. *Nokalakevi, Georgia: Interim Report on the Pottery from the 2010 Season*. Unpublished AGEN report

Tsetskhladze, G. 1999. *Pichvnari and its environs 6th century BC – 4th century AD*. Institut des Sciences et techniques de l'Antiquité. Presses Universitaires Franc-Comtoises

Tsetskhladze, G. and Vnukov, S. 1992. Colchian amphorae: typology, chronology and aspects of production, *Annual British Sch Athens* 87: 357-86

Vickers, M. and Kakhidze, A. 2004. *Pichvnari. Results of excavations conducted by the joint British-Georgian Pichvnari expedition 1998-2000. Vol 1*. Batumi /Oxford

Vnukov, S. 2010. Problems of 'brown clay' (Colchian) amphora studoes. Typology, chronology, production centres, distribution, in Tezgör, D. and Inaishvili, N. (ed) *PATABS: production and trade of amphorae in the Black Sea: actes de la table ronde international de Batoumi et Trabazon, 27-29 avril 2007, Varia Anatolica*, 21: 29-32

CHAPTER SEVEN

The conservation-restoration and analysis of artefacts 2001-2010

By Nino Kebuladze

Introduction

The excavations at Nokalakevi from 2001 to 2010 produced a wide variety of archaeological materials (ceramics, metal, glass and etc.). The material discovered in the seasons before 2006 were carefully transported to the Simon Janashia Georgian State Museum in Tbilisi and treated in the chemical-restoration laboratory. In 2006 Prof. Lomitashvili established a field conservation-restoration laboratory at the expedition base in Nokalakevi. This well-stocked, modern field laboratory is fitted with an extraction system and other equipment necessary for scientific analysis including chemical wares, reagents and chemicals, and tools for the mechanical cleaning of artefacts (Figure 7.1.1).

From the foundation of the laboratory in Nokalakevi, material from the local archaeological excavation has been treated here (Figure 7.1.2-4) alongside finds from other archaeological excavations in west Georgia, such as Pichvnari. Work at the laboratory also includes the conservation-restoration of exhibits from a number of west Georgian museums, including Nokalakevi, Senaki, Martvili, Chkhorotsqu and others.

The work of the on-site restorers at Nokalakevi includes the lifting of fragile and damaged objects revealed during the excavation season. Artefacts are lifted individually with the surrounding soil matrix, which is later carefully removed in laboratory conditions guaranteeing that as much information as possible can be retrieved (Figure 7.1. 5-8).

Cleaning and restoration–conservation of ceramics

During the excavation season ceramic material is processed on site. Following washing, drying and specialist analysis, fragments of ceramics are gathered according to context, sorted and where there are multiple sherds of vessels they are glued.

At the end of the excavation season some ceramic material is deposited in the Nokalakevi archaeological museum. The rest of it, along with the metal, glass, bone finds etc, is transported to the stores of the Georgian National Museum in Tbilisi following conservation in the Nokalakevi laboratory.

Ceramic material that is covered with soil, and a white-grey layer of carbonates, has sediment removed before being sorted by condition to ensure that fragile finds are not washed with water or acids. To remove sediments fragments are soaked in water for 2-3 hours and afterwards every piece is washed under running water and is cleaned by brush. Clean fragments are put in distilled water before being dried at room temperature.

Material covered with carbonates are put in diluted (5%) hydrochloric acid (HCl) until carbonates are fully dissolved. After the removal of the carbonate layer, the ceramic is washed with a brush under running water and is put in a bath where it stays until the next day, when it is washed again with a brush under running water before finally being put in distilled water. The water is regularly changed until the pH indicator shows pH=7.0, meaning the water has neutral reaction. Finally the material is shelf-dried at room temperature.

The lifting, cleaning and restoration-conservation of ceramic material found in graves is conducted differently. Vessels are retrieved from site with the soil inside, and are taken to the laboratory. Here the soil is removed from the vessel and is placed in a clean, labelled plastic-bag in preparation for paleobotanical and palynological analysis. After this the cleaning, drying and restoration are conducted similarly as the other ceramic material, however ceramic vessels recovered from graves are almost always fully reconstructed.

The vessels are restored with PVA (polyvinyl acetate[1]), with missing sherds replaced using different methods:

1. The missing pieces are partially or completely filled with plaster of Paris (Figures 7.3, 7.4), which if nessessary is covered by water-color, acrylic or oil paint (Figure 7.4. 1, 15).
2. Missing pieces are filled with plaster of Paris which is mixed with the appropriate colour dry pigment (Figure 7.4. 5, 8, 19). If the original vessel and the plaster are exactly the same colour, the surface of filled area must be slightly lowered so that the difference is obvious.

During this process photographs are taken before, during, and after restoration (Figure 7.3. 1, 2). Ceramic material recovered and treated from 2001-10 includes some very interesting domestic and ritual material (Figures 7.3, 7.4, 7.5).

Cleaning and restoration-conservation of metal

Excavations at Nokalakevi between 2001 and 2010 have produced a wide variety of metals and alloys (gold, bronze, zinc, iron), including material made for household and military use, as well as jewellery (Figures 7.2, 7.6-7.12). In terms of quantity, however, it represents a smaller assemblage than that of ceramic finds.

Metal is far more unstable than ceramic. Nokalakevi is located on the edge of the Colchian lowland and consequently the ground is very wet and rich with oxygen, which damages metal. Iron artefacts, in particular, are often damaged beyond saving by rust.

The surface of bronze artefacts recovered at Nokalakevi was, as a rule, covered with soil, mechanical (i.e. unbonded) coating and patina. This material was, therefore, often cleaned using modern mechanical techniques, treated and conserved (Figure 7.1. 3).

To separate mechanical sediment and soil from an artefact, metal objects are placed in alcohol, and are cleaned with a soft brush. Afterwards it is treated under a microscope, using a lancet, a rubber-tipped drill, or a diamond abrasive in order to reveal the original form and surface of the artefact.

To remove bad patina from bronze material, artefacts are placed in Titriplex 4% solution, before being cleaned with a brush in water. After this it is placed in distilled water and the water is regularly changed until its pH is neutral. After drying it is covered with 5% Paraloid B-72[2] in acetone[3].

In Trench B, in 2003, a fragment of a gold artefact was found, with a Greek inscription inlaid with blue and white enamel (Figure 7.2. 1). The artefact was dated by the letter forms to the 6th century A.D. It was cleaned very carefully with alcohol cotton and was conserved with 5% Paraloid B-72 solution in acetone. The same methods were used for the cleaning and conservation of a gold earring found in Trench B in 2004 (Figure 7.2. 2).

Analysis of metal finds

All metals, with the exception of gold, are unstable and prone to corrosion. Corrosion is the process by which a metal breaks down and combines with other elements to form metallic compounds, known as corrosion products. These products differ from the metal in shape, colour, appearance, density and volume. Some artefacts are made of pure metal. Frequently they are made from the alloy of two or more metals. Metals are often used in conjunction with each other as coatings, decorations or jointing materials.

Depending upon the composition of a metal or alloy and the nature of its corrosion, the products of corrosion contain information concerning the metal grain structure and the position of its original surface. This information can be used to reveal technological information about the object and may aid its authentication. For this reason spectral analysis was undertaken on all bronze and lead artefacts found from 2001-10.

The analyses have been done on *ElvaX,* a desktop energy-dispersive X-ray fluorescence (EDXRF) spectrometer which does not require liquid nitrogen cooling of the solid state X-ray detector. Energy-dispersive X-ray fluorescence (XRF) spectrometry is a modern method for quantitative determination of elemental composition. Within the available analytical methods, XRF techniques are noted for their universality and excel in a number of characteristics. Unlike most of the analytical methods, which require sampling, the XRF technique is non-destructive.

The aim of the XRF method is to determine the concentration of an analyte in the sample using the intensity of its characteristic lines in the spectrum. Analyses were conducted on 40kv, 81 second live time and the results are presented below (Table 7.1). Analysis of other metal finds from Nokalakevi is ongoing, and the results will be published soon.

Cleaning and restoration-conservation of glass

Glass material from Nokalakevi is mainly fragmentally represented. To remove dirt and other sediments from glass, the artefact is placed in alcohol and is cleaned with a soft brush. Glass is very often irisated so, if it is necessary, the material is cleaned mechanically, using a variety of soft tools and solutions, or they are put in pH<7 solution and washed under running water. Finally the artefact is placed in distilled water until it is pH neutral. Well dried glass fragments are covered with a solution of Paraloid B-72 in acetone. Fragments of a variety of glassware were produced by the excavations at Nokalakevi from 2001-10 including cup bases and rims, fragments of windows, and jewellery, such as necklaces and pendants (Figures 7.13-7.15).

Cleaning and restoration-conservation of stone

During the excavations a variety of stone artefacts were found, representing religious (part of a cross) (Figure 7.2. 7), ritual (a seal) (Figure 7.2. 5), domestic (hand-mill [Figure 7.2.8], touchstones [Figure 7.16. 1, 2, 8, 12], spindles [Figure 7.16. 3], hand-axes [Figure 7.16. 13] and beads [Figure 7.15. 1, Figure 7.16. 9]), and military/hunting activity (arrow-heads [Figure 7.16. 11], sling shot). Stone artefacts were cleaned in distilled water with a soft brush and, after drying, were packed for storage.

In Nokalakevi's field laboratory the photo-fixation of ceramics, metal, glass, and stone artefacts, before and after restoration, was constantly in progress. Ultimately, all the conserved items were wrapped and placed in a sealed box, with appropriate specific humidity (RH)[4], controlled by silica gel and a humidity indicator card (Figure 7.1. 4).

All documentation, without which the artefacts are archaeologically useless, and material that was gathered from 2001 to 2010 is kept in Nokalakevi's Archaeological Museum and in storage rooms at the National Museum of Georgia specifically set aside for the Nokalakevi project.

Specialist Glossary

[1] **PVA - polyvinyl acetate resin solution** – *a number of polyvinyl acetate resins are available as emulsion in water, which can used in restoration work.*
[2] **Paraloid B-72** – *a methyl methacrylate co polymer, a clear acrylic resin supplied in bead form. When dissolved in an appropriate solvent the solution can be used as a consolidant for fragile materials.*
[3]**Acetone** – *a colourless volatile liquid used as a solvent for some adhesives and consolidants.*
[4] **Relative humidity** – *is the amount of water that the air can hold at a given temperature.*

N	Object	Inv. N	Ca	Cr	Fe	Ni	Cu	Zn	As	Ag	Sn	Sb	Pb
1	clasp for shroud	12-974:5180	10.267		2.148	0.000	0.127	0.000	0.000	0.863	0.000	0.000	86.595
2	slag	12-974:5181	4.888		15.887		71.420		6.019	0.436			
3	stick	12-974:5182			2.489		55.668			0.732	28.295		12.816
4	ear-ring	12-974:5183			6.460		40.377			0.699	51.326		1.138
5	ear-ring with pendant	12-974:5184			2.616		69.275			0.621	25.021		2.466
6	ear-ring (fragment)	12-974:5184			5.704		63.228		0.970	0.571	29.428		0.099
7	ear-ring shaft	12-974:5184			0.127		87.837			0.354	9.407		2.274
8	bracelet (1)	12-974:5185					70.437			0.554	21.319		7.690
9	bracelet (2) broken	12-974:5185			1.656		46.017		1.801	0.666	49.617		0.243
10	bracelet (3) broken	12-974:5185			1.090		36.244			0.808	48.410		10.448
11	bracelet (4)	12-974:5185			0.444		60.851			0.862	37.843		
12	bracelet (5)	12-974:5185			0.452		72.840		0.733	0.563	25.051		0.361
13	bracelet (6)	12-974:5185			0.270		80.346			0.427	17.026		1.932
14	ear-ring with bead	12-974:5482			0.358		73.420			0.573	24.535		1.114
15	bracelet	12-974:5484		10.127	1.146		69.810	2.995		0.388	13.377		2.217
16	bracelet (1)	12-974:5588			0.196		75.105			1.263	22.199		1.237
17	bracelet (2)	12-974:5588			0.733	3.265	48.625			0.919	42.449		4.009
18	bracelet	12-974:5590			0.181	0.663	78.582		0.913	0.402	19.156		0.103
19	ear-ring	12-974:5591			6.529		26.936	0.385	2.854	0.806	60.833		1.669
20	buckle	12-974:4251					26.427	1.500		0.874	19.117		52.082
21	fibula	12-974:3906			0.079		88.830	32.352		0.259			0.481
22	ear-ring	12-974:5422					92.061			0.494	5.241	0.723	
23	coin	12-974:4325					98.843			0.268			0.889
24	arrow-head (small)	12-974:4326			0.713		98.917		0.116	0.253			
25	arrow-head	12-974:4327	2.471		3.467		89.861			0.331	0.685	0.264	2.921
26	pendant	12-974:4328	8.137		7.396		77.180	1.251		0.774	0.952	3.219	1.091
27	bracelet (fragment)	12-974:4329			2.522		56.066			2.234	25.428		13.761
28	coin (bent)	12-974:4333			0.192		98.939						0.869
29	bent plate	12-974:4337	1.623		97.763		0.120	0.075		0.262			0.122

Table 7.1: Results of spectral analysis of bronze and lead finds

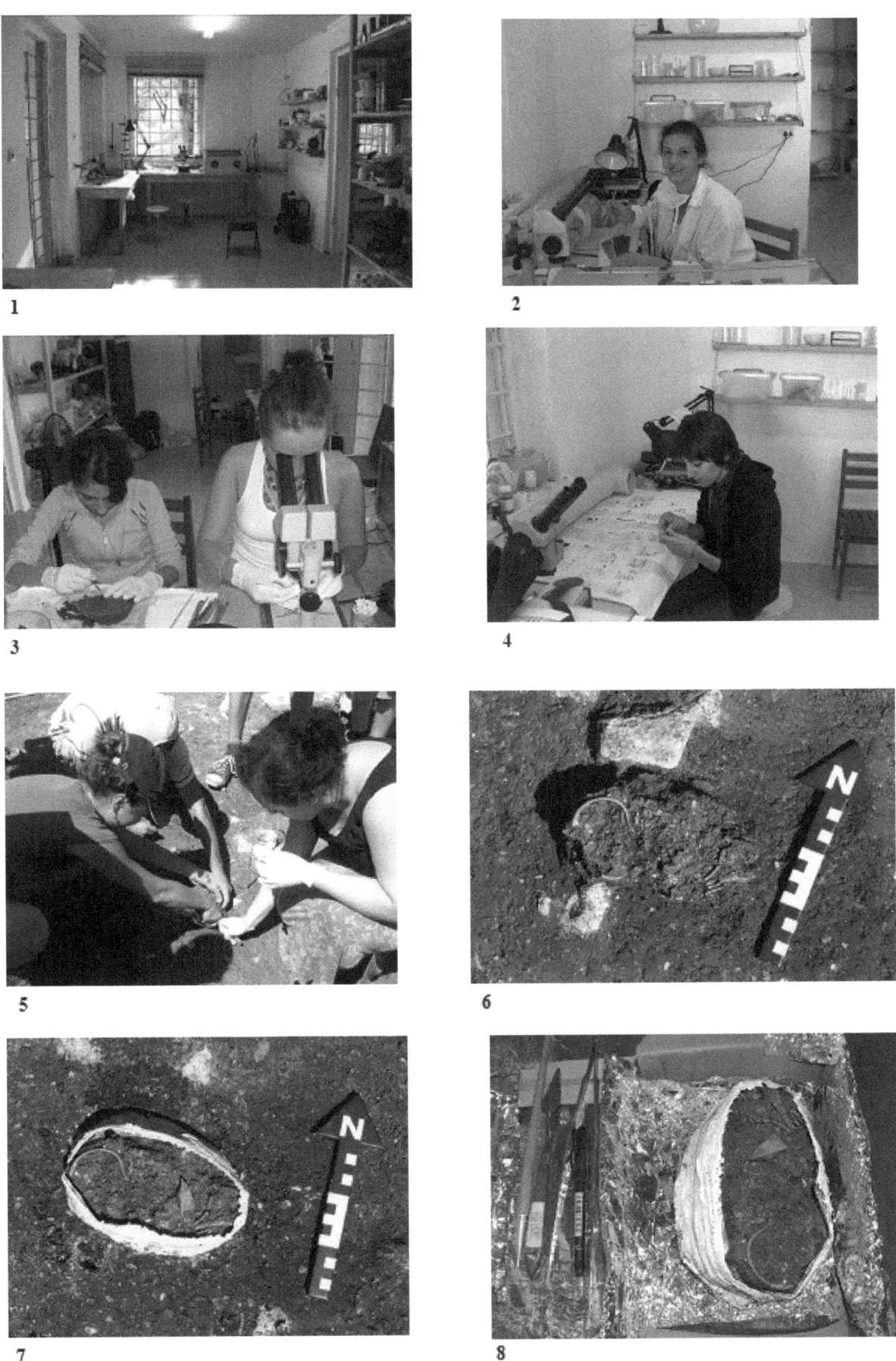

Figure 7.1: 1 *Field laboratory in Nokalakevi;* **2-4** *Processes of restoration-conservation treatment;* **5** *Isolation of the bracelet in a block of earth;* **6** *Bracelet exposed on earth matrix;* **7** *Matrix undercut at edges and supported with bandage;* **8** *Lifted earth block with bracelet*

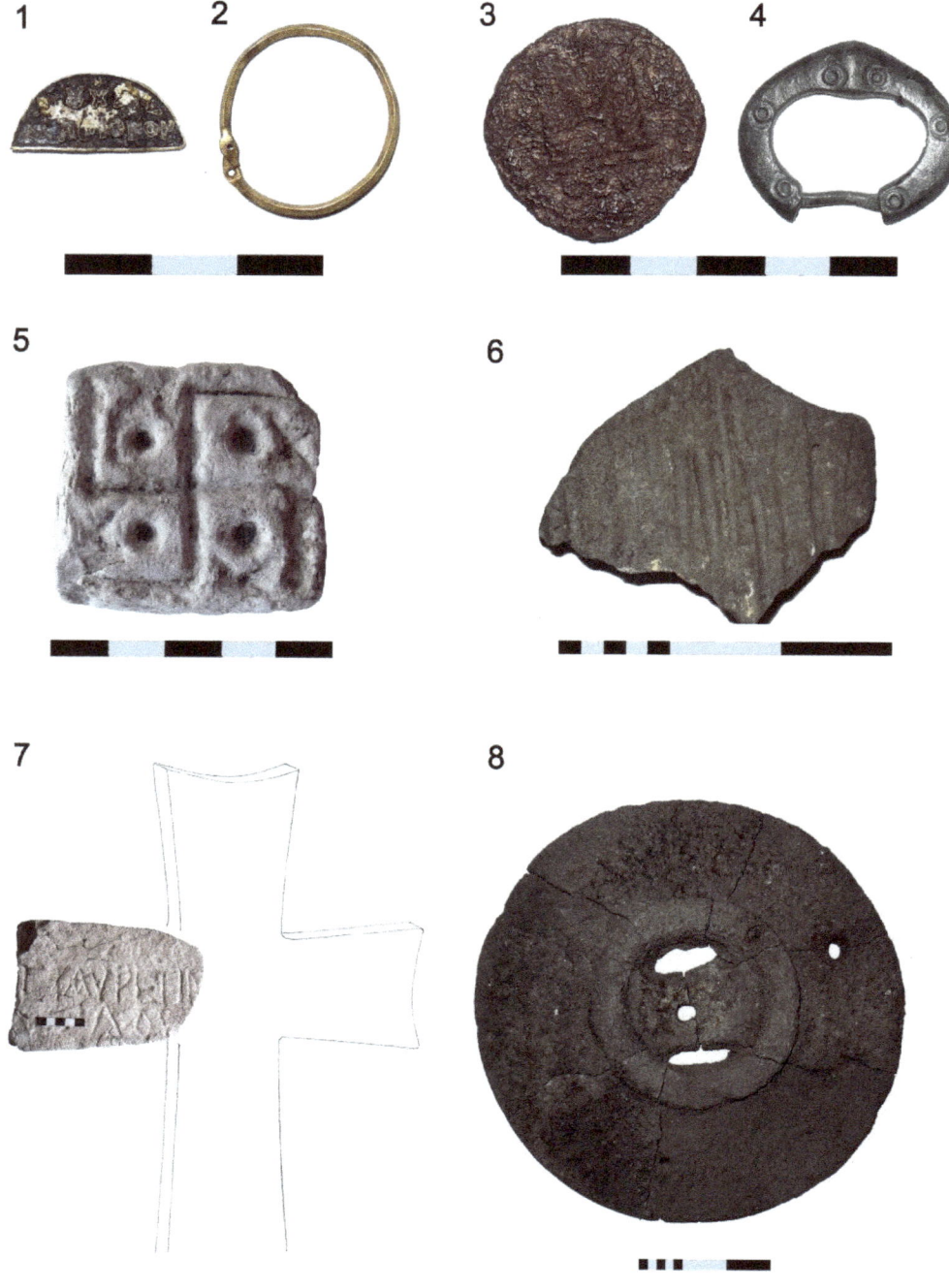

Figure 7.2: 1 12-974:4219 Enamel. Gold. Trench B, cont. 303. 2003; *2* 12-974:4220 Ear-ring. Gold. Trench B. 2004; *3* 12-974:4325 Coin. Copper; *4* 12-974:3905 Buckle. Bronze. Trench A, cont. 111. 2001; *5* 12-974:5829 Seal. Stone. Trench B. 2010; *6* 12-974:5739 Stone for abrasive and polishing beads. Trench A, cont. 268. 2010; *7* 12-974:3912 Part of the cross. Stone. Trench A, cont.122. 2001; *8* 12-974:5705 Hand-mill. Stone. Trench A, cont.267. 2010

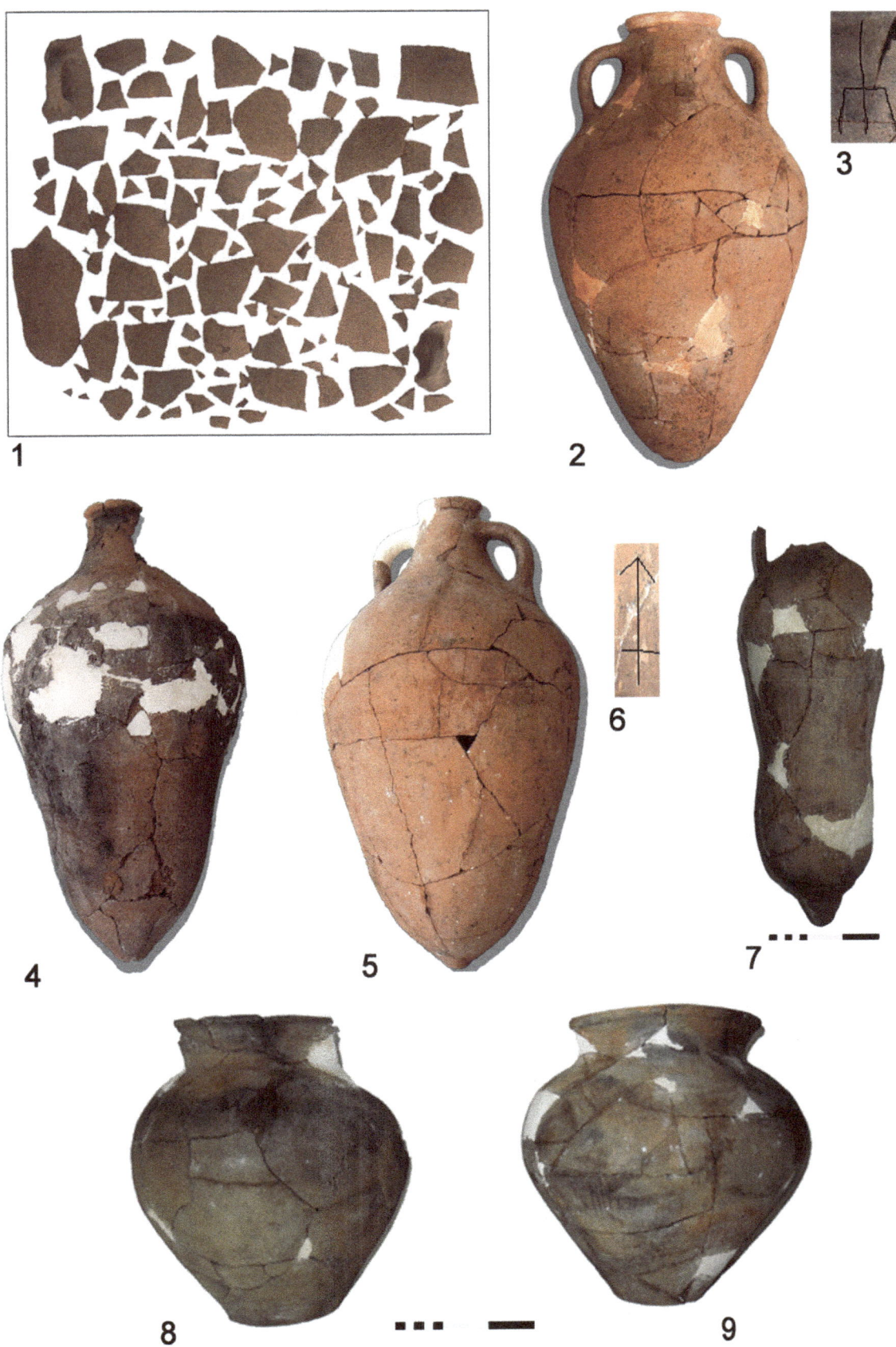

Figure 7.3: 1 *12-974:5199 Amphora before restoration; 2 12-974:5199 Amphora. Clay. Trench A, cont. 189. 2007; 3 12-974:5199 Inscribed image of trident on amphora; 4 12-974:5200 Amphora. Clay. Trench A, cont 220. 2007; 5 12-974:5198 Amphora. Clay.Trench A, cont 205. 2007; 6 12-974:5198 Inscribed image of crossed arrow on amphora; 7 12-974:5704 Amphora. Clay. Trench A, cont 267. 2010; 8 12-974:4513 Jar. Clay. Trench A, cont 181. 2006; 9 12-974:5780 Jar. Clay. Trench A, cont 276. 2010*

Figure 7.4: 1 *12-974:4939 Jug. Clay. Trench A, cont 136. 2004;* **2** *12-974:5461 Jug. Clay. Trench A, cont 235. 2008;* **3** *12-974:4194 Jug with handle. Clay. Trench A. 2003;* **4** *12-974:5176 Jar. Clay. Trench A. 2005;* **5** *12-974:5587 Jug. Clay. Trench A, cont 260. 2009;* **6** *12-974:5478 Jug. Clay. Trench A, cont 252. 2008;* **7** *12-974:4195 Jug with handle. Clay. Trench A. 2003;* **8** *12-974:5559 Pot. Clay. Trench A, cont 254. 2009;* **9** *12-974:4197 Pot. Clay. Trench A. 2003;* **10** *12-974:5475 Pot. Clay. Trench A, cont 246. 2008;* **11** *12-974:5177 Pot. Clay. Trench A, cont 226. 2007;* **12** *12-974:4196 Jug with handle. Clay. Trench A, cont 226,227. 2007;* **13** *12-974:4193 Amphoriskos. Clay. Trench , cont . 2003;* **14** *12-974:5767 Amphoriskos. Clay. Trench A, cont 267. 2010;* **15** *12-974:4946 Bowl. Clay. Trench A, cont 171. 2006;* **16** *12-974:4332 Bowl. Clay. Trench A. 2005;* **17** *12-974:5533 Bottom of the cup. Clay. Trench A, cont 235. 2009;* **18** *12-974:5707 Cup. Clay. Trench A, cont 268;* **19** *12-974:5544 Cup. Clay. Trench A, cont 235. 2009;* **20** *12-974:5521 Cup. Clay. Trench A, cont 235. 2009*

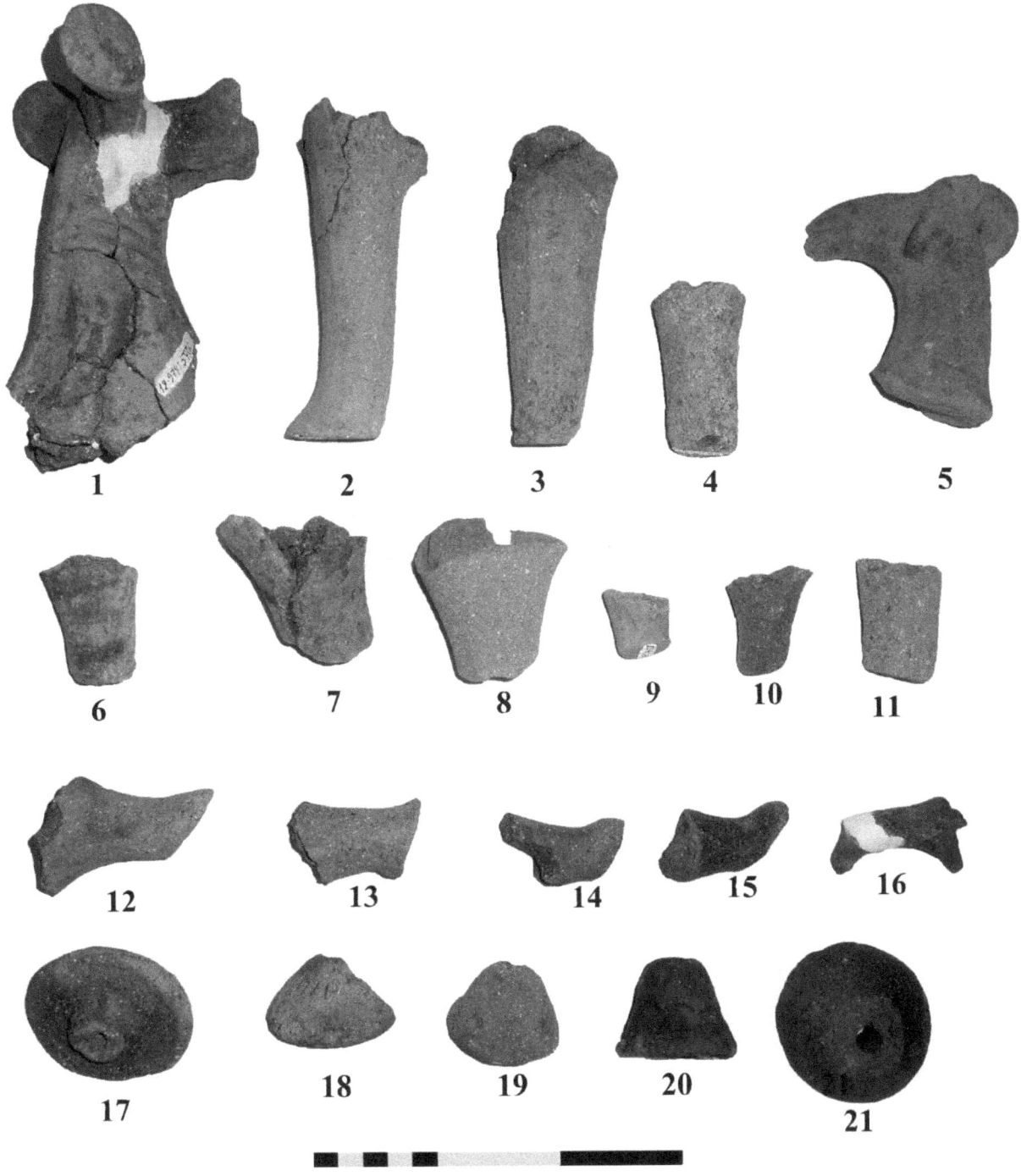

Figure 7.5: 1 *12-974:5776 Head of zoomorphic figurine. Clay. Trench A, cont. 272. 2010;* ***2*** *12-974:5775 Leg of zoomorphic figurine. Clay. Trench A, cont. 272. 2010;* ***3*** *12-974:5775 Leg of zoomorphic figurine. Clay. Trench A, cont. 272. 2010;* ***4*** *12-974:5738 Leg of zoomorphic figurine. Clay. Trench A, cont. 268. 2010;* ***5*** *12-974:4331 Head of ram. Clay. Trench A, cont. 166. 2005;* ***6*** *12-974:5775 Leg of zoomorphic figurine. Clay. Trench A, cont. 272. 2010;* ***7*** *12-974:5775 Leg of zoomorphic figurine. Clay. Trench A, cont 272. 2010;* ***8*** *12-974:5670 Leg of zoomorphic figurine. Clay. Trench A. 2010;* ***9*** *12-974:5670 Leg of zoomorphic figurine. Clay. Trench A. 2010;* ***10*** *12-974:5145 Leg of zoomorphic figurine. Clay. Trench A, cont. 216. 2007;* ***11*** *12-974:5464 Leg of zoomorphic figurine. Clay. Trench A. 2008;* ***12*** *12-974:5670 Horn of zoomorphic figurine. Clay. Trench A. 2010;* ***13*** *12-974:5738 Horn of zoomorphic figurine. Clay. Trench A, cont. 272. 2010;* ***14*** *12-974:5738 Horn of zoomorphic figurine. Clay. Trench A, cont. 272. 2010;* ***15*** *12-974:5509 Horn of zoomorphic figurine. Clay. Trench A;* ***16*** *12-974:5714 Small zoomorphic figurine (not full). Clay. Trench A, cont 268. 2010;* ***17*** *12-974:5513 Model of wheel. Clay. Trench A, cont 235. 2009;* ***18*** *12-974:5830 Sinker. Clay. Trench A, cont. 235. 2010;* ***19*** *12-974:5671 Sinker. Clay. Trench A, cont. 232. 2010;* ***20*** *12-974:5759 Sinker. Clay. Trench A, cont. 268. 2010;* ***21*** *12-974:5577 Spindle whorl. Clay. Trench A, cont. 259. 2009*

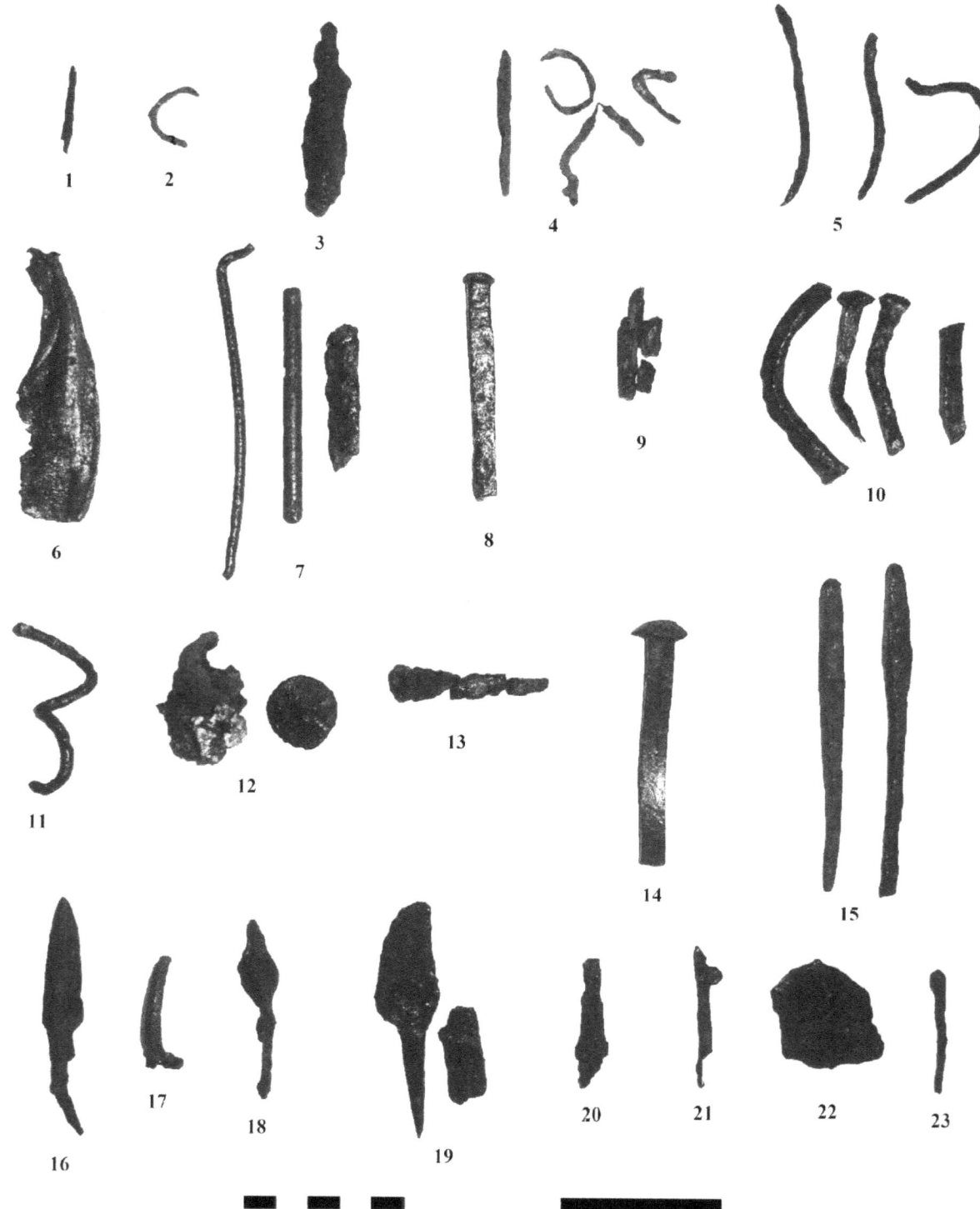

Figure 7.6: *1 12-974:3793 Ear-ring (fragment). Iron. Trench A, cont. 104. 2001; 2 12-974:3794 Arrow-head (fragment). Iron. Trench A, cont.104. 2001; 3 12-974:3795 Arrow-head. Bronze. Trench A, cont.104. 2001; 4 12-974:3821 Object (fragments). Bronze. Trench A, cont. 104. 2001 ; 5 12-974:3840 Object (fragment). Iron. Trench A, cont.100. 2001; 6 12-974:3843 Vessel (fragment). Copper. Trench A, cont.102. 2001; 7 12-974:3845 Object (fragment). Iron. Trench A, cont.102. 2001; 8 12-974:3846 Nail. Iron. Iron. Trench A, cont.102. 2001; 9 12-974:3880 Arrow-head. Iron. Trench A, cont.108. 2001; 10 12-974:3882 Nail. Iron. Trench A, cont. 101. 2001; 11 12-974:3883 Object (fragment). Trench A, cont. 101. 2001; 12 12-974:3885 Object (fragment). Iron. Trench A, cont. 101. 2001; 13 12-974:3886 Arrow-head. Iron. Trench A, cont. 103. 2001; 14 12-974:3897 Nail. Iron. Trench A, cont. 105. 2001; 15 12-974:3898 Arrow-head. Iron. Trench A, cont. 105. 2001; 16 12-974:3899 Arrow-head. Iron. Trench A, cont. 107. 2001; 17 12-974:3906 Brooch. Copper. Trench A, cont. 111. 2001; 18 12-974:3907 Arrow-head. Iron. Trench A, cont. 112. 2001; 19 12-974:3908 Arrow-head. Iron. Trench A, cont. 114. 2001; 20 12-974:3911 Arrow-head. Iron. Trench A, cont. 122. 2001; 21 12-974:3919 Pin. Iron. Trench A, cont. 104. 2001; 22 12-974:3920 Plate. Iron. Trench A, cont. 104. 2001; 23 12-974:3925 Object (fragment). Iron. Trench A, cont. 110. 2001*

Figure 7.7: 1 12-974:3957 Nail. Iron. Trench B, cont. 101. 2002; *2* 12-974:3958 Bracelet (fragment). Iron. Trench B, cont. 101. 2002; *3* 12-974:3959 Object (fragment). Iron. Trench B, cont. 101. 2002; *4* 12-974:4041 Nail. Iron. Trench B, cont. 101. 2002; *5* 12-974:4042 Arrow-head. Iron. Trench B, cont. 101. 2002; *6* 12-974:4043 Bowl (fragments). Copper. Trench B, cont. 101. 2002; *7* 12-974:4044 Arrow-head. Iron. Trench B, cont. 101. 2002; *8* 12-974:4046 Vessel (fragments). Copper. Trench A, cont. 108. 2002; *9* 12-974:4046^2 Phalera. Bronze. Trench A, cont. 108. 2002; *10* 12-974:4046^1 Cut coin. Copper. Trench A, cont. 108. 2002; *11* 12-974:4047 Nail. Bronze. Copper. Trench B, cont. 108. 2002; *12* 12-974:4048 Nails (4). Iron. Trench A, cont. 108. 2002; *13* 12-974:4049 Arrow-head. Iron. Trench A, cont. 108. 2002; *14* 12-974:4050 Pins (segments). Trench A, cont. 108. 2002; *15* 12-974:4051 Pendant. (segment). Copper. Trench A, cont. 108. 2002; *16* 12-974:4052 Object (fragments 2). Iron/Bronze. Trench A, cont. 108. 2002; *17* 12-974:4058 Bowl (fragments). Copper. Trench A, cont. 110. 2002; *18* 12-974:4063 Knife. iron. Trench A, cont. 125. 2002; *19* 12-974:4064 Nail. Iron. Trench A, cont. 125. 2002; *20* 12-974:4065 Knife (fragments). Iron. Trench A, cont. 125. 2002; *21* 12-974:4066 Spearhead (fragment). Iron. Trench A, cont. 125. 2002; *22* 12-974:4067 Object. Iron. Trench A, cont. 125. 2002; *23* 12-974:4069 Arrow-head. Iron. Trench A, cont. 132. 2002; *24* 12-974:4070 Pin. Iron. Trench A, cont. 132. 2002; *25* 12-974:4071 Object. Iron. Trench A, cont. 132. 2002

Figure 7.8

1. 12-974:4143 Bracelet (fragment). Copper. Trench B, cont. 136. 2003
2. 12-974:4144 Bell. Copper. Trench B, cont. 136. 2003
3. 12-974:4145 Bowl (part). Trench B, cont. 136. 2003
4. 12-974:4151 Clasp of shroud. Lead. Trench A, cont. 139. 2003
5. 12-974:4156 Object (fragment). Copper. Trench A, cont. 136. 2003
6. 12-974:4157 Object (fragments – 4). Copper. Trench A, cont. 136. 2003
7. 12-974:4159 Bracelets (fragment). Bronze. Trench A, cont. 136. 2003
8. 12-974:4161 Arrow-head. Iron. Trench A, cont. XXX. 2003
9. 12-974:4162 Bracletes (fragments). Bronze. Trench A, cont.138. 2003
10. 12-974:4163 Bracelet (fragment). Bronze. Trench A, cont. 137. 2003
11. 12-974:4164 Ear-rings (3). Bronze. Trench A, cont. 137. 2003
12. 12-974:4165 Nails (2). Iron. Trench B. 2003
13. 12-974:4166 Arrow-head. Iron. Trench B. 2003
14. 12-974:4180 Ear-ring. Copper. Trench A, cont. 154. 2003
15. 12-974:4181 Ear-ring. Bronze. Trench A, cont. 151. 2003
16. 12-974:4183 Ear-ring Copper. Bronze. Trench A. 2003
17. 12-974:4185 Hangers (3). Bronze. Trench A, cont. 154. 2003
18. 12-974:4186 Bracelet. Bronze. Trench A, cont. 154. 2003
19. 12-974:4187 Spherical object. Bronze. Trench B, cont. 303. 2003
20. 12-974:4188 Bracelet (fragment). Bronze. Trench B, cont. 303. 2003
21. 12-974:4189 Object (fragment). Copper. Trench B, cont. 315. 2003
22. 12-974:4191 Pin. Copper. Trench B, cont. 318. 2003
23. 12-974:4192 Buckle. Copper. Trench B, cont. 322. 2003

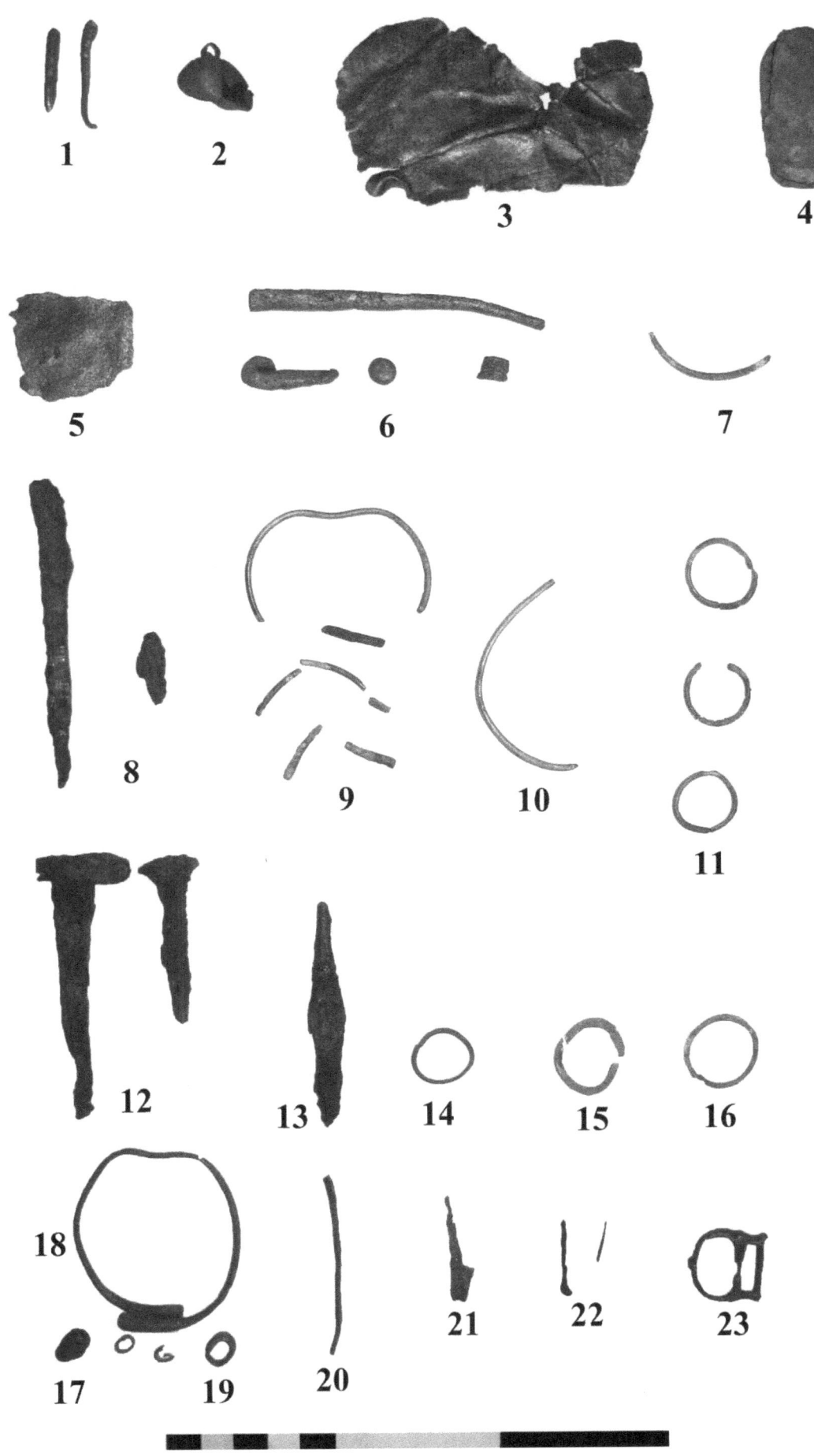

Figure 7.8: *Captions opposite*

Figure 7.9

1. 12-974:4246 Object (fragments 2). Iron. Trench A, cont. 108. 2004
2. 12-974:4251 Buckle. Copper. Trench A. 2004
3. 12-974:4256 Chain. Bronze. Trench B, cont. 326. 2004
4. 12-974:4257 Object (fragments 2). Bronze. Trench A, cont. 108. 2004
5. 12-974:4258. Object (fragment) Trench B, cont. 106. 2004
6. 12-974:4261 Nail. Iron. Trench B, cont. 106. 2004
7. 12-974:4268 Ring. Bronze. Trench B, cont. 108. 2004
8. 12-974:4270 Nail. Iron. Trench B, cont. 108. 2004
9. 12-974:4272 Knife. Iron. Trench B, cont. 108. 2004
10. 12-974:4276 Knife. Iron. Trench A, cont. 125. 2004
11. 12-974:4277 Knife. Iron. Trench A, cont. 125. 2004
12. 12-974:4278 Spearhead. Iron. Trench B, cont. 125. 2004
13. 12-974:4279 Object (fragment). Bronze. Tench A, cont. 108. 2004
14. 12-974:4280 Brooch. Bronze. Trench A, cont. 108. 2004
15. 12-974:4281 Bell. Bronze. Trench B, cont. 339. 2004
16. 12-974:4283 Arrow-head. Iron. Trench A, cont. 151. 2004
17. 12-974:4285 Nail. Iron. Trench A, cont. 151. 2004
18. 12-974:4286 Bracelet (3). Bronze. Trench A, cont. 151. 2004
19. 12-974:4288 Object (pieces). Iron. Trench B, cont. 325. 2004
20. 12-974:4289 Object fragments (5). Copper.. Trench B, cont. 325. 2004
21. 12-974:4291 Ring. Copper. Trench B, cont. 328. 2004
22. 12-974:4290 Knife (fragments). Iron. Trench B, cont. 325. 2004
23. 12-974:4292 Horseshoe. Iron. Trench A, cont. 108. 2004
24. 12-974:4294 Pins. Bronze (2). Trench B, cont. 339. 2004
25. 12-974:4295 Blade (fragment). Bronze. Trench B, cont. 106. 2004
26. 12-974:4296 Arrow-head (pieces) (5). Iron. Trench A, cont. 108. 2004
27. 12-974:4297 Nail. Iron. Trench B, cont. 106. 2004
28. 12-974:4298 Arrow-head. Iron. Trench A, cont. 108. 2004
29. 12-974:4301 Object (fragment). Bronze. Trench A, cont. 108. 2004
30. 12-974:4302 Pin. Bronze. Trench A, cont. 108. 2004
31. 12-974:4303 Bracelet (fragment). Bronze. Trench A, cont. 108. 2004

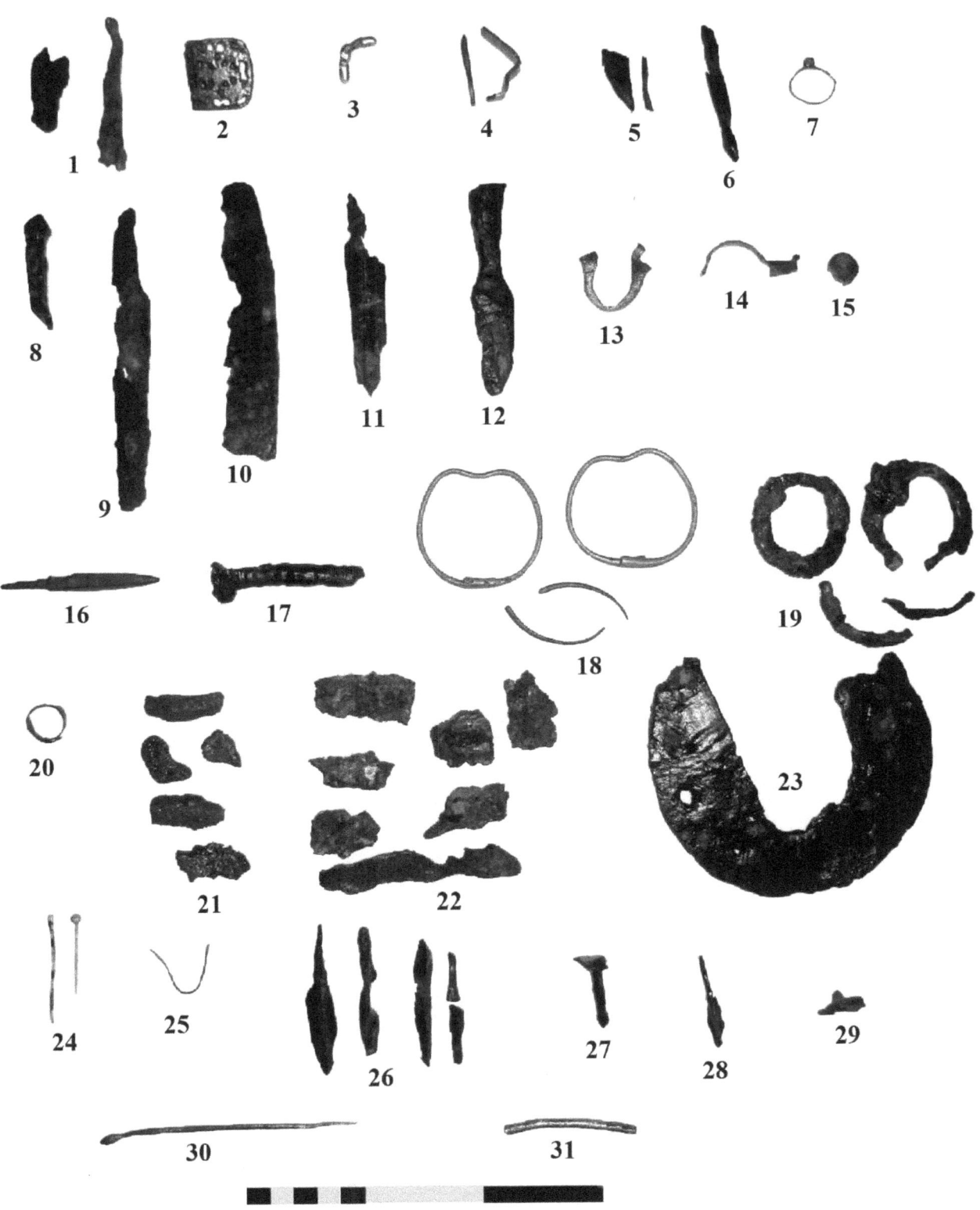

Figure 7.9: *Captions opposite*

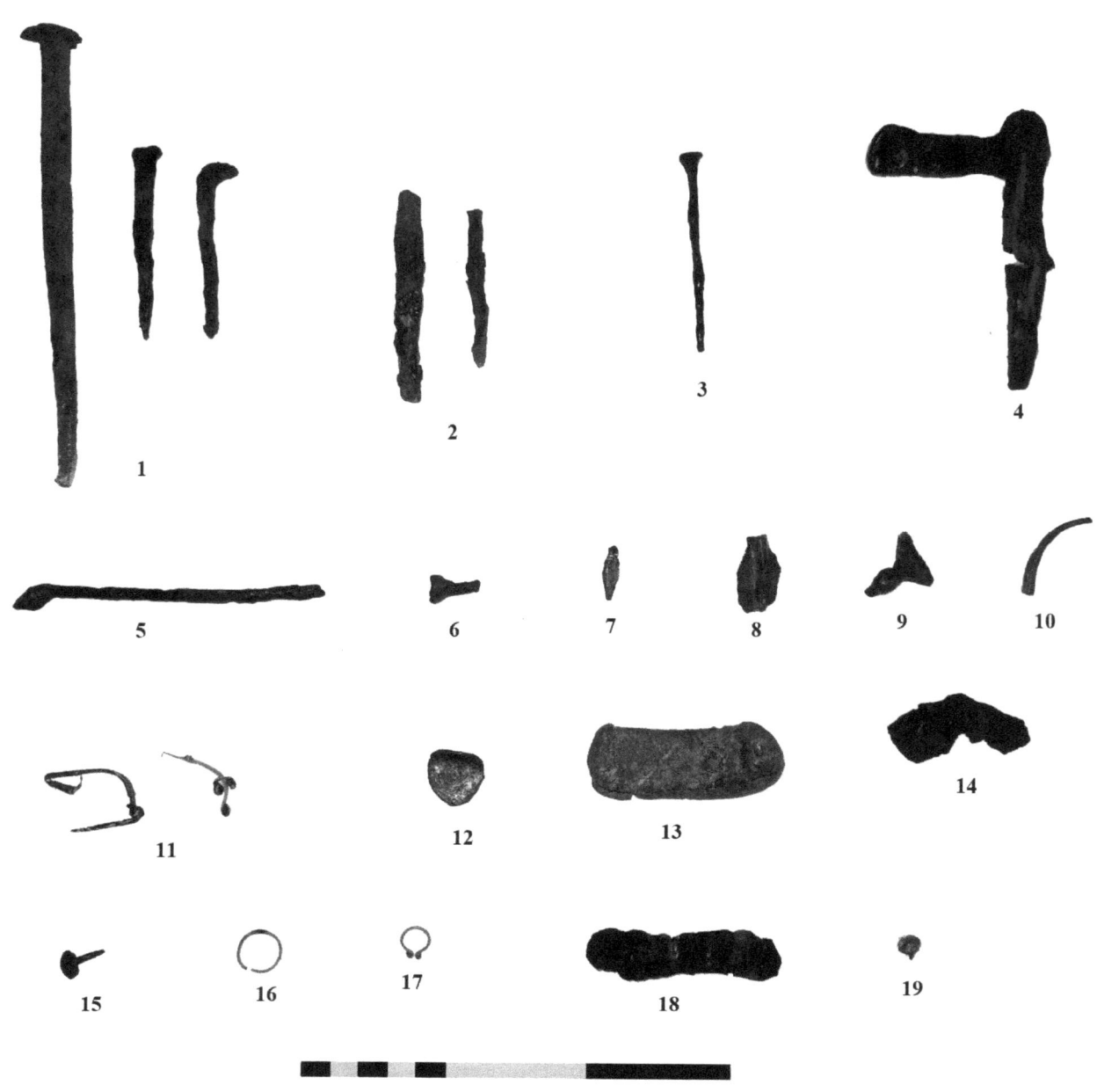

Figure 7.10: 1 12-974:4316 Nail. Iron. Trench A, cont. 111. 2005; *2* 12-974:4317 Arrow-head. Iron. Trench A, cont. 166. 2005; *3* 12-974:4318 Nail. Iron. Trench A, cont. 171. 2005; *4* 12-974:4319 Fastener. Iron. Trench A, cont. 171. 2005; *5* 12-974:4322 Earspoon. Iron. Trench A, cont. 164. 2005; *6* 12-974:4324 Nail. Iron. Trench A, cont. 163. 2005; *7* 12-974:4326 Arrow-head. Bronze Trench A, cont. 166. 2005; *8* 12-974:4327 Spearhead. Bronze. Trench A, cont. 166. 2005; *9* 12-974:4328 Object (fragment). Bronze. Trench A, cont. 166. 2005; *10* 12-974:4329 Bracelet (fragment). Bronze. Trench A, cont. 166. 2005; *11* 12-974:4330 Brooch. Bronze. Trench A, cont. 166. 2005; *12* 12-974:4333 Coin (?). Copper. Trench B, cont. 382. 2005; *13* 12-974:4334 Clasp of shroud. Lead. Trench B, cont. 303. 2005; *14* 12-974:4337 Object (fragment). Copper. Trench B, cont. 303,326. 2005; *15* 12-974:4338 Object. Copper. Trench B, cont. 303,326. 2005; *16* 12-974:4339 Ear-ring. Bronze. Trench B, cont. 303,326. 2005; *17* 12-974:4340 Object (fragment). Trench B, cont. 303,326. 2005; *18* 12-974:5020 Plate. Iron. Trench A, cont. 174. 2006; *19* 12-974:5021 Small nail. Iron. Trench A, cont. 173. 2006.

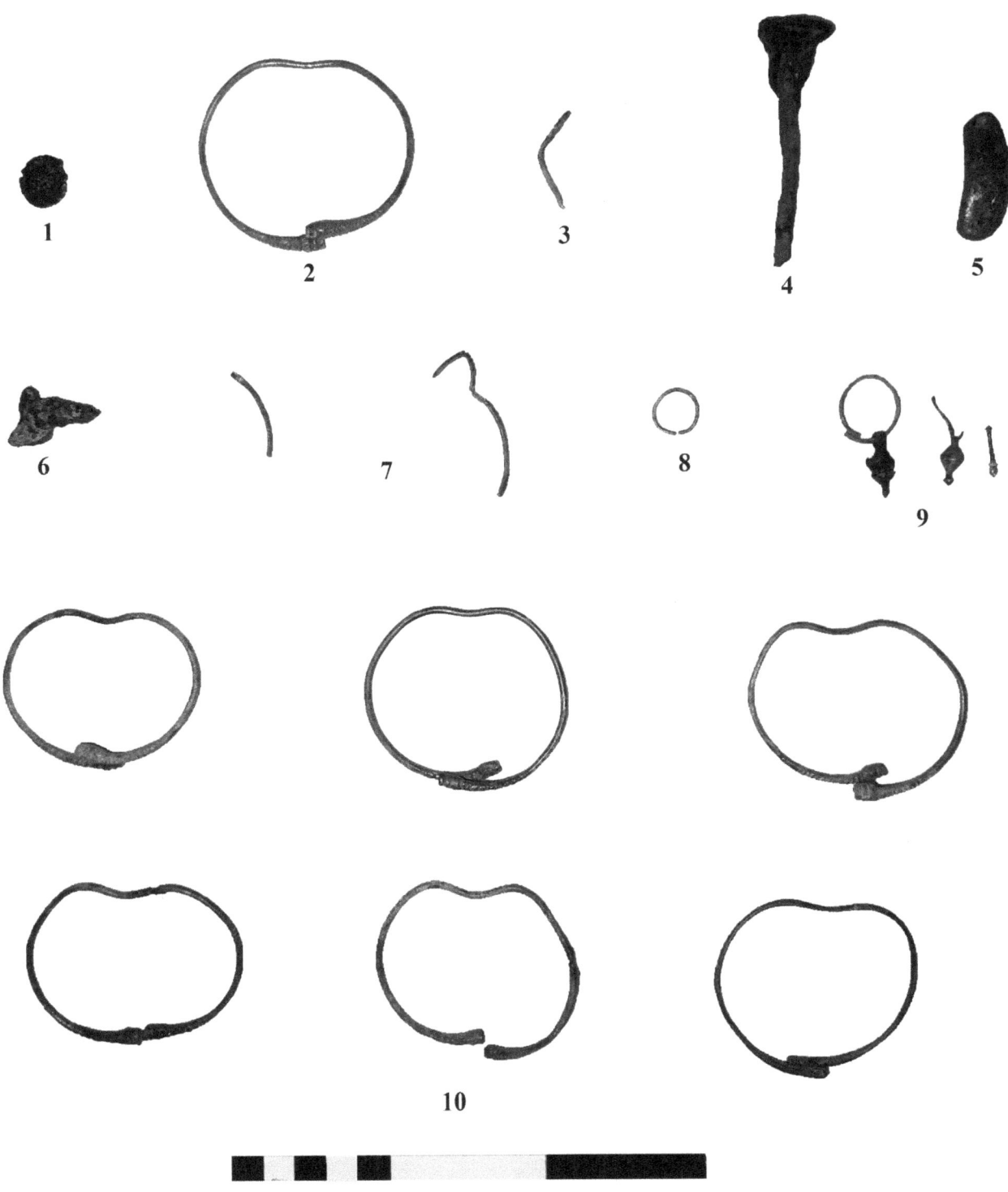

Figure 7.11: *1* *12-974:5081 Coin. Bronze. Trench A, cont. 174. 2007*; *2* *12-974:5089 Bracelet. Bronze. Trench A, cont. 198,199. 2007*; *3* *12-974:5120 Bracelet (fragment). Bronze. Trench A, cont. 211. 2007*; *4* *12-974:5162 Nail. Iron. Trench A, cont. 217. 2007*; *5* *12-974:5180 Clasp of shroud. Lead. Trench A, cont. 226. 2007*; *6* *12-974:5181 Object (fragments). Bronze. Trench A, cont. 226. 2007*; *7* *12-974:5182 Object (fragments) (2). Bronze. Trench A, cont. 226. 2007*; *8* *12-974:5183 Ear-ring. Bronze. Trench A, cont. 226. 2007*; *9* *12-974:5184 Ear-ring (fragments) (3) Bronze. Trench A, cont. 226. 2007*; *10* *12-974:5185 Bracelet (6). Bronze. Trench A, cont. 227. 2007*

Figure 7.12

1. *12-974:5422 Object (fragment). Copper. Trench A, cont. 217. 2008*
2. *12-974:5423 Bracelet (fragment). Bronze. Trench A, cont. 217. 2008*
3. *12-974:5468 Object (fragment). Copper. Trench A, cont. 240. 2008*
4. *12-974:5422 Ear-ring (2). Bronze. Trench A, cont. 253. 2008*
5. *12-974:5484 Bracelet. Bronze. Trench A, cont. 253. 2008*
6. *12-974:5499 Bracelet (fragment). Copper. Trench A, cont. 217. 2009*
7. *12-974:5515 Awl. Bronze. Trench A, cont. 235. 2009*
8. *12-974:5517 Bracelet (fragment). Copper. Trench A, cont. 235. 2009*
9. *12-974:5518 Object (fragment). Copper. Trench A, cont. 235. 2009*
10. *12-974:5561 Object (fragment). Copper. Trench A, cont. 254. 2009*
11. *12-974:5563 Bracelet (fragment). Copper. Trench A, cont. 254. 2009*
12. *12-974:5564 Bracelet (fragment). Copper. Trench A, cont. 254. 2009*
13. *12-974:5565 Ear-ring (2). Bronze. Trench A, cont. 254. 2009*
14. *12-974:5588 Bracelet (2). Bronze. Trench A, cont. 261. 2009*
15. *12-974:5590 Bracelet. Bronze. Trench A, cont. 261. 2009*
16. *12-974:5591 Ear-ring (2). Bronze.. Trench A, cont. 260. 2009*
17. *12-974:5613 Pendant. Bronze. Trench B, cont. 398. 2009*
18. *12-974:5614 Ear-ring (fragment). Bronze. Trench B, cont. 399. 2009*
19. *12-974:5638 Ear-ring. Bronze. Trench B, cont. 402. 2009*
20. *12-974:5641 Pendant. Bronze, glass. Trench B, cont. 407. 2009*
21. *12-974:5673 Small ring. Bronze. Trench A. cont. 232. 2010*
22. *12-974:5687 Object (fragment). Bronze. Trench A, cont. 267. 2010*
23. *12-974:5764 Object (fragment). Bronze. Trench A, cont. 268. 2010*
24. *12-974:5667 Object (fragment). Trench A, cont. 217. 2010*
25. *12-974:5770 Bracelet. Bronze. Trench A, cont. 270. 2010*
26. *12-974:5771 Bracelet. Bronze. Trench A, cont. 270. 2010*
27. *12-974:5765 Bracelet (fragments) Bronze. Trench A, cont. 268. 2010*
28. *12-974:5777 Bracelet. Bronze. Trench A, cont. 276. 2010*
29. *12-974:5778 Ear-ring. Bronze. Trench A, cont. 276. 2010*
30. *12-974:5819 Fastener (piece). Bronze. Trench B, cont. 424. 2010*
31. *12-974:5821 Ring (fragment). Bronze. Trench B, cont. 426. 2010*
32. *12-974:5822 Bracelet. Bronze. Trench B, cont. 426. 2010*
33. *12-974:5848 Object (fragment). Bronze. Trench A, cont. 270. 2010*

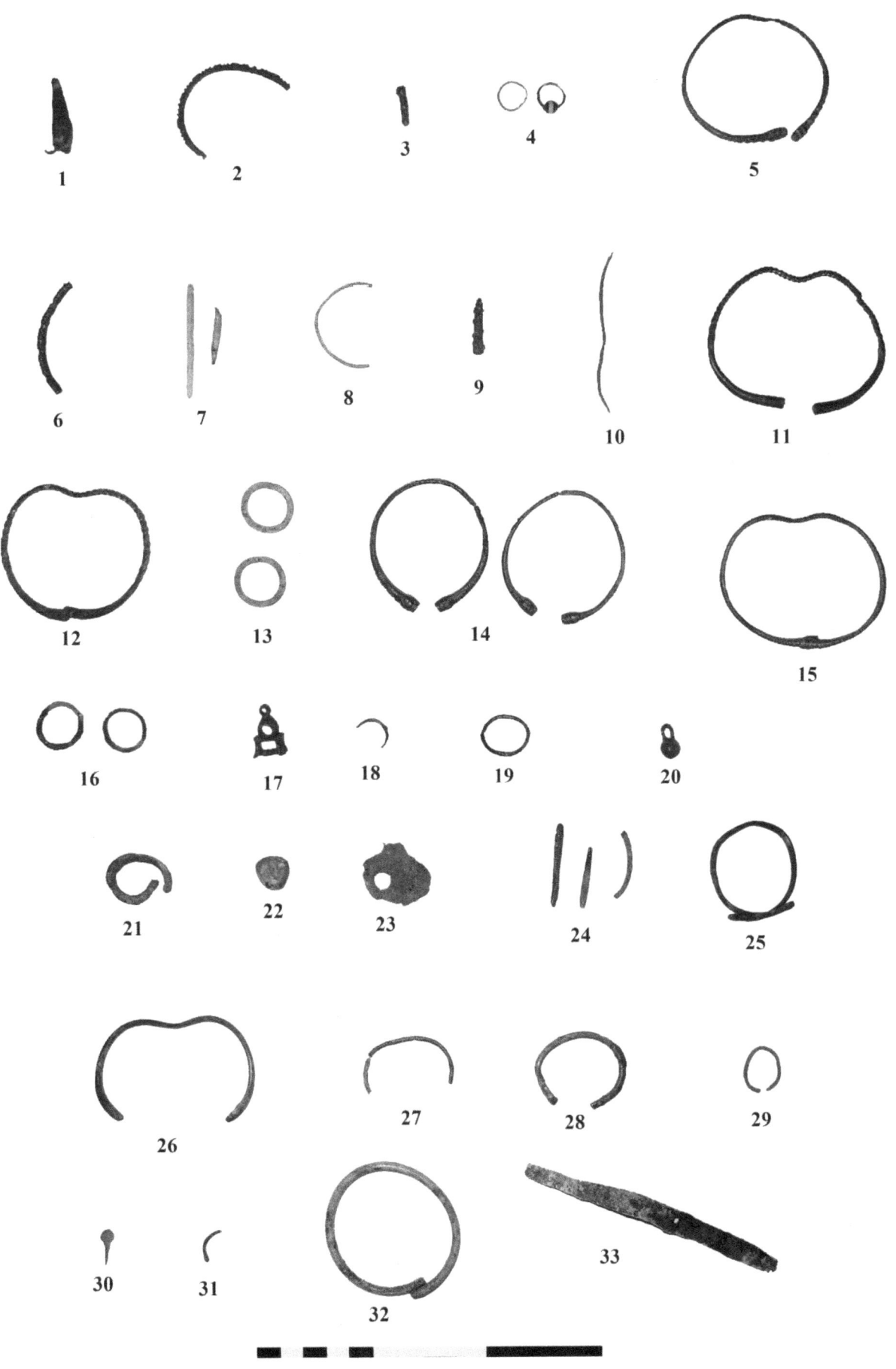

Figure 7.12: Captions over

Figure 7.13: 1 12-974:3917 Glass ring setting. Trench A. cont. 102. 2001; **2** 12-974:3923 Bases of drinking vessels. Glass. Trench A. cont. 104. 2001; **3** 12-974:3949 fragments of vessel. Glass. Trench B. cont. 101. 2002; **4** 12-974:4040 Bases of drinking vessels. Glass. Trench B. cont. 101. 2002; **5** 12-974:4054 Bases of drinking vessels. Glass. Trench A. cont. 108 2002; **6** 12-974:4068 fragments of vessels. Glass. Trench A. cont. 125. 2002

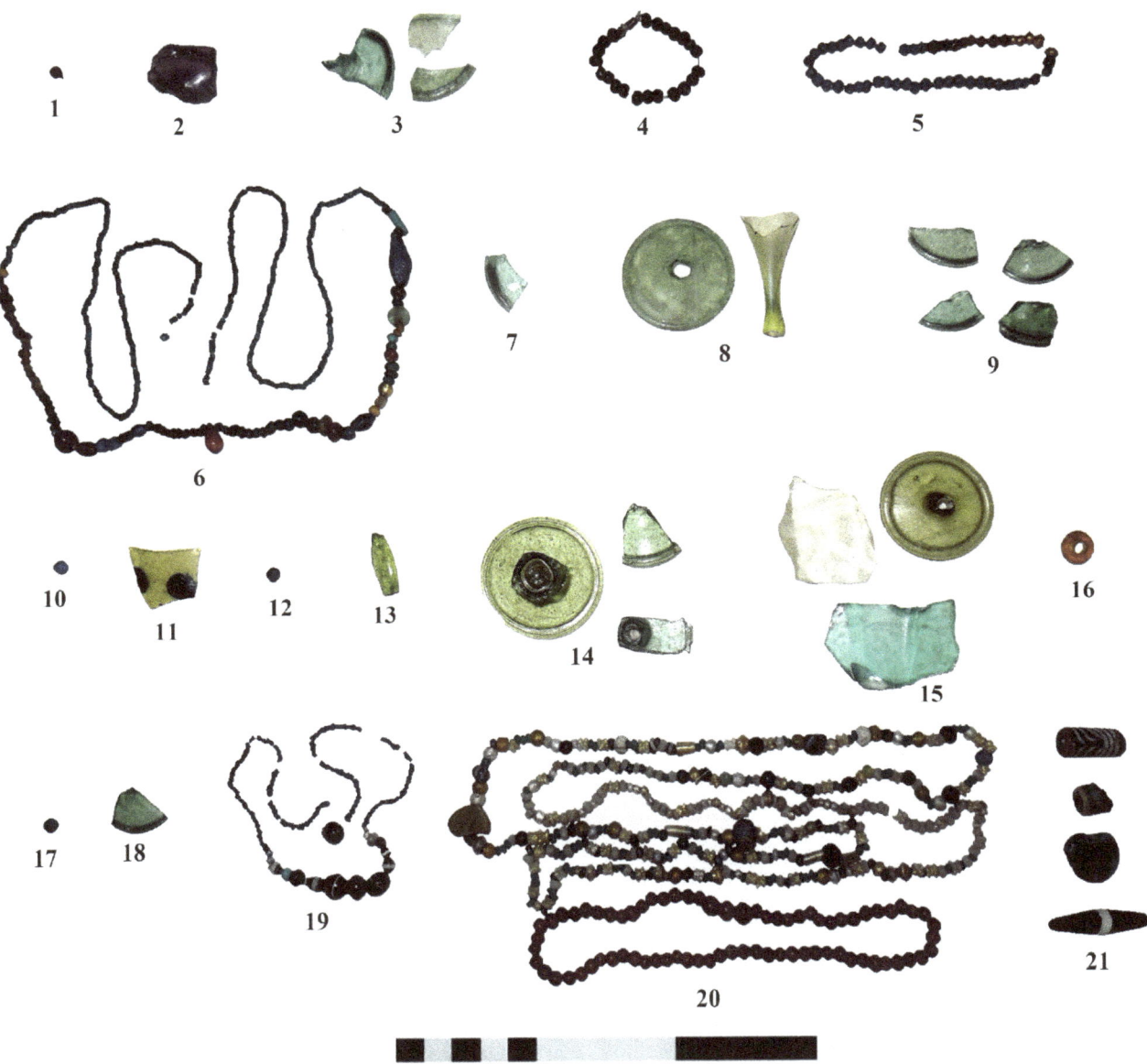

Figure 7.14: 1 12-974:4147 Pendant. Glass. 2003; **2** 12-974:4148 Bases of vessel. 2003; **3** 12-974:4150 Bases of drinking vessels. Glass. 2003; **4** 12-974:4160 Bead. Glass. Trench A, cont. 138. 2003; **5** 12-974:4182 Bead. Glass. Trench A, cont. 151. 2003; **6** 12-974:4184 Bead. Glass. Trench A, cont. 154. 2003; **7** 12-974:4190 Bases of drinking vessel. Glass. Trench B, cont. 318. 2003; **8** 12-974:4248 Fragment of perfum vessel. Glass. Trench A. 2004; **9** 12-974:4247 Bases of drinking vessels. Glass. Trench A. 2004; **10** 12-974:4254 Bead. Glass. Trench B, cont. 335. 2004; **11** 12-974:4255 Vessel with spot (fragment). Glass. Trench A, cont. 123 2004; **12** 12-974:4252 Bases of drinking vessel. Glass. 2004; **13** 12-974:4269 Bead. Glass. Trench B, cont. 106 2004; **14** 12-974:4315 Drinking vessels (fragments) Glass. 2004; **15** 12-974:4414 Drinking vessels (fragments). Glass. Trench B, cont. 379. 2005; **16** 12-974:4415 Bead. Glass. Trench B, cont. 379. 2005; **17** 12-974:5022 Bead. Glass. Trench A, cont. 173. 2006; **18** 12-974:5062 Bases of drinking vessel (fragments). glass. Trench A, cont. 137. 2007; **19** 12-974:5088 Bead. Glass. Trench A, cont. 198-199. 2007; **20** 12-974:5178 Bead. Glass. Trench A, cont. 226. 2007; **21** 12-974:5179 Bead. Glass. Trench A, cont. 226. 2007

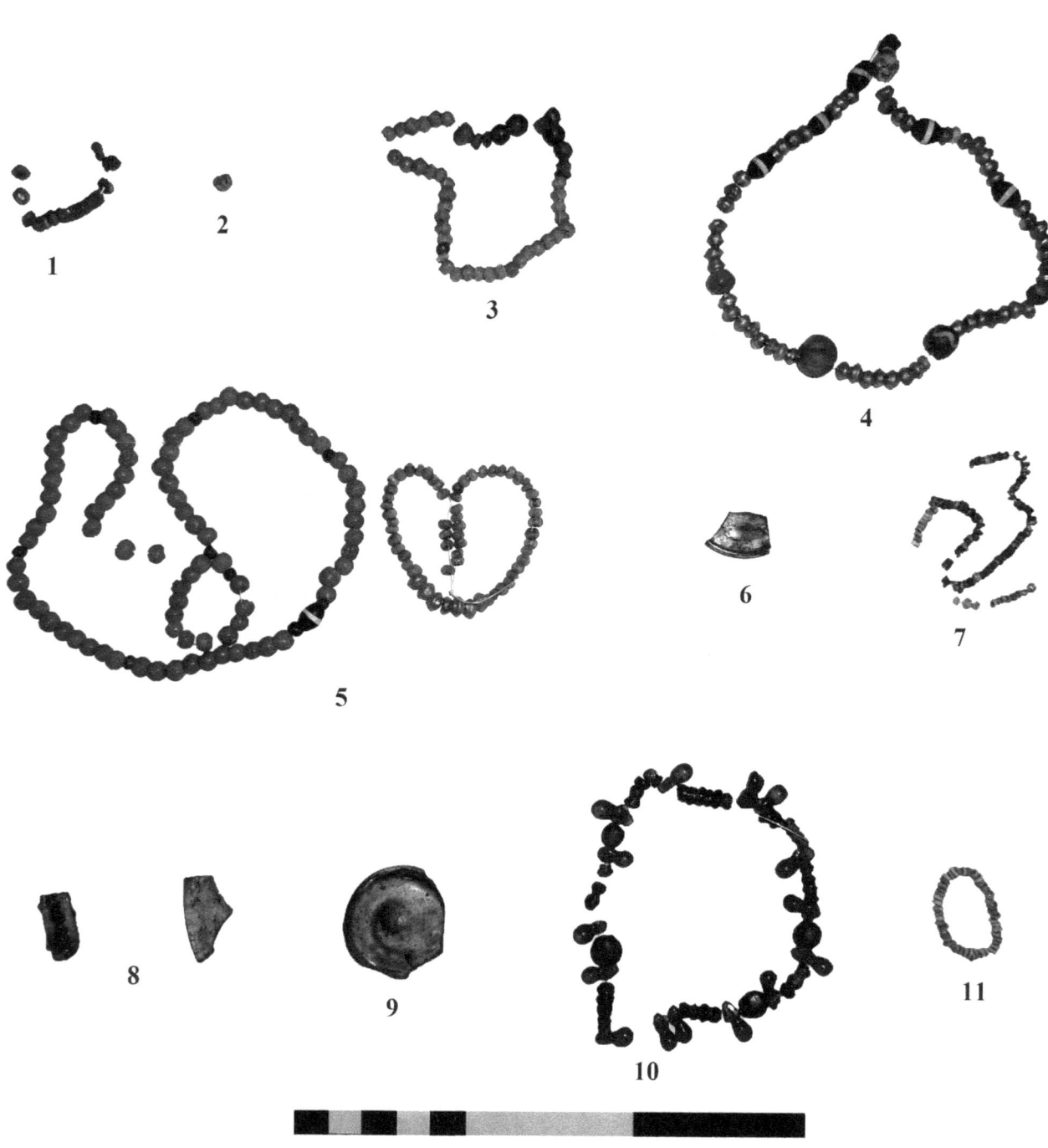

Figure 7.15: 1 *12-974:5473 Bead. cornelian, Glass. Trench A, cont. 240. 2008;* **2** *12-974:5476 Bead. Paste. Trench A, cont. 246. 2008;* **3** *12-974:5483 Bead. Glass. Trench A, cont. 253. 2008;* **4** *12-974:5562 Bead. Glass. Trench A, cont. 254. 2009;* **5** *12-974:5589 Bead. Glass. Trench A, cont. 261. 2009;* **6** *12-974:5686 Base of drinking vessel (fragments). Glass. Trench A, cont. 235. 2010;* **7** *12-974:5779 Bead. pasta. Trench A, cont. 276. 2010;* **8** *12-974:5799 Vessel (fragments). Glass. Trench B, cont. 417. 2010;* **9** *12-974:5800 Base of vessel (fragments). Glass. Trench B, cont. 417. 2010;* **10** *12-974:5820 Bead. Glass. Trench B, cont. 426. 2010;* **11** *12-974:5848 Bead. Paste. Trench B, cont. 417. 2010*

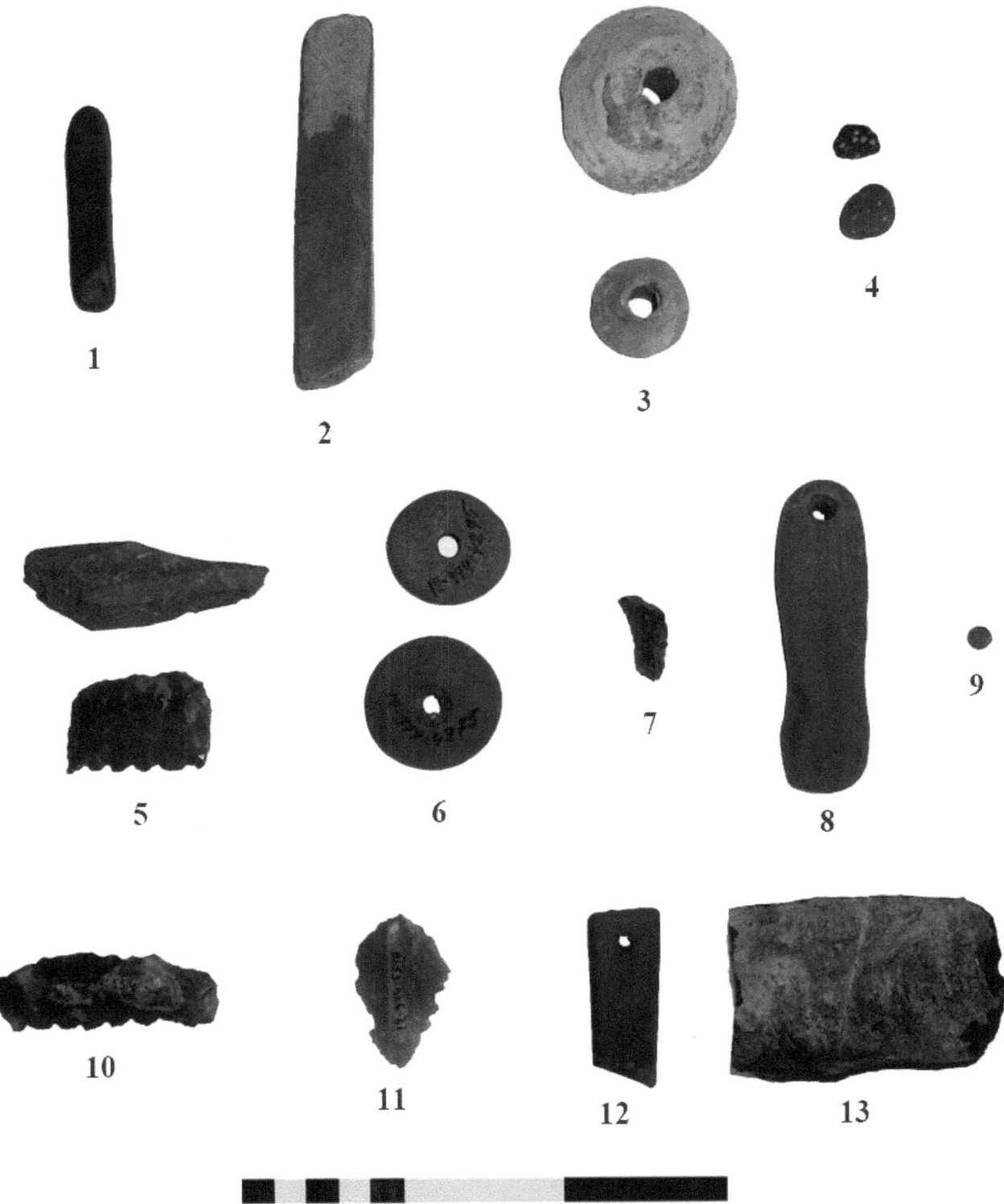

Figure 7.16: *1 12-974:4158 Touchstone. Stone. Trench A, cont. 136. 2009; 2 12-974:4176 Touchstone. Stone. Trench A, cont. 145. 2009; 3 12-974:4178 Spindle whorls (2). Stone. Trench A, cont. 145-148. 2009; 4 12-974:4179 Stone with red inclusions. Trench A, cont. 154. 2009; 5 12-974:4264 Sickle blade (2). Stone. Trench B, cont. 340. 2009; 6 12-974:5275 Spindle whorls (2). Stone. Trench A, cont. 125. 2009; 7 12-974:5163 Sickle blade. Stone. Trench A, cont. 217. 2007; 8 12-974:5202 Touchstone. Stone. Trench A, cont. 211. 2009; 9 12-974:5498 Decoration (fragment). Stone. Cornelian. Trench A, cont. 217. 2009; 10 12-974:5714 Sickle blade. Flint. Trench A, cont.235. 2009; 11 12-974:5516 Arrow-head. Flint. Trench A, cont. 235. 2009; 12 12-974:5519 Worked drilled stone. Trench A, cont. 235. 2009; 13 12-974:5636 Hand-axe. Stone. Trench B, cont. 401. 2009*

CHAPTER EIGHT

Archaeobotanical analysis of samples from Nokalakevi

By Marine Bokeria

Introduction

The site of Nokalakevi, located on the edge of the Colchian plain some 40km from the Black Sea, is characterised by a subtropical climate, with mild winters and hot summers. Annual precipitation averages between 1500-1700 mm, with subtropical landscapes of Colchian vegetation and yellow, red and humus-carbonate soils (Maruashvili 1971). Colchis represents part of the Caucasian refuge, where thermophilous plants survived the cold and aridity of the glacial periods (Kikvidze and Ohsawa 2001). During the last Glacial Maximum, Colchis was an important refuge for the flora of Tertiary, sub-mediterranean, temperate and boreal relict species (Klerk *et al* 2009).

In the piedmonts and central mountain belt, broad-leaved forests consist of Georgian oak, oriental beech, hornbeam, sweet chestnut, several local endemics of oak and hazel, Imeretian buckthorn, wild grapevine etc. Common yew, which was widespread here in the past, now occurs as single trees in an undergrowth of beech and oak forests. Evergreen bushes, such as pontian rhododendron, cherry laurel, holly, burglass, butcher's broom, daphne, colchian ivy, colchian boxwood etc, contribute to the subtropical expression of Colchian forests. Today the relict Colchian forest is fragmentarily preserved, particularly in the limestone gorges such as those found within the basin of the river Tekhuri at Nokalakevi (394 m above s.l.), Eki (461 m), and Abedati (623 m). Oak forests on the rocky and erosive lower mountain slopes are rare, and secondary formation often includes hornbeam. In the gorges of the river basins of the Tekhuri and the Abasha, Colchian forests dominated by hornbeam and beech often include oak and wild pear. The wider environment of Nokalakevi consists of secondary vegetation cover, and in disturbed areas black and common thorn, medlar, date plum, caucasian persimmon, and pomegranate are very common. Within and around extant settlements the land is more commonly cleared for gardening, and is occupied almost entirely by cultivated plants with cereals being imported (Nakhutsrishvili 1999).

Materials and methods

This archaeobotanical study deals with carbonised fruits and seeds recovered from the Hellenistic and early Byzantine deposits at Nokalakevi between 2007 and 2010. More than 130 samples were taken from Trench A and B for archaeobotanical investigation. Most of the samples were from Hellenistic and early Byzantine period graves, including both Hellenistic cremation and inhumation burials, and included human skeletal material, artefacts, remnants of animal bones and vegetal material (Table 8.1). Several samples were analysed from layers in both trenches, including a significant deposit of burnt daub from Trench A (context **216**) representing a collapsed wall that sealed a Hellenistic structure.

The samples were water sieved through 0.35-4mm meshes in accordance with standard procedure. Plant remains were identified by microscope (magnification range x6-x50). Cultivated species were measured according to the criteria given by Jacomet (2006), Zohary and Hopf (2000). Uncarbonised seeds recovered in samples from Trench B are considered to be contaminants of the modern site environment and are not recorded.

The relevant material was identified and compared with the reference collections of modern seeds and fruits housed at the Georgian National Museum and with identification manuals and atlases (Beijerinck 1947; Cappers *et al* 2009; Keller *et al* 1935; Neef *et al* 2012). Photographs were taken with a digital camera (SONY DSC-W200).

While samples were characterised by a low density of plant species – most of the samples include single species (taxon) from one botanical genus – some samples contained a relatively wide spectrum of plant remains. Fossilised macro remains recovered from the samples are shown in Table 8.1, where the quantity identified is indicated as follows: x=one item (seed/fruit/nut), xx=2-10, xxx=>10. Crop plants are categorised by their economic use.

Results

Ninety species, belonging to 67 genera, were identified and recorded. The quantity and structure of the archaeobotanical samples are diverse. The botanical remains associated with Hellenistic inhumation burials are more rich and diverse than those associated with the cremations. Several samples from the early Byzantine period Christian graves are relatively poor in botanical remains. All material was preserved by charring apart from the fragments of textiles, which were preserved through mineralisation. The majority of samples contained charcoal. Single seeds of grape and Italian millet were found within a very small ceramic vessel. The assemblages of macro remains recovered are represented by cereals, legumes, fruits and nuts, oil/fibre plants and wild/weed taxa. Some unidentified wild fruit seeds and the mineralised remains of textile, possibly flax, were also recovered.

Cereals

Several kinds of wheat were identified: einkorn *(Triticum monococcum)*, spelt *(Tr. spelta)* and timopheevii wheat *(Tr. timopheevii)* were present as single grains. Emmer *(Triticum dicoccum)* was more abundant, and a few grains of barley *(Hordeum vulgare)* were found as well. Charred grains of naked wheat *(Triticum aestivum* s.l.*)* dominate the Hellenistic grave samples. Charred seeds of hulled wheat and barley are more numerous in early Byzantine grave samples, prior to the free threshing species. The chaff of wheat and barley was missing in all samples so it was not possible to identify free threshing cereal grains to species level (Jacomet 2006). Broomcorn *(Panicum miliaceum)* and Italian millet *(Setaria italica)* are also common in the charred seed assemblage.

Pulses

Pulses are represented by the seeds of lentil *(Lens culinaris)*, celtic bean *(Vicia faba)* and bitter vetch *(Vicia ervilia)* as well as grass pea *(Lathyrus sativus)*. The complete range of legume species, both cultivated and weed varieties, are revealed only in samples from the Hellenistic burial **227** (grave fill **226**).

Oil and fibre plants

The archaeobotanical assemblage contained charred seeds of flax *(Linum usitatissimum/ bienne)*, as well as a single seed and seed coat of hemp *(Cannabis sativa)*. The remains of mineralised textiles were revealed in both Hellenistic (grave fill NOK08/A **226)** and early Byzantine (grave fill NOK10/B **417)** burials.

Cultivated fruits/nuts

Several whole and some fragmented grape seeds *(Vitis vinifera)* were found in the samples along with fragments of several walnuts *(Juglans regia)*.

Wild plants

Wild plants are represented by several fruits, nuts, ruderal and weed species. Wild fruits are represented in the charred seed spectrum by wild grape *(Vitis silvestris)*, elderberry *(Sambucus ebulus)*, and single fruits of blackberry *(Rubus sp.)*, wild apple *(Malus sp.)*, raspberry *(Rubus idaeus)* and cherry *(Prunus* sp.). Hazelnut *(Corylus avellana)* is found as fragments of charred nutshell. There is some evidence indicating a possible grape stem and charred pine *(Pinus sp.)* needles. The amount and frequency of wild herbs and grasses are very low per samples, and predominantly survived as single charred seeds. Only barnyard grass *(Echinochloa frumentacea)* grains are abundant in many samples.

The remains of charred, processed meal were revealed, most likely millet porridge. Unidentified seed/fruit and fruit flesh remnants were also found, and require further investigation.

Discussion

To summarise the data above, most of the archaeobotanical samples were typical of the Hellenistic and early Byzantine periods. Previous archaeobotanical work has identified burnt cereals, pulses, fruits, and cereal cakes as offerings associated with burials (Zach 2002; Palmer *et al* 2002; Megaloudi 2005, 2007; Bakels and Jacomet 2003; Preiss *et al* 2005; Cooremans 2008).

One of the most important questions relating to the interpretation of plant remains from graves deals with their stratigraphic position and the possible reason for their appearance in funeral contexts. Plant remains may have been deliberately deposited in burials for reasons such as funerary feasts, food for the deceased, grave goods, sacrifice, or perceived magic properties (Bakels and Jacomet 2003; Robinson 2002; Rottoli and Castiglioni 2011). They may also be accidentally included during the backfill of graves, and simply represent residual material from layers through which graves were dug. Most charred remains recovered from the Nokalakevi samples are of economic importance. The presence of a variety of species, including cereals, pulses, oil/fibre plants, nuts and fruits as well as textile remnants indicates deliberate human action. They were probably intentionally selected for funerary rituals and should be interpreted as plant offerings.

In the samples analysed pulses are best preserved, in contrast to cereal grains and wild grape. All samples contained a significant quantity of wheat grain fragments. The large quantity of wheat and broomcorn millet in the Hellenistic burials underlines their particular importance in funerary offering, and a possible remnant of millet porridge seems to be a component of a funerary meal. Archaeobotanical evidence of wheat and grape are well documented from the Early Antique burials from Ergeta (7th-6th centuries BC) and Gienos (8th-7th centuries BC) (Rusishvili 1990). Millets played a central role in the rituals associated with fertility deities and are still used in Svaneti (west Georgia). Millets were also found in a ritual context in the Early Antique city of Vani, where amphorae were filled with broomcorn millet grains and placed under the altar (Lordkipanidze 1966).

The tradition of ritual consumption or offering of special dishes made from einkorn wheat, millets and lentils, particularly at funerals, is still maintained and is very well documented ethnographically. Hard wheat (emmer, spelt and einkorn) were more suitable for making porridge and flat bread and were preferred in ritual and funeral feasts (Rukhadze 1976). Fragmented cereal grains, revealed in the burial samples, may represent prepared foods rather than post-depositional damage (Palmer and Van der Veen 2002). The consumption of cracked wheat and bulgur, observed archaeologically at prehistoric sites in Greece, is a tradition still alive in modern Greece in daily, festive and ritual meals alike. The boiled wheat is prepared and offered in relation to funerary rituals in modern southeastern Europe, just as it was in ancient Greece (Megaloudi *et al* 2007).

The huge quantity of charred, fragmented (possibly crushed) grape seeds and whole grape pips may represent consumption, wine production or its use as a plant offering. The remnants of wild grape stem perhaps indicates its use in a ritual context.

Within the Nokalakevi assemblage, other potentially ritual plant species are lentil and celtic bean. From the written sources it is known that the flowers of celtic bean were a symbol of death and their seeds were eaten during the funerary feast (Pliny the elder: in Kreus 2000; Palmer and Van Der Veen 2002**)**.

The most interesting finds from the Nokalakevi grave samples are charred seeds of flax and hemp and mineralised flax textile fragment. Fibre plants are rarely found in archaeobotanical samples containing charred plant assemblages (Connor and Kvavadze 2007; Robinson 2002). Fruits and seeds of hemp are underrepresented in charred plant macrofossil assemblages from Georgia. The pollen grains of hemp are recorded from the southwestern coast of the Black Sea sediment zone, dated to 830–1300 AD (Klerk *et al* 2009), and flax seeds were observed elsewhere in west Georgia (Rukhadze *et al* 1988; Bokeria 2007, 2010). Pale flax and hemp may have been widely used in ancient Colchis for oil, fibre, and medicine. The oil provided fuel for lamps, while the fibres were used for textiles, ropes, nets, and warp threads (Javakhishvili 1934; Zhukovskii 1971; Molodini 1963; Lomitashvili 2003). Hemp seeds were utilised for their perceived magic properties, and stalks of linseed and hemp were added to a pyre to protect against malicious spirits (Javakhishvili 1934; Rukhadze 1976).

Clothes made of linen and hemp fabrics had a ritual importance, and fibre of vegetal origin was associated with purity and fidelity, and had a special significance from ancient times (Lomitashvili 2003). According to the Book of the Law of Moses, in ancient Egypt it was prohibited to enter temples dressed in woollen clothes. Instead garments spun from flax were considered sacred, and the cerement for the deceased was made from linen and hemp fibres. Ethnographic data suggests that, in west Georgia (Samegrelo, Svaneti), people used to dip the flax cerement in candle wax and roll it around the deceased before burial (Rukhadze 1976). The privilege and importance of vegetal fibre is confirmed by archaeological evidence. Textile remains, possibly of fragments of linen cerements

were revealed from several Early Antique burials in west Georgia (e.g. at Vani, Kobuleti, and Dablagomi).

Most of the archaeological evidence connected with early flax cultivation is related to Bronze Age settlement. Many archaeological finds, historic sources and linguistic studies also point to flax cultivation in ancient Colchis (Molodini 1963; Rukhadze 1976; Lordkipanidze 1966; Lomitashvili 2003). The earliest mention of flax cultivation in ancient Greek and Roman sources is from the 5th century BC, when Herodotus stated that the finest linen cloth spun in Colchis was comparable to that of Egypt. Xenophon reported that the tribes that inhabited the eastern coast of the Black Sea utilised flax fabric, and Strabo noted that the export of linen clothes, hemp, pitch, wax, agricultural produce and timber was of particular commercial importance. Colchians in the ancient East were considered to be the best weavers (Lordkipanidze 1966, 2000).

The presence of charred nuts and seeds of edible berries in some assemblages may indicate that those graves were filled in late summer or autumn, when most edible nuts and berries are ripe. Plant species such as hazelnut and walnut were possibly consumed as only fragmented shell was found. Some grape vines may have been eaten before burning, or been offered entire.

Small pieces of charred grape branches and pine needles might represent the remnants of fuel burned at the grave-side. They may have been deliberately selected for their symbolic importance as grapevines, like oak trees, were related to immortality, wealth and hope. The pine, like figs and palms, was linked to fertility and fecundity. Such interpretations are often problematic, as the boundary between religion, magic and superstition in ancient times was very slight (Robinson 2002; Rovira and Chabal 2008; Kreuz 2000).

Within the archaeobotanical spectra there were revealed annual and perennial plant species associated with crop weeds, especially wheat and millet, such as several varieties of vetch, grass pea, corn salad, mustard, bedstraw, lucerne, medic, rye-grass etc. Species such as cinquefoil, creeping buttercup, crabgrass, hollow root etc, may have been derived from the edge of woodland and clearings close to Nokalakevi. In the charred seed assemblage there is evidence of grasses, sedges and herbs that would have grown near the Tekhuri river edge. Ruderals of disturbed habitats, such as broadleaf plantain, bird eye, spearwort, alkali bulrush, wood sorrel, ribwort plantain, sheep's sorrel, knotgrass, fat hen, speedwell etc, would have grown in the vicinity of the site, and characterise the humid habitat of Nokalakevi.

The wild plant seed assemblage was considered as part of the site environment. The charred remains of weeds, ruderals and meadow plant species recovered in burial assemblages represent functional data of the graves (Kreus 2000), as they were probably deposited in the grave unintentionally.

	NOK07/A				NOK08/A					NOK09/A			NOK10/A		NOK09/B				NOK10/B			NOK07/A			NOK 08/A	NOK09/B		NOK 10/A
Context	198 199	208 209	205	220	226	239 240	247	236	252	260	254	264	270	276 277	395	402	407	410	414	417	426	214-216	218	223	235	401	340	267
Arch. Period	Hell.	Hell.	Hell.	Hell.	Hell.	Hell.	Hell.	Hell.	Hell.	Hell.	Hell.	Hell.	Hell.	Hell.	E. By	E. By	E. By	E. By	E. By	E. By	E. By	Hell.	Hell.	Hell.	Hell.	E. By	E. By	E. By
Burial type	Crem	Crem	Inhu.	Inhu.	Inhu.	Crem	Crem	Inhu.	Inhu.	Inhu.	Inhu.	Inhu.	Inhu.	Inhu.	Inhu.	Inhu.	Inhu.	Inhu.	Inhu.	Inhu.	Inhu.	-	-	-	-	-	-	-
Cereals																												
Triticum aestivum			x			x			x					x								x		x				
Tr. compactum	x	x	x	x	x					x	x	x				x			x	x			x	x	x		x	
Tr. dicoccum	x	x	x				x			x		x		x			x				x		x	x	x			
Tr. monococcum		x							x	x	x	x	x			x	x						x			x		x
Tr. spelta					x						x					x	x	x	x	x					x		x	
Tr. timofeevii											x	x		x					x									
Tr. fragments		x	x		xx			x	x		x	x		x		x				x		x			x			
Hordeum distichon		x																	x	x								
Hordeum sp.										x	x	x		x					x	x								
Cerealia fragm.	xxx	xxx	x	x	x	x	x		x	x	x	x		x						x		x	x	x	x			
Panicum milliaceum	xx	xxx	xxx	x	xx	xx	x		x	x	x	x			x	x	x						x	x	x			
Setaria italica	x	x	x	x	x	x			x	x	x	x	x		x	x	x	x		x			x	x			x	x
Millets fragm.	x					x			x	x	x	x		x			x		x	x		x			x			x
Pulses																												
Lens culinaris			x	x	x					x				x						x		x	x					
Pisum sativum																												
Pisum fragm.					x				x																			
Vicia ervilia					x					x	x							x										
Vicia faba	x																											
Oil / fibre plants																												
Cannabis sativa					x									x											x			
Linum ussitatissimum	x													x										x				
Cultivated fruits / nuts																												
Vitis vinifera/fragm.			x		x	x			x	x	x					x						x					x	
Juglans regia						x			x					x														
Wild fruits and nuts																												
Vitis sylvestris / fragm.	x		x	x	x	x			x		x			x		x						x		x			x	x
Vitis sp. fragm.																							x				x	x
Corylus avellana				x	x				x			x				x			x									
Prunus sp.	x	x	x	x	x	x		x	x	x	x	x		x		x						x						

	NOK07/A					NOK08/A				NOK09/A			NOK10/A		NOK09/B				NOK10/B			NOK07/A			NOK 08/A	NOK09/B		NOK 10/A
Context	198 199	208 209	205	220	226	239 240	247	236	252	260	254	264	270	276 277	395	402	407	410	414	417	426	214-216	218	223	235	401	340	267
Arch. Period	Hell.	Hell.	Hell.	Hell.	Hell.	Hell.	Hell.	Hell.	Hell.	Hell.	Hell.	Hell.	Hell.	Hell.	E. By	E. By	E. By	E. By	E. By	E. By	E. By	Hell.	Hell.	Hell.	Hell.	E. By	E. By	E. By
Burial type	Crem	Crem	Inhu.	Inhu.	Inhu.	Crem	Crem	Inhu.	Inhu.	Inhu.	Inhu.	Inhu.	Inhu.	Inhu.	Inhu.	Inhu.	Inhu.	Inhu.	Inhu.	Inhu.	Inhu.	-	-	-	-	-	-	-
Sambucus ebulus		x							x													x						
Rubus idaeus																							x					
Malus sp.					x																							
Pinus sp.	x			x	x																							
Sorbus sp.										x																		
Wood edges, clearings																												
Coridalis cava													x	x														
Dianthus barbatus														x														
Lepidium heteropyullum																				x								
Silene dioica														x														
Ononis repens														x														
Weeds																												
Amaranthus lividus																x												
Asparagus officinalis														x														
Asperula arvensis																											x	
Brassica rapa												x	x	x														
Carduus acanthoides														x														
Cirsium/Seratula																		x										
Chenopodium album											x			x			x											
Chenop. hybridum														x														
Chenopodium ficifolium														x														
Digitaria sanguinalis														x						x								
Echinochloa frument./cruss-galii		x									x			x														
Echinochloa cruss-galii																		x										
Echinochloa sp.											x	x		x		x												
Eleusine indica												x				x												
Eleusine coragana						x																	x					
Elymus sp.																					x							
Erodium cicutarium					x															x								
Geranium molle																												

101

Context group	NOK07/A					NOK08/A					NOK09/A		NOK10/A			NOK09/B			NOK10/B			NOK07/A			NOK 08/A	NOK09/B		NOK 10/A
Context	198 199	208 209	205	220	226	239 240	247	236	252	260	254	264	270	276 277	395	402	407	410	414	417	426	214-216	218	223	235	401	340	267
Arch. Period	Hell.	Hell.	Hell.	Hell.	Hell.	Hell.	Hell.	Hell.	Hell.	Hell.	Hell.	Hell.	Hell.	Hell.	E. By	E. By	E. By	E. By	E. By	E. By	E. By	Hell.	Hell.	Hell.	Hell.	E. By	E. By	E. By
Burial type	Crem	Crem	Inhu.	Inhu.	Inhu.	Crem	Crem	Inhu.	Inhu.	Inhu.	Inhu.	Inhu.	Inhu.	Inhu.	Inhu.	Inhu.	Inhu.	Inhu.	Inhu.	Inhu.	Inhu.	-	-	-	-	-	-	-
Geranium sp.					x																							
Lathyrus palustris					x																							
Lathyrus pratensis													x															
Leucojum aestivum											x																	
Lolium remosum																												x
Lolium temulentum		x			x									x														
Lotus corniculatus														x														
Malva silvestris													x															
Medicago lupulina													x															
Oxalis corniculata														x							x							
Persicaria hydropiper / capitata																				x								
Plantago lanceolata											x			x	x													
Polygonum aviculare													x				x											
Polygonum hidropiper														x														
Scleranthus annuus											x			x						x								
Setaria verticillata			x			x					x	x	x	x						x								x
Silene dioica																										x		
Sinapis alba																					x							
Sinapis arvensis														x														
Spergula arvensis		x			x				x																			
Thymelaea passerina											x																	
Trifolium sp.										x																		
Valerianella rimosa													x		x			x										
Vicia ervilia			x																									
Vicia hirsuta					x																							
Vicia lensisperma					x									x														
Vicia sativa subsp. sativa					x					x																		
Vicia/lathyrus type													x															
Vicia lensisperma														x						x						x		
Vicia sepium					x																							
Vicia tetrasperma					x																							

Group	NOK10/A	NOK09/B	NOK09/B	NOK08/A	NOK07/A	NOK07/A	NOK07/A	NOK10/B	NOK10/B	NOK10/B	NOK09/B	NOK09/B	NOK09/B	NOK09/B	NOK10/A	NOK10/A	NOK09/A	NOK09/A	NOK09/A	NOK08/A	NOK08/A	NOK08/A	NOK08/A	NOK07/A	NOK07/A	NOK07/A	NOK07/A	NOK07/A
Context	267	340	401	235	223	218	214-216	426	417	414	410	407	402	395	276 277	270	264	254	260	252	236	247	239 240	226	220	205	208 209	198 199
Arch. Period	E. By	E. By	E. By	Hell.	Hell.	Hell.	Hell.	E. By	E. By	E. By	E. By	E. By	E. By	E. By	Hell.	Hell.	Hell.	Hell.	Hell.	Hell.	Hell.	Hell.	Hell.	Hell.	Hell.	Hell.	Hell.	Hell.
Burial type	-	-	-	-	-	-	-	Inhu.	Inhu.	Inhu.	Inhu.	Inhu.	Inhu.	Inhu.	Inhu.	Inhu.	Inhu.	Inhu.	Inhu.	Inhu.	Inhu.	Crem.	Crem.	Inhu.	Inhu.	Inhu.	Crem.	Crem.
Vicia villosa																								×				
Ruderals/wet meadows																												
Aristolochia clematis																								×				
Carex extensa	×																							×		×	×	
Chenopodium hybridum																								×				
Chenopodium album																								×				
Deschampsia caespitosa																										×		
Elymus sp.	×																								×			
Oxalis corniculata		×																							×			
Plantago lanceolata						×																		×				
Polygonum sp.							×																					×
Sinapis alba			×																					×				
Spergularia sp.	×																							×				
Wet meadows/ Pastures																												
Bolboschoenus maritimus			×							×																		
Carex extensa					××				×																			
Carex pilulifera								×	×																			
Cyperus fuscus					×													×										
Dechampsia caespitosa																												
Epilobium pariflorum								×	×																			
Fabaceae									×				×	×														
Galium vernum									×				×			×												
Genista pillosa									×			×	×															
Medicago sativa																						×		×				
Myosotis sp.																								×				
Myosotis discolor	×										×																	
Persicaria bistorta									×																			
Persicaria capitata	×																											
Potentilla reptens											×					×												
Ranunculus bulbosus									×																			

103

	NOK 10/A	NOK09/B	NOK09/B	NOK 08/A	NOK07/A	NOK07/A	NOK07/A	NOK10/B	NOK10/B	NOK10/B	NOK09/B	NOK09/B	NOK09/B	NOK09/B	NOK10/A	NOK10/A	NOK09/A	NOK09/A	NOK09/A	NOK08/A	NOK08/A	NOK08/A	NOK08/A	NOK07/A	NOK07/A	NOK07/A	NOK07/A	NOK07/A
Context	267	340	401	235	223	218	214-216	426	417	414	410	407	402	395	276 277	270	264	254	260	252	236	247	239 240	226	220	205	208 209	198 199
Arch. Period	E. By	E. By	E. By	Hell.	Hell.	Hell.	Hell.	E. By	E. By	E. By	E. By	E. By	E. By	E. By	Hell.	Hell.	Hell.	Hell.	Hell.	Hell.	Hell.	Hell.	Hell.	Hell.	Hell.	Hell.	Hell.	Hell.
Burial type	-	-	-	-	-	-	-	Inhu.	Inhu.	Inhu.	Inhu.	Inhu.	Inhu.	Inhu.	Inhu.	Inhu.	Inhu.	Inhu.	Inhu.	Inhu.	Inhu.	Crem	Crem	Inhu.	Inhu.	Inhu.	Crem	Crem
Ranunculus muricatus		x					x																					
Ranunculus repens									x		x																	
Rosaceae																x		x										
Rumex crispus								x									x											
Scrophularia nodosa																								x				
Spergularia media															x				x									
Trifolium hybridum															x			x						x				
Trifolium sp.																									x		x	
Veronica sp.																				x	x	x	xx					x
Ononis repens ssp. repens																								x				
Dry habit																												
Erodium cicutarium																												
Rhinanthus minor																	x								x			
Sagina procumbens														x			x											
Salvia viridis																x												
Veronica sp.				x																								
Textile fragm.																								x	x			
Unidentif. fruit fragm.		x																						x	x			
Bones		x	xx																	xxx				xxx	xxx			
Charcoal				x	xxx						xxx	xxx	xxx	x	x	x			x	xxx		x	x	xxx	x	x	x	x

Table 8.1 Results of the palaeobotanical study of contexts from Trenches A and B

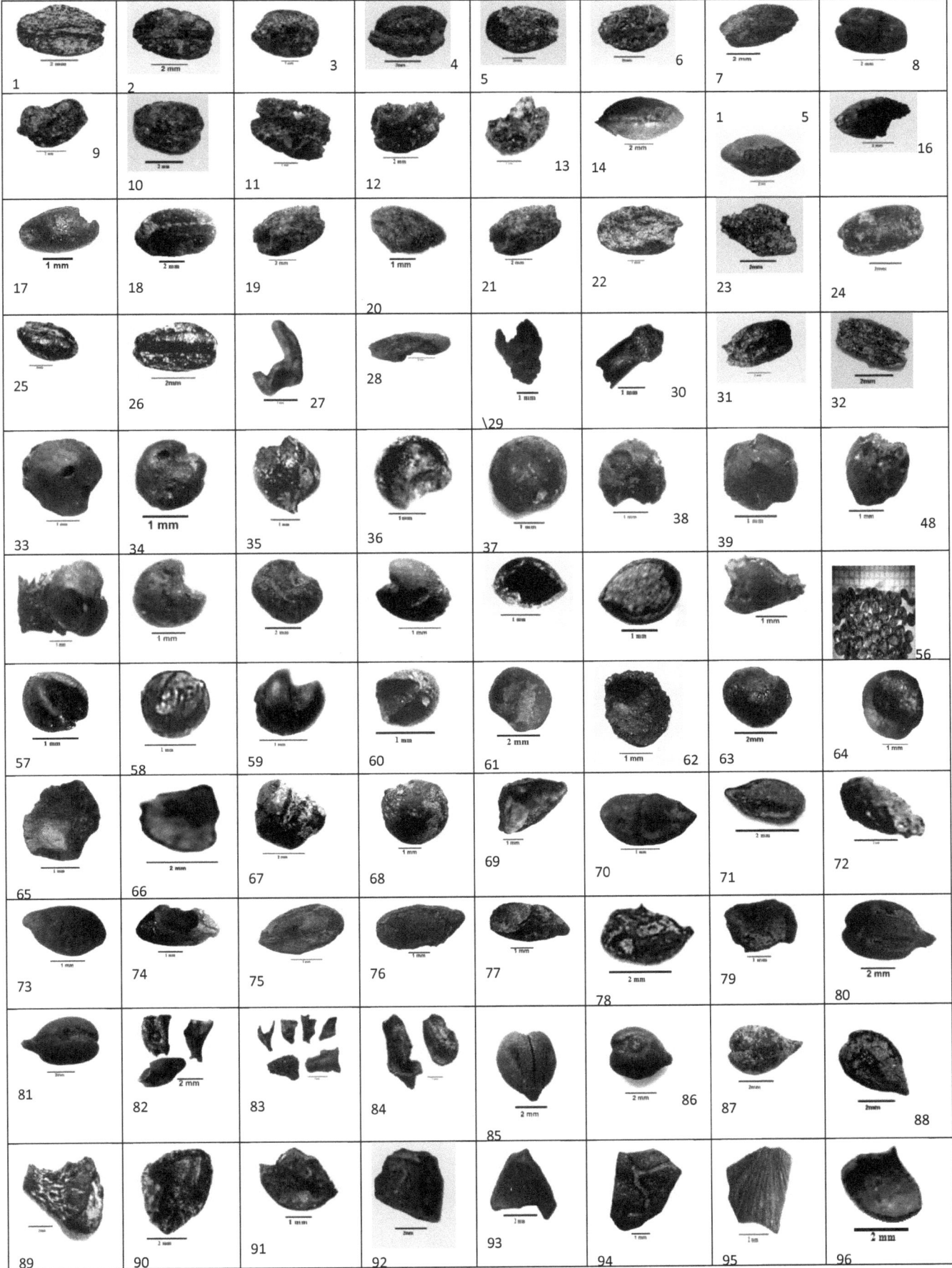

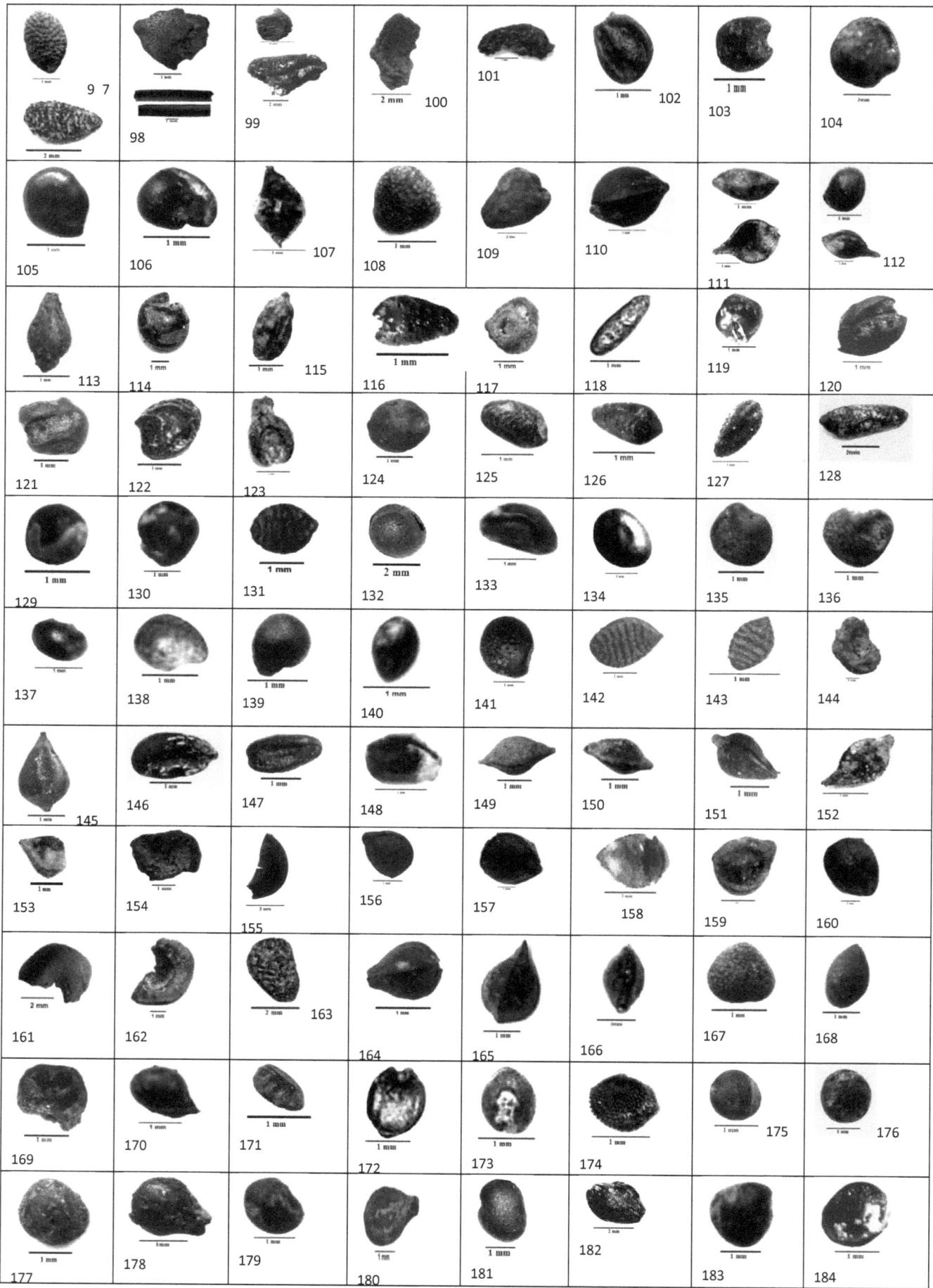

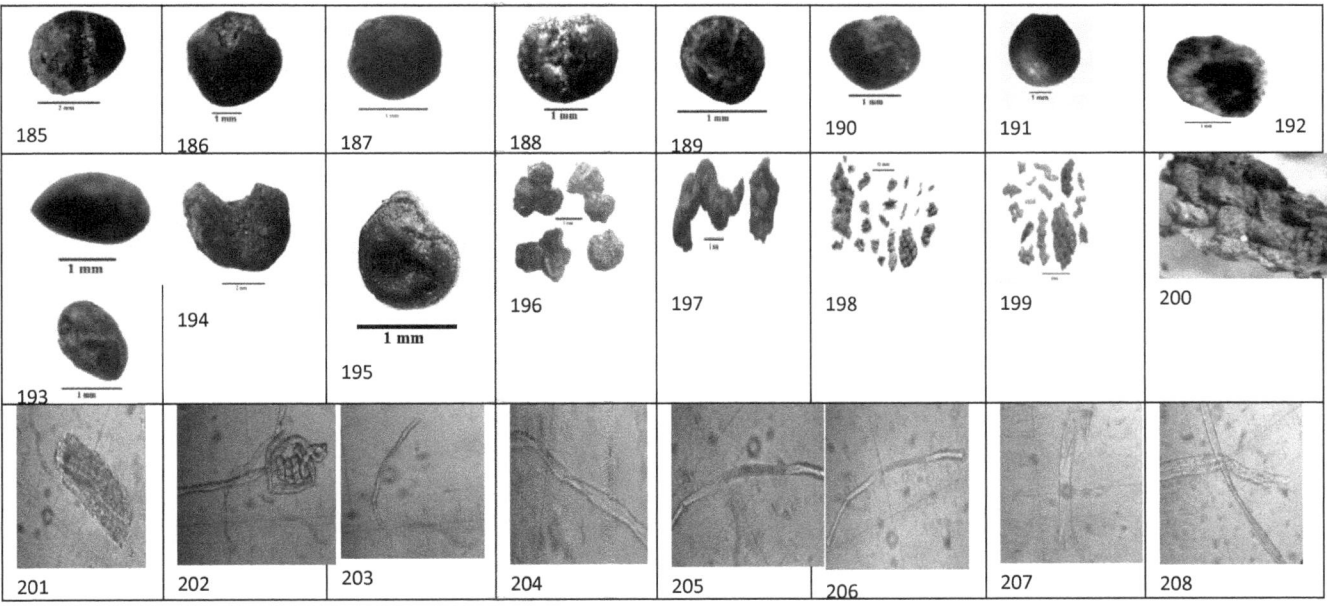

Figure 8.1 Macrobotanical remains from Nokalakevi

1-6 Naked wheat *(Triticum aestivum s.l.)*; 7-13 Emmer (*T. dicoccum); 14-17 Einkorn *(T. monococcum); 18-24 Wheat (Triticum sp.)*; 25-27 Spelt wheat *(T. spelta)* fruit, spikelet; 28 Timopheevii wheat (*T. timofeevii*); 29-30 Wheat chaff ; 31-37 Barley (*Hordeum distichum*); 38 Witch grass (*Panicum capillare*); 39-52;55-6 Broomcorn millet (*Panicum miliaceum*); 53-54 Hulled caryopsis; 57-60 Setaria italica (*Setaria italica*); 61-66 Lentil *(Lens culinaris)*; 67 Celtic bean *(Vicia faba)*; 68 Hemp (*Canabis sativa)* fruit, 69 fruit coat; 70-78 Flax (*Linum usittatisimum*);79 unidentif. Fruit fresh; 80-84 Grape wine (*Vitis vinifera*); 85-88 Wild grape (*V. sylvestris*) 89 charred stem remnant; 90-94 Walnut (*Juglans regia*) shell fragm.; 95-96 Hazelnut (*Corylus avellana*) shell fragm.; 97 Elderberry (*Sambucus ebulus*); 98 Pine (*Pinus sp.*); 99-100 unidentified seed *Cerealia;* 101 common Thistle (*Cirsium vulgare*); 102 Rough pigweed (*Amaranthus paniculatus*); 103 Sweet vernal grass (*Anthroxantum odoratum*); 104 Asparagus *(Asparagus officinalis*); 105 Fat-hen (*Chenopodium album); 106 Oak-leaved goosefoot *(Chenopodium glaucum)*; 107 Alkali bulrush (*Bolboschoenus maritimus*); 108 Rapeseed *(Brassica silvestris*); 109 Spiny thistle (*Carduus acanthoides*); 110 Long bract sedge (*Carex extensa*); 111 Pill sedge (*C. pilulifera*) fruit, fruit with utricle; 112 Woodland sedge (*C. sylvatica*) fruit, fruit with utricle; 113 Brown flat sedge (*Cyperus fuscus*); 114 Hollow root (*Corydalis cava*); 115 Orchard grass (*Dactylis glomerata*); 116 Tufted hair grass (*Deschampsia caespitosa*); 117 Sweet william *(Dianthus barbatus*); 118 Hairy crabgrass (*Digitaria sanguinalis*); 119 Water grasses (*Echinichloa sp.*); 120 Barnyard millet (*Echinochloa frumentaceae*); 121-124 Barnyard grass (*Echinochloa crus-gallii*); 125-127 Goose grass (*Eleusine indica*); 128 Pinweed (*Erodium cicutarium*); 129 Pea family (*Fabaceae);* 130 Wood waxen (*Genista pillosa*); 131 Dove foot geranium (*Geranium molle*); 132 Marsh pea (*Lathyrus palustris*); 133 Field pepper weed (*Lepidium heterophullum*); 134 Summer snowflake (*Leucojum aestivum*); 135 Birdsfoot (*Lotus corniculatus*); 136 Common mallow (*Malva silvestris*); 137 Black medick (*Medicago lupulina*); 138 Lucerne (*M. sativa*); 139 Creeping cinquefoil (*Potentilla reptens);* 140 'Forget me not' (*Myosotis discolor*); 141 Restharrow (*Ononis repens*); 142-143 Creeping wood sorrel (*Oxalis corniculata*); 144 Cherry (*Prunus sp.*); 145 Common bistort *(Persicaria bistorta*); 146-148 Narrow leaf plantain (*Plantago lanceolata*); 149-151 Knotgrass bird weed (*Polygonum aviculare*); 152-153 Smartweed (*Polygonum hydropiper*); 154 unidentified fruit flesh; 155 Lungwort (*Pulmonaria sp.*); 156-157 Corn buttercup (*Ranunculus arvensis*); 158 Bulbous buttercup (*Ranunculus bulbosus*); 159-160 Creeping buttercup *(Ranunculus repens*); 161-162 Hay rattle (*Rhinanthus minor*); 163 Raspberry (*Rubus idaeus*); 164-165 Curled dock (*Rumex crispus*); 166 Broad-leaved dock (*R. obtusifolia*); 167 Bird eye pearlwort (*Sagina procumbens*); 168 Annual clary sage (*Salvia viridis);* 169-170 Annual knawel (*Scleranthus annus*) fruit with periant and seed; 171 Water figwortis (*Scrophularia auriculata*); 172 Bristly foxtail (*Setaria verticillata);* 173 Cockspur grass *(Echinochloa crus-galii*); 174 Campion (*Silene dioica*); 175 White mustard. (*Sinapis alba);* 176 Wild mustard *(Sinapis arvensis);* 177 Mustard (*Sinapis desserta*); 178 Passerine annuelle (*Thymelaea passerine*); 179 Alsike clover (*Trifolium hybridum*); 180 Corn salad *(Valerianella officinalis*); 181 Cow vetch (*Vicia angustifolia*); 182 Tufted vetch (*V. cracca*) ; 183 bitter vetch (*V. ervilia*); 184 Lentil vetch (*V. lensisperma);* 185-187 Common vetch (*Vicia sativa*)(*V. sativa ssp. sativa*); 188 Bush vetch (*V. sepium*); *189* Sparrow vetch (*V. tetrasperma*); 190 Vetch (*Vicia sp.*); 191 Fodder vetch (*Vicia villosa*); 192 Woodruff *(Asperula arvensis*); 193-195 unidentified fruit/seed ; 196 burnt porridge residue; 197-208 Linen textile fibre fragments.

Conclusion

According to data recovered from the samples analysed we can conclude that the cultivation of summer crops played an important role in subsistence strategies in Nokalakevi. The prevalence of broomcorn millet, and evidence of flax and hemp requiring abundant moisture during the growing seasons, reflect a damp climate in the Hellenistic period. The high quantity of barnyard millet (*Echinochloa frumentacea*) and common weeds of damp fields found in samples is also related to high humidity in the Hellenistic period.

The decrease of broomcorn millet, and prevalence of hard wheat and barley, by the early Byzantine period probably reflects a more favourable climate for wheat cultivation including a dryer summer. However the low number of samples from the early Byzantine period makes it difficult to draw detailed conclusions. The presence of several wetland plant species, such as wood sedge, pill sedge, bulrush, common knotweed, and dock, found in the early Byzantine period assemblage may indicate vegetation from the river edge next to the settlement.

The widest spectrum of archaeobotanical remains was found in the Hellenistic inhumation graves, including a great variety of cereals, legumes, flax, fruits and nuts. The samples from the early Byzantine period graves presented an atypical spectrum, with the near absence of pulses (only one item), and complete absence of broomcorn millet, grape and flax, however this might be for taphonomic reasons.

The majority of plants recovered, such as cereals, pulses, fruits and nuts are interpreted as funerary offerings, widely used in the Hellenistic period. Evidence for hemp was the first recorded from Nokalakevi. Cereals and pulses were exposed to fire, and the cereal grains were cleaned before offering. The recovery of grape, hazelnut and walnuts, berries, and some unidentified fruit and shell fragments, indicates the consumption of fruit and nuts and that fruit may also have been offered whole as part of a funerary ritual. In some samples burnt material could be attributed to millet porridge, possibly an element of funeral meals.

Some wild species recovered from the samples are interpreted as indicators of the natural landscape of the surrounding area. The presence of wild plants, such as arable weeds and ruderals, may be indicative of the local vegetation or may derive from dried straw used for kindling. Of particular interest were the fragments of linen textile, which may have been deposited in the grave as clothing, or the wrapped cerement of the deceased.

Bibliography

Bakels, C. and Jacomet, S. 2003. Access to luxury foods in Central Europe during the Roman period: The archaeobotanical evidence. In: Van der Veen, M. (ed) *Luxury foods. World Archaeology* 34: 543-557

Beijerinck, W. 1947. *Zadenatlas der Nederlandsche Flora*. H. Veenman et Zonen, Wageningen: 304

Bokeria, M., Rukhadze, L., Ammann, B., Masserey, C., Lomitashvili, D., Tvalchrelidze, Z., Kebuladze, N. 2009. Archaeobotanical evidence from West Georgia (South Caucasus). *Moambe, Georgian National Museum bulletin*, Natural Science Prehistory 1 :140-150

Bokeria, M. 2010. West Georgia: history and diversity of vegetation and the use of plants through Archaeobotany. *News of ancient Colchis*. Tbilisi: Adamantis-press: 21-31.

Cappers, R.T.J., Neef, R. and Bekker, R.M. 2009. *Digital atlas of economic plants 2a, 2b*. Groningen Archaeological Studies, Vol.9. Barkhuis & Groningen University Library, Groningen

Connor, S., Thomas, I., Kvavadze, E. 2007. A 5600 year history of changing vegetation, sea levels and human impacts from the Black Sea coast of Georgia. *The Holocene* 17, 1:25-36

Cooremans, B. 2008. The Roman cemeteries of Tienen and Tongeren: results from the archaeobotanical analysis of the cremation graves. *Veget. Hist. Archaeobot.* 17:3-13

Gorgidze, A.D. 1955. *Flax in Georgia: Philogenetical research*. Tbilisi (in Russian)

Jacomet, S. 2006. *Identification of cereal remains from archaeological sites*, 2, IPNA, Basel

Jacomet, S. 2007. Plant macrofossil methods and studies. Use in environmental archaeology: 1, *Encyclopedia of Quaternary Science*: 2384-2412

Javakhishvili, I. 1934. *Economic History of Georgia* 2, "Federatsia". Tbilisi (in Georgian)

Keller, B.A., Lyubimenko, V.N., Maltsev, A.I., Fedtshenko, B.A., Shishkin, B.K., Rodzevich, Yu, R. and Kamenskii, K.V. (eds) 1934-1935. *Weed plants of the USSR, A guide to the determination of the weeds of USSR* . Vol.1-4. Moscow - Leningrad: AN USSR (in Russian)

Kikvidze, Z., Ohsawa, M. 2001. *Richness of Colchic vegetation: a comparison between refugia of south-western and East Asia*. BMC Ecology,1,6

Klerk, P., Haberl, A., Kaffke, A., Krebs, M., Matchutadze, I., Minke, M., Schulz J. and Joosten H. 2009. Vegetation history and environmental development since ca 6000 cal yr BP in and around Ispani 2 (Kolkheti lowland, Georgia). *Quaternary Science Reviews* 28:890–910

Kreuz, A. 2000. Functional and conceptual archaeobotanical data from Roman cremations. In: Pearce, J., Millett, M. and Struck, M. (eds) *Burial Society and Context in the Roman World*. Oxford, Oxbow Books: 45-51

Lomitashvili, D. 2003. *Central Colchida in 8th century BC - 6th century AD. Cixegoji- Archeopolis-Nokalakevi*. Tbilisi (In Georgian)

Lordkipanidze, O.D. 1966. *Antique world and ancient Colkhis*. Tbilisi (in Georgian)

Lordkipanidze, O. 2000. *Phasis: The river and city in Colkhis*. Stuttgart, Franz Steiner Verlag

Maruashvili, L. 1971. *Geomorphology of Georgia*. Metsniereba, Tbilisi: 263-271 (in Georgian)

Megaloudi, F. 2005. Burnt plant offerings in Hellenistic times: An archaeobotanical case study from Messene, Peloponnese, Greece. *Veget . Hist. Archaeobot.* 14: 329-340

Megaloudi, F., Papadopoulos, S., Sgourou, M. 2007. Plant offerings from the classical necropolis of Limenas, Thasos, northern Greece. *Antiquity* 81: 933-943

Molodini, L. 1963. *Oil crops in Georgia*. Tbilisi: 7-25 (in Georgian)

Nakhutsrishvili, G. 1999. Evergreen broad-leaved vegetation in Colchis. In: Kloetzli, F. and Birkhaeuser, G. R. W (eds.) *Recent shifts in vegetation boundaries of deciduous forests, especially due to general global warming*. Basel, Boston, Berlin, Verlag: 167-179

Neef, R., Cappers, R.T.J. and Bekker, R.M. 2012. *Digital atlas of economic plants in archaeology*. Groningen Archaeological Studies,vol.17, Barkhuis & Groningen University Library, Groningen

Palmer, C. and van der Veen, M. 2002. Archaeobotany and the social context of food. *Acta Palaeobot*. 42, 2:195-202

Preiss, S., Matterne, V. and Latron, F. 2005. An approach to funerary rituals in the Roman provinces: plant remains from a Gallo-roman cemetery at Faulquemont (Moselle,France). *Veget . Hist. Archaeobot*. 14: 362-372

Robinson, M. 2002. Domestic burnt offerings and sacrifices at Roman and pre-roman Pompeii. Italy. *Veget. Hist. Archaeobot*. 11: 93-99

Rottoli, M. and Castiglioni, E. 2011. Plant offerings from Roman cremations in northern Italy: a review. *Veget. Hist. Archaeobot*. 20: 495-506

Rovira, N. and Chabal, L. 2008. A foundation offerings at the Roman port of Lattara (Lattes, France): the plant remains. *Veget. Hist. Archaeobot*. 17 (Suppl. 1): S191-S200

Rukhadze, L., Kvavadze, E. and Shamba, G. 1988. Dynamics of the vegetation of the environs of Eshera settlement (Abkhasia). *Proceed. Acad. Sci. GSSR*, ser.Biol., 14, 6: 406-412 (in Russian)

Rusishvili, N. 1990. *Cultivated plants from early settlements of Georgia according to palaeoetnobotanical investigations*. Ph.D. thesis, Kishiniov (in Russian)

Vandorpe, P. and Jacomet, S. 2011. Remains of burnt vegetable offerings in the temple area of Roman Oedenburg (Biesheim-Kunheim, Haut-Rhin, Alsace). First results. *Carpologia*: 87 -101

Zach, B. 2002. Vegetable offerings on the Roman sacrifical site in Mainz, Germany ,short report on the first results. *Veget. Hist. Archaeobot*., 11: 101-106

Zhukovskii, P.M. 1971. *Crops and their wild relatives*. Izdatelstvo Nauka. Leningrad (in Russian)

Zohary, D. and Hopf, M. 2000. *Domestication of Plants in the Old World: The origin and spread of cultivated plants in West Asia, Europe and Nile Valley*. Oxford, Oxford University Press

CHAPTER NINE

Palynological analysis of samples taken from vessels and burials in 2009

By Maia Chichinadze and Eliso Kvavadze

Introduction

More than forty samples for palynological analysis were obtained from Trenches A and B in the course of excavations carried out by the Anglo-Georgian Expedition to Nokalakevi in 2009. The palynological analysis revealed that more than half of the material contained nearly no pollen or spores, and that their quantity was not sufficient for drawing palaeoecological or other kinds of conclusions. From the authors' point of view, this could be explained by the fact that the chemical and mechanical composition of limestone and its soil is not favourable for preservation of pollen grains. At the same time, pollen and other kinds of palynomorphs were well represented in surviving residues on the kitchen vessels where food – cooked with fat on fire – was kept. In this case thermal processing and fat worked as sterilising agents on the food kept in the vessel, therefore bacteria, microbes or fungi could not reproduce and, therefore, they could not destroy pollen grains of plants.

There were many pollen grains and spores in the abdominal area of the human remains and under the skull. Being first saturated with saliva and then with gastric juice, food residues that reached the abdomen were well preserved (Berg 2002; Kvavadze and Narimanishvili 2010). The thin layer created by the organic residues found under the skull frequently represented the partial survival of hair fragments. Human hair attracts and contains various organic particles, including the pollen of those plants which were nearby (Kvavadze 2011). Correspondingly, the palynological spectrum of human hair represents a perfect marker for the reconstruction of those environmental conditions in which the deceased lived, since the hair spectrum contains numerous significant details of human activities and his/her lifestyle (Kvavadze et al, 2010; Bitadze et al, 2011; Chikhladze and Kvavadze 2011; Sikharulidze et al, 2012). It should also be noted that the palynological material obtained from human hair is predominantly studied in forensic medicine and in criminology (Jamieson and Moenssens 2009). In terms of palaeoecology, analysis of this type has seldom been undertaken previously.

In some cases a rich spectrum was revealed near the lower extremities of the deceased (Kvavadze et al 2010). This can most likely be explained by organic residues that remained on socks and shoes where pollen were easily collected and well preserved.

Results and discussion

1. Palynological properties of the ceramic vessel dated to the Hellenistic period.

Residues of four kitchenware sherds obtained from contexts **235** and **254** in Trench A (dated from the end of the 4th – 2nd century BC) were studied palynologically (Lomitashvili et al 2010). The samples in question represent organic residues surviving on the walls and the bottom of the vessel. Four samples were obtained from unwashed vessels. Their laboratory numbers are: 1, 2, 3, and 4. Palynological spectra of the material obtained from vessels are represented on the first diagram (Figure 9.1). As might be expected from kitchenware, pollen of edible and medicinal plants dominated in the spectra of organic residues found in the vessel.

Sample No 1. The palynological spectrum of the vessel residue revealed that the pollen of arboreal plants prevailed over herbaceous ones (Figure 9.1). Pollen of walnut (*Juglans regia*), hazel (*Corylus*), beech (*Fagus*) and cereals (*Cerealia*) were well-represented. Of medicinal plants, there were found many pollen grains of yarrow (*Achillea*), knot-grass (*Polygonum*), clover (*Trifolium*), lime (*Tilia*) and alder-tree (*Alnus*). There were many spores of medicinal plants such as maidenhair fern (*Adiantum capillus-veneris*). Moss remains were also observed.

Carbonised cells of barks and phytoliths of plants dominated in the group of non-pollen fossils (Figure 9.2). There were many microscopic remains of moss. Bone crystals were well-represented in the spectrum and probably represent traces of meat boiled in this vessel. A significant number of cotton and flax fibres were present, including dyed cotton fibres and unidentified textile fibre. The quantity of cotton fibres was much greater than that of flax. Spores of fungi, the bristles and claws of mites and ticks (*acari indumenta*), feathers and salt crystals were found in small quantities (Figure 9.2).

Sample No 2. In the palynological spectrum of the residues from the second vessel there were found less pollen than in the first one. Pollen of pine (*Pinus*) – a medicinal plant (Odisharia and Sabakhtarishvili 1993) – dominated. There were numerous pollen grains of edible plants such as hazel (*Corylus*), sowing cereals (*Cerealia*) and goosefoot (*Chenopodium*). Medicinal plants other than pine were represented by the pollen of great plantain (*Plantago*), knot-grass (*Polygonum*), chicory (*Cichorium*) and fragrant

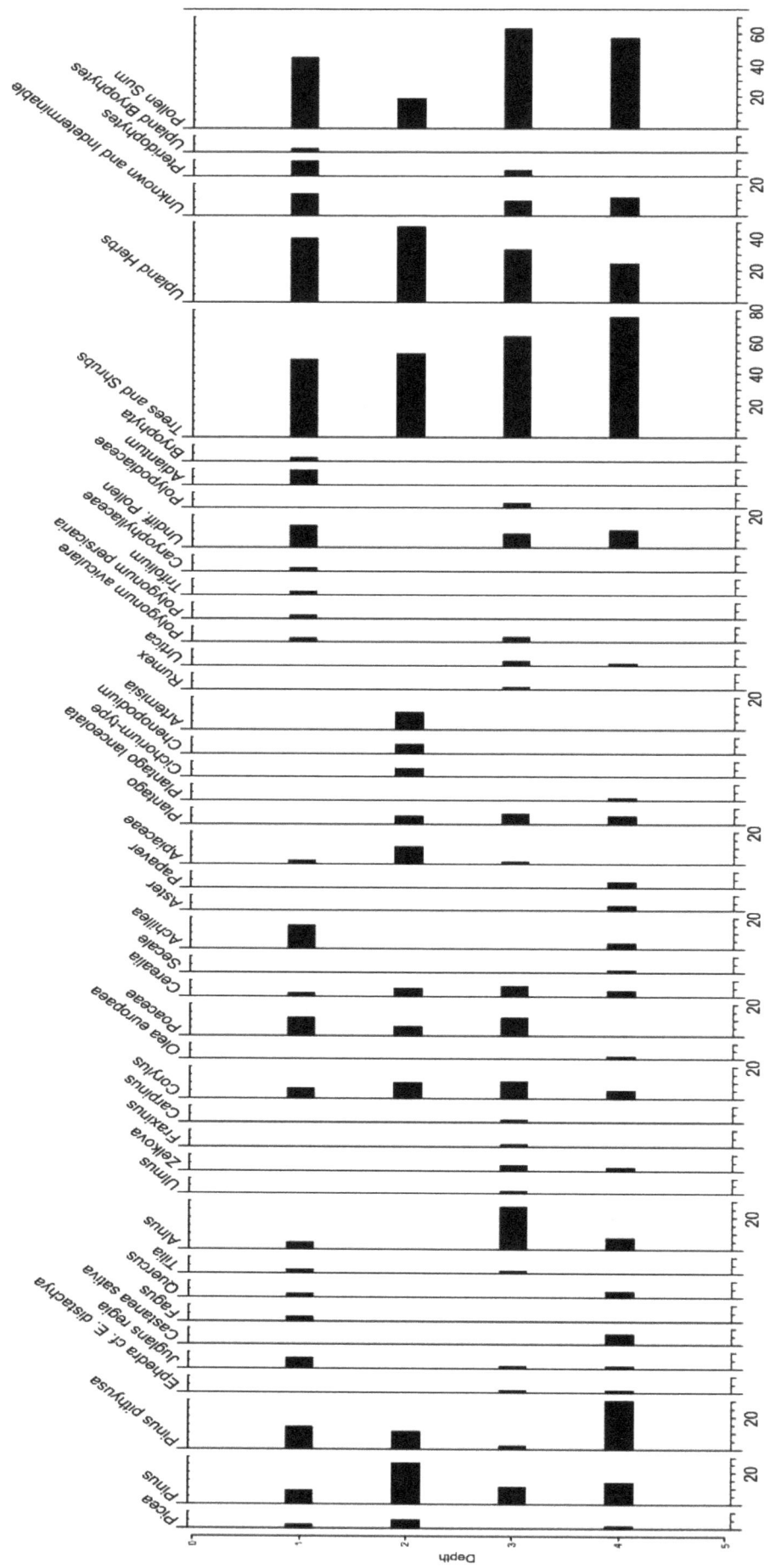

Figure 9.1: Pollen diagram of the material obtained from the pottery

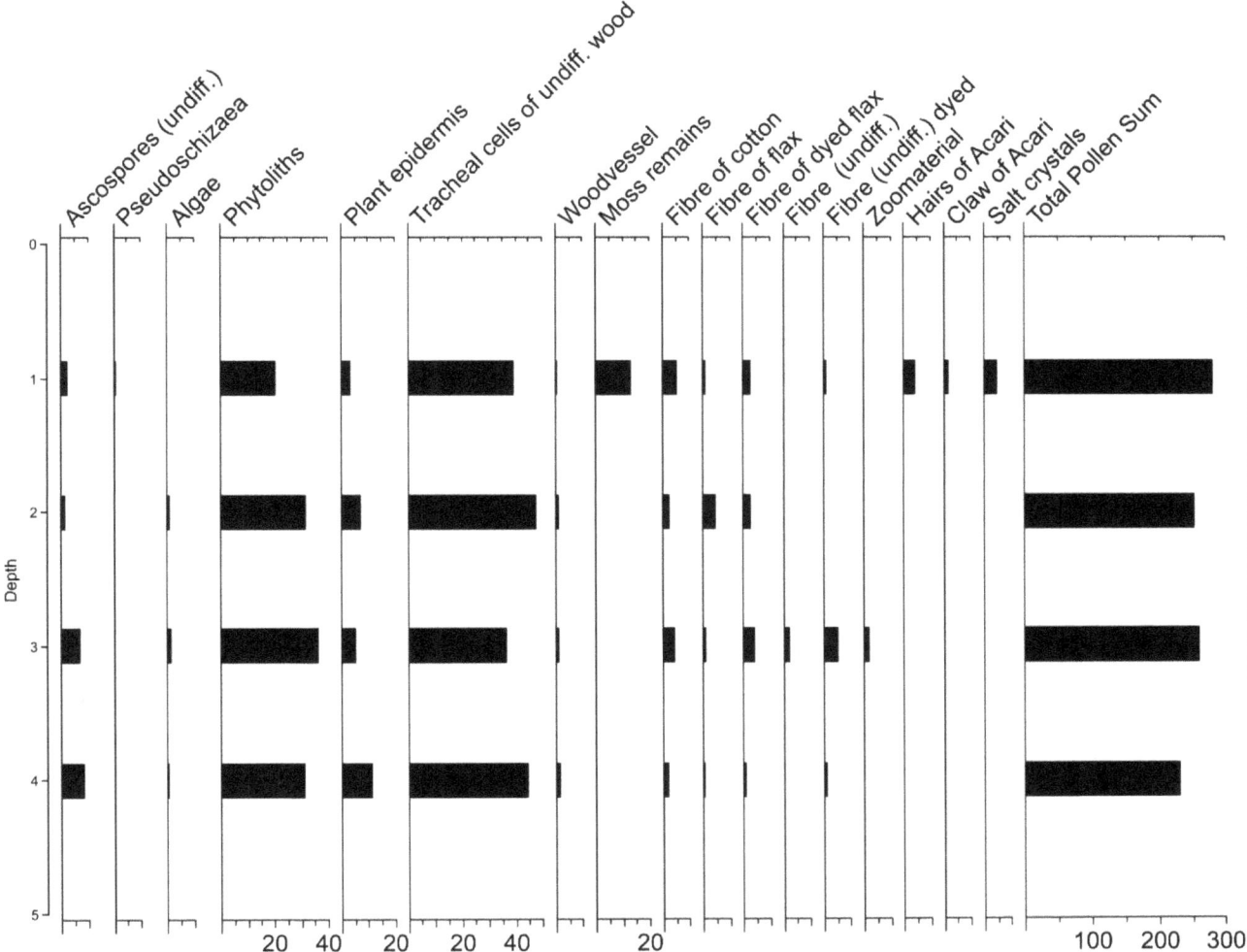

Figure 9.2: Non-pollen palynomorph diagram of the material obtained from the pottery

wormwood (*Artemisia*). Of non-pollen palynomorphs, phytoliths of herbaceous plants (mainly of cereals) and carbonised parenchimal cells of barks – traces of wood fired in the kitchen – dominated. There were lots of cotton and flax fibres (Figure 9.2), with the former dominating. Dyed cotton fibres were well-represented. Spores of fungi and vascular cells of bark were found in small quantities.

Sample No 3. The palynological spectrum of this vessel was rich. There were found many pollen grains of alder-tree (*Alnus*). Hazel (*Corylus*) and cultivated cereals were well-represented. Pollen of pine (*Pinus*), joint-pine (*Ephedra*), walnut (*Juglans*), lime (*Tilia*), elm (*Ulmus*), zelkova (*Zelkova*), hornbeam (*Carpinus*) and ash (*Flaxinus*) were identified. There were many wild cereals (*Poaceae*) and great plantain (*Plantago*) in the group of herbaceous plants. Pollen of umbelliferae, sorrel, nettle and knot-grass were found in small quantities. There was a small quantity of fern spores. Of non-pollen remains, herbaceous phytoliths and parenchimal cells of bark prevailed. Lots of spores of fungi, textile fibres and epidermis of plants were also identified. It is notable that in the residues of the vessel in question flax fibres prevailed over those of cotton. There were many dyed fibres of flax and cotton. Fibre of unidentified textile was also represented (Figure 9.3).

Sample No 4. The palynological spectrum of this vessel was rich. The pollen of arboreal plants dominated the sample. Of edible plants, the pollen of chestnut were identified for the first time (Figure 9.4) and their quantity was rather remarkable. The pollen of hazel and walnut was observed as well. It should be noted that the pollen of olive (*Olea europeae*) were found only in this vessel. The palynological spectrum contained the pollen of rye (*Secale cerealia*) and of other sowing cereals. Of the herbaceous group the pollen of edible plants such as nettle (*Utrica*) and poppy (*Papaver*) were identified. Of medicinal plants, there were found pollen of yarrow and great plantain. Non-palynological remains were represented with herbaceous phytoliths and carbonised tracheal cells of bark. There were a number of spores of fungi and plant epidermis. Bark vascular cells, cotton, flax and fibre of unidentified textile were found in small quantities. Dyed fibres were not observed in this sample.

The palynological analysis of the organic residues of the ceramic vessels appears to indicate a predominantly vegetarian diet. Cereals, nettle, goosefoot, lime, poppy and other edible greens were cooked. Walnut (*Juglans regia*) and hazel (*Corylus*) were perhaps used for the seasoning of food, possibly including meat. The sample from vessel 1 might support such a suggestion (Sample

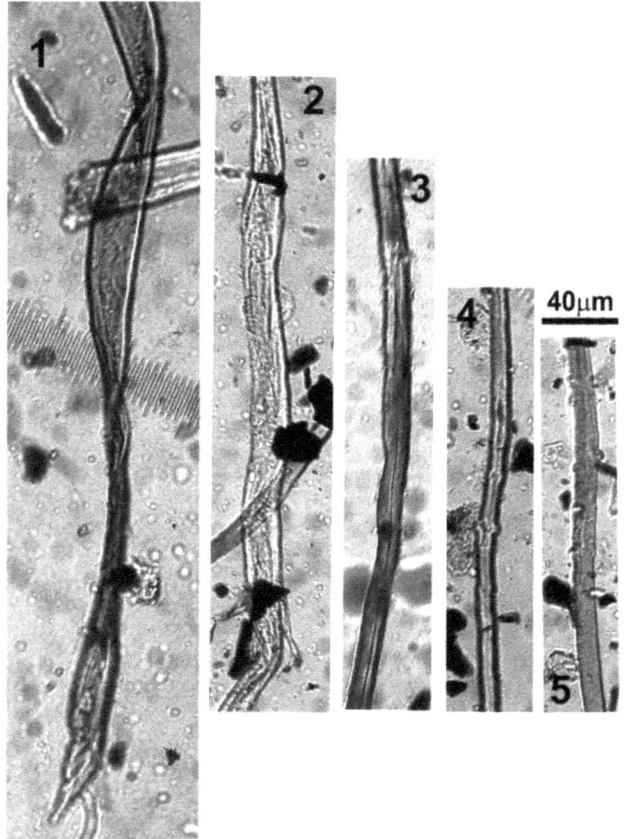

Figure 9.3: Textile fibres found in Sample No 3 (1,2 cotton; 3,4,5 linum)

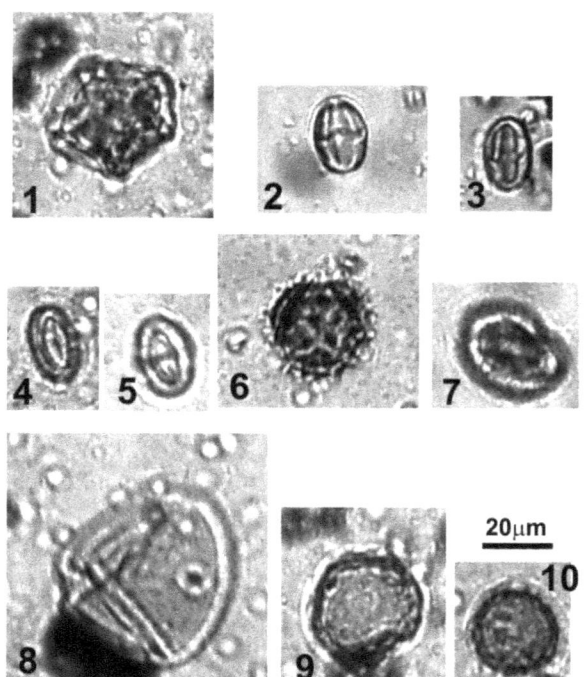

Figure 9.4: Plant pollen found in Sample No 4 (1 – alder (Alnus); 2,3,4,5,- chesnut (Castanea sativa); 6 – yarrow (Achillea); 7 - poppy (Papaver); 8 – rey (Secale); 9 – great plantain (Plantago); 10 – great plantain (Plantago m/m)

1, Figures 9.1 and 9.2). Here pollen of walnut and hazel were found along with bone crystals (Figure 9.5). It seems that chestnut, walnut, hazel, acorn and beech nuts were popular food since their pollen were found in the Hellenistic period kitchenware from Nokalakevi. Despite the apparent contradiction, pollen is known to survive in significant quantities on the host plant, and appears on the surface of nuts etc produced later in the year. It is therefore a good indicator of both environment and plants exploited for food.

As well as predominantly medicinal plants that were also used for culinary purposes, there were species of plants that only had a medicinal function and the inhabitants of ancient Nokalakevi used them in the preparation of medicines. In accordance with the palynological spectra of the vessel, goosefoot, yarrow, great plantain, absinth (wormwood), clover, chicory, knot-grass, and maiden hair fern belonged to this group of plants. Of arboreal plants, lime, alder, joint-pine, pine, zelkova, oak, hornbeam, ash and elm also had a medicinal usage. A quantity of phytoliths were found in the residues supporting the supposition that plants were mainly cooked in pots (Figure 9.6).

2. Peculiarities of palynological spectra of the samples obtained from the abdominal area of the human remains found at Nokalakevi.

Along with the palynological spectrum of the kitchenware, the samples obtained from the abdominal area of the deceased contained great information for closer definition of the palaeo-diet of the 4th-3rd centuries BC. The abdominal area always contains microscopic remains of the food which the deceased received in the last days of life (Berg 2002; Reinhard and Bryanth 2008; Kvavadze and Narimanishvili 2010). This could be explained by the fact that any organic remains are well preserved in the saliva and gastric juice of humans and other mammals (Berg 2002; Kvavadze and Narimanishvili 2010; Kvavadze and Shatberashvili 2010). As a result, human and animal coprolites are rich in pollen grains of plants (Reinhard *et al* 1991; Araujo and Ferreira 2000; Chaves and Reinhard 2006). At Nokalakevi, the abdominal areas of four burials from the early Byzantine period (4th – 6th centuries A.D.) were palynologically studied (Figure 9.7, samples No 5, 6, 7 and 8).

Sample No 5 was obtained from the grave fill (**394**) around skeleton **395** from Trench B. The palynological spectra of the abdominal area of the burial was characterised as containing pollen grains of only edible (wheat and rye) and medicinal (great plantain, knot-grass and alder) plants (Figure 9.7). There was a small amount of wild cereal pollen, caryophylaceae, dead white nettle and pine. The

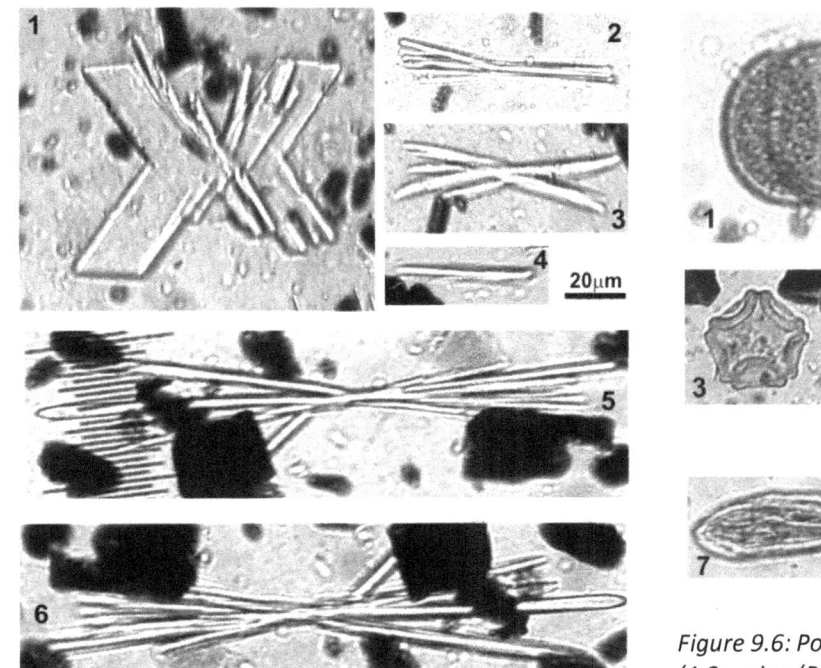

Figure 9.5: Crystals observed in Sample No 1 (1- Salt crystals; 2,3,4,5,6 – Bone crystals)

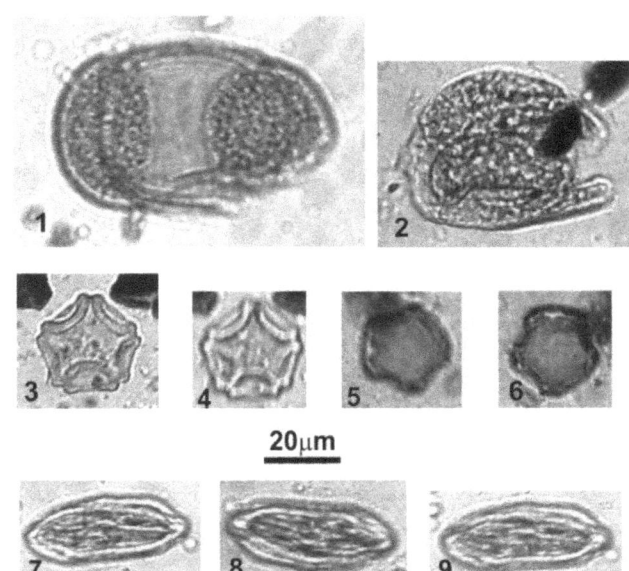

Figure 9.6: Pollen of edible plants observed in Sample No 2 (1,2 – pine (Pinus); 3,4 – alder (Alnus barbata); 5,6 – alder (Alnus glutinosa); 7,8,9 – joint-pine (Ephedra)

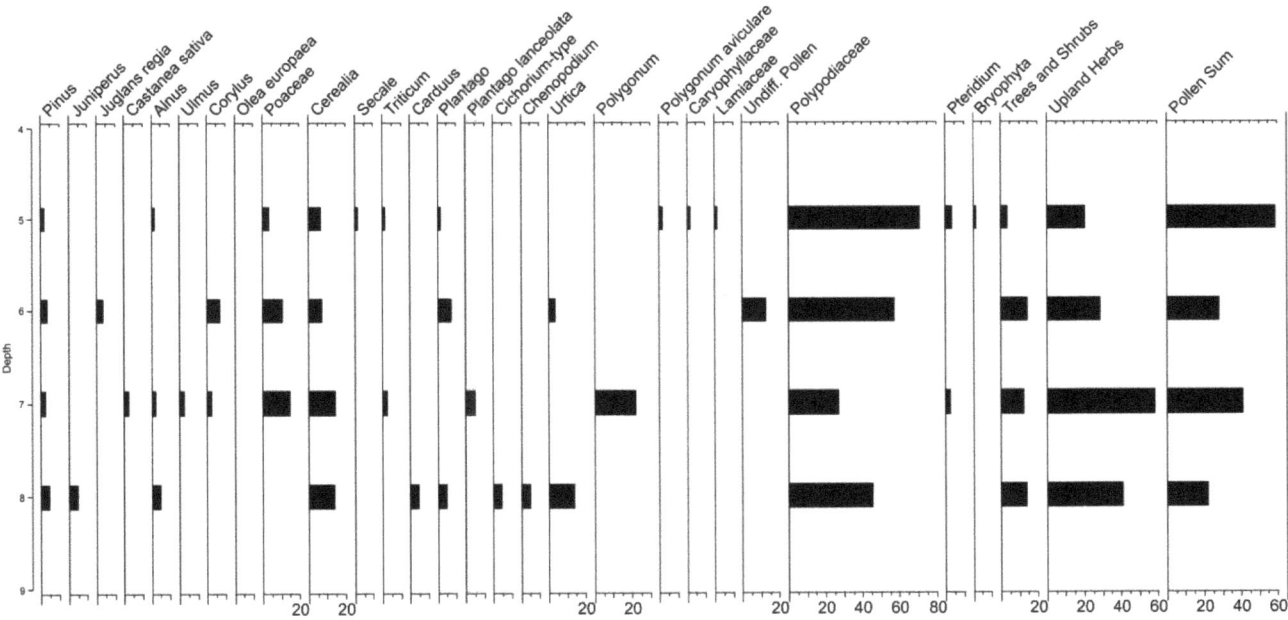

Figure 9.7: Pollen diagram of the material obtained from the abdomenal area of the burials

palynological spectrum contained a large quantity of fern spores (Figure 9.8), all of which are medicinal. Bark cells and phytoliths of cereals dominated among non-palynological residues (Figure 9.9). Plant epidermis and spores of fungi were well represented. Also observed were dung fungus *Sordaria*, *Chaetomium* and *Neurospora*. There were spores of *Ustulina* and *Coniocheta* growing on the bark (van Hoeve and Hendrikse 1998; Geel 2008; Geel and Aptroot 2007). Small quantities of cotton and flax textile were observed, as well as a small number of microscopic remains of ticks and insects.

Sample No 6. was obtained from the grave fill (**410**) around skeleton **411** from Trench B. Analysis of this sample revealed pollen grains of edible (hazel, walnut and wheat) and medicinal (great plantain and knot-grass) plants in the spectrum (Figure 9.7). A large quantity of fern spores was also observed. Tracheal and vascular cells of wood prevailed among non-pollen palynomorphs (Figure 9.10). There were many cereals and other phytoliths. Spores of fungi, such as fungus *Brachiosporium* and *Ustulina* (Figure 9.11) were well-represented (van Hoeve and Hendrikse 1998; Geel and Aptroot 2006). Spores of dung fungus

115

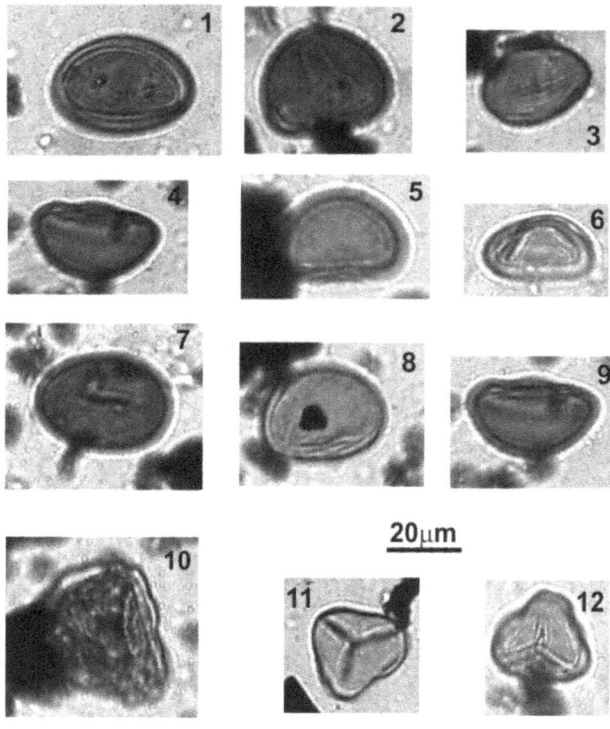

Figure 9.8: Fern spores observed in Sample No 5 from the abdominal area of burial **395** (1,2,3,4,9 – Polypodiaceae; 10 – Pteris cretica; 11,12 – Pteridium aquilinum)

Sordaria, Cercophora and Chaetomium were observed. Those species of fungi grow on the dung of ruminant animals and their spores attest to the development of cattle-breeding (Geel et al 2003). Spores of the fungus Glomus, which grows on friable soil, were found and represent a good indicator for the development of agriculture. Residues of fresh-water aquatic plants, such as Pseudoshcizae and Dinoflagellata, were also observed. A small quantity of flax and unidentified textile fibres were found, along with small quantities of bristles (indumenta) and claws of insects.

Sample No 7. Similarly to the palynological spectrum of the abdominal areas of other burials, pollen grains of edible plants and pollen of medicinal plants dominated in the palynological spectrum of the seventh sample. Pollen of chestnut, hazel and wheat were found. Pollen grains of such medicinal plants as great plantain, knotgrass, alder, etc were also observed. There were many phytoliths of cereals and tracheal cells of bark among the non-pollen residues of the sample. Plant epidermis was well represented. There were remains of aquatic plants. As for spores of fungus, they were few. Representatives of dung fungus were not observed. There were spores of fungus Ustulina growing on bark. Fibres of cotton textile were present in a greater quantity in this sample, while fibres of flax and unidentified textile were fewer. There were also fewer remains of insects and ticks.

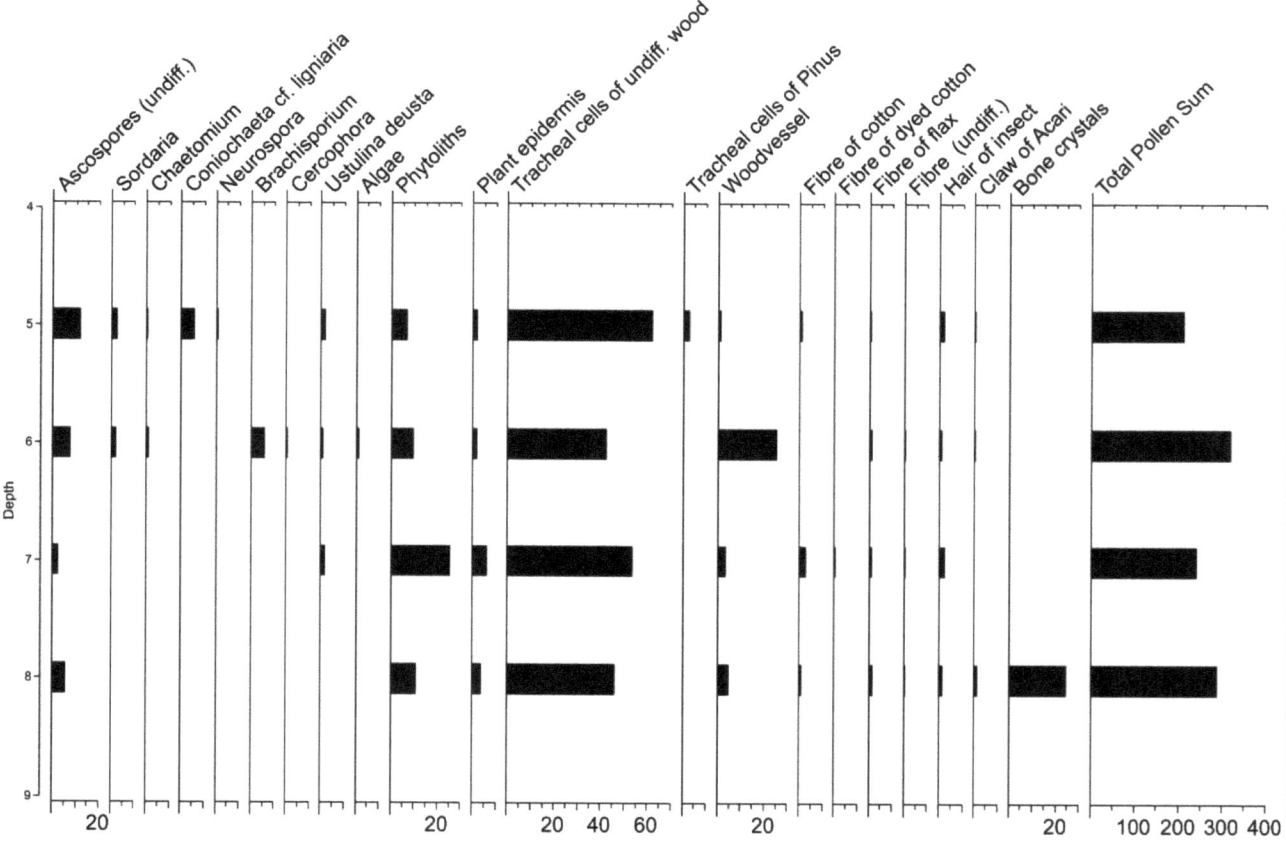

Figure 9.9: Non pollen palynomorph diagram of the material obtained from the abdomenal area of the burials

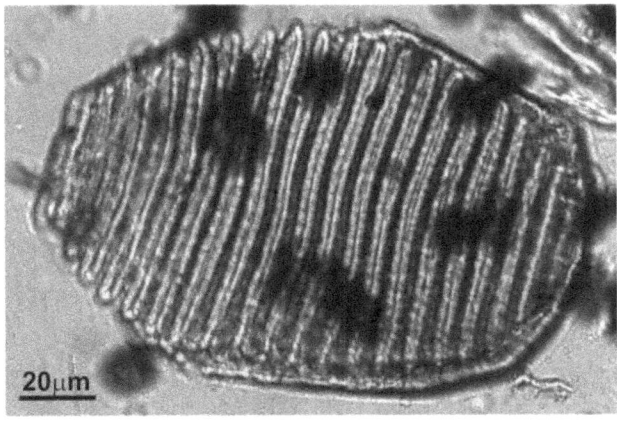

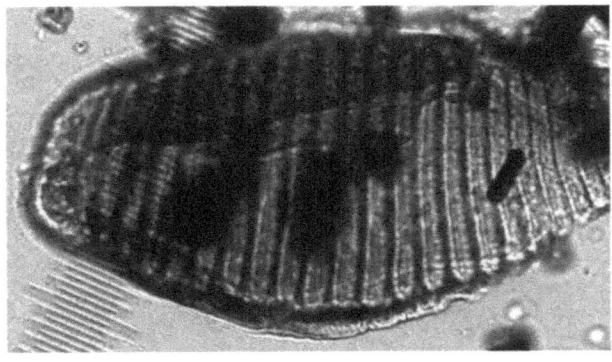

Figure 9.10: Vascular cells of wood bark from Sample No 6 (grave fill **410** around skeleton **411** from Trench B)

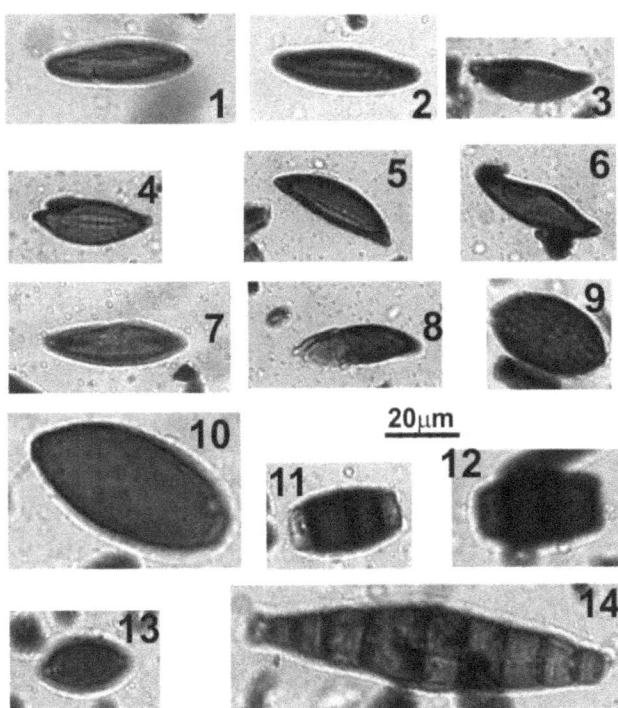

Figure 9.11: Spores of fungi from Sample No 6 (1-8 – Ustulina; 9 – Neurospora; 10 – Cercophora; 11,12 – Brachysporium; 13 – Sordaria; 14 – Clasterosporium)

Sample No 8 Context **394** around skeleton **395**. The palynological spectrum of the eighth sample mainly contained pollen of medicinal arboreal and herbaceous plants. Pollen grains of edible plants were found in small quantities, representing only pollen of cultivated cereals. There were many pollen grains of nettle. However, this plant could be used for both medicinal and edible purposes, as can Goosefoot (Grossgeim 1946) which was also observed. Great plantain (*Plantago*), juniper (*Juniperus*), alder (*Alnus*) and thistle (*Carduus*) represent the purely medicinal plants found. There were many spores of ferns in the palynological spectrum. Parenchimal cells of bark prevailed among non-pollen remains. Bone crystals were the second dominant of the sample. There were many phytoliths. Plant epidermis of fresh water aquatic plants (Pseudoschizea) were well-represented. Spores of fungi *Glomus* and *Ustulina* and small quantities of fibres of cotton, flax and unidentified textile were observed. Fossils of ticks and insects were represented in small quantities.

It is evident that great similarity exists between palynological spectra of samples obtained from the abdominal areas of deceased and the ones estimated in residues taken from kitchenware. In both cases there was great amount of pollen of sowing cereals. They seem to be residues of cereal porridge and remains of wheat and rye bread, which seem to be also very popular (Figure 9.7).

As for the funeral rite, all deceased seem to be lying in wooden constructions (coffin). This speculation is based on the existence of great amount of tracheal and vascular cells of bark. Such remains of wood prevailed in spectra of all deceased. Since the active phase of ticks, insects and other zoological material is marked only in summer, the small amount of their microscopic remains might indicate that all four deceased were interred in a cold season of the year. In addition, the great quantities of fern spores (which, as pollen, survives well beyond the season in which they are produced) gives grounds for supposition that wooden constructions and burial floor, or one of them, was covered with bunches of fern.

3. Peculiarities of pollen spectra obtained from the skull and lower limb samples of the Nokalakevi burials

Samples 9, 10 and 11 (from Trench B contexts **394**, **402** – the grave fills of burials **395**, **403** and **406**) have been studied. They were obtained under the skulls of three burials. Sample No 12 was extracted from the feet area of burial **395**, within grave fill **394**. A palynological diagram (Figure 9.12) shows that, in comparison with spectra from vessels, samples obtained from under skulls contained much less pollen of arboreal plants, while herbaceous ones were found in abundance. Their taxonomical composition, however, is lower. Here cereals prevail, both cultivated and wild species. It is worth noting that no pollen of medicinal plants have been identified from these samples.

Sample No.9 was obtained from burial **395**. It seems to reflect the complete palynological spectrum of the hair of the deceased. Of arboreal plants, the pollen of hazel (*Corylus*) prevail. Pollen of pine (*Pinus*), beech (*Fagus*) and alder (*Alnus*) were found in smaller quantities (Figure 9.12). The herbaceous group contained lots of weed pollen including goosefoot (*Chenopodiaceae*), knot-grass (*Polygonum*), wild succory (*Cichoriodeae*), and fragrant wormwood (*Artemisia*). There was a significant quantity of forest fern pollen, including woolly bracken (*Pteridium aquilinum*) and tabula (*Pteris cretica*). Among non-pollen

remains, cells of wood bark (Figure 9.13) and phytolith predominate. Fungus spores are found in considerable quantity, among which are those of dung fungi (*Sordaria*). Of interest is the fact that in this sample spores of *Ustulina* and *Coniocheta,* which form on wood bark, were identified. The remains of some freshwater plants (*Pseudischizea*) were revealed. The sample contained microscopic remains of plant epidermis. Fibre of cotton and flax was also present (Figure 9.13). A small amount of zoological material was represented in the shape of bristles (*indumenta*) of insects and ticks, as well as their epidermis.

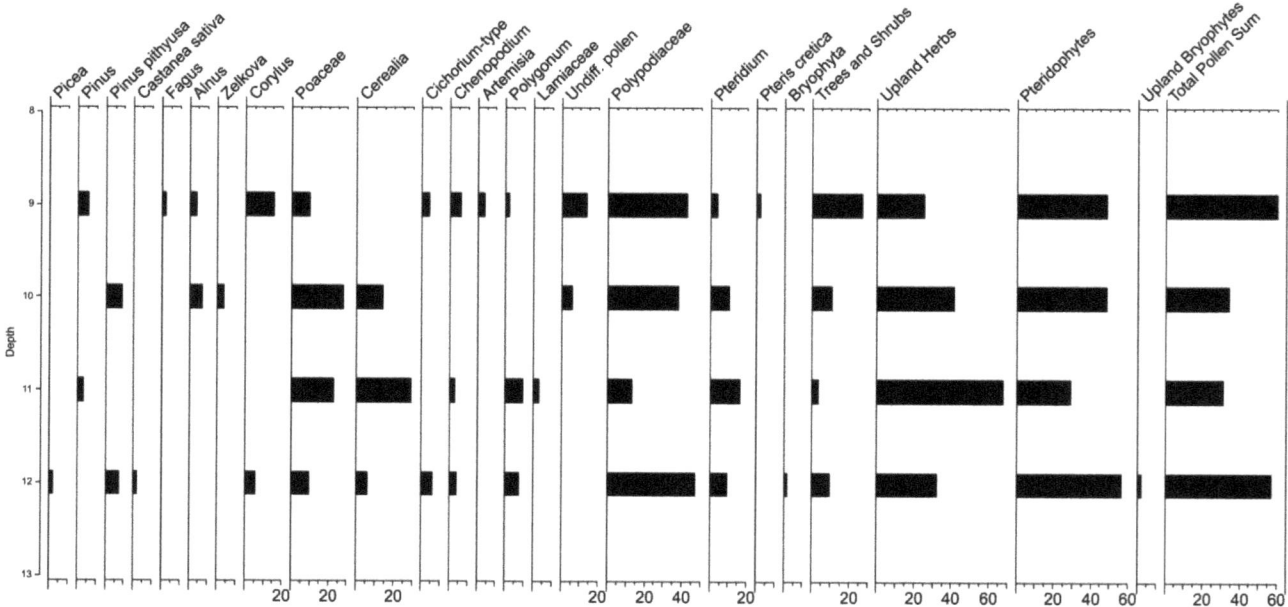

*Figure 9.12: Pollen diagram of the material obtained from under the skulls of Trench B burials **395, 403** and **406** (Samples 9, 10 and 11 respectively) and from the feet of burial **395** (Sample 12)*

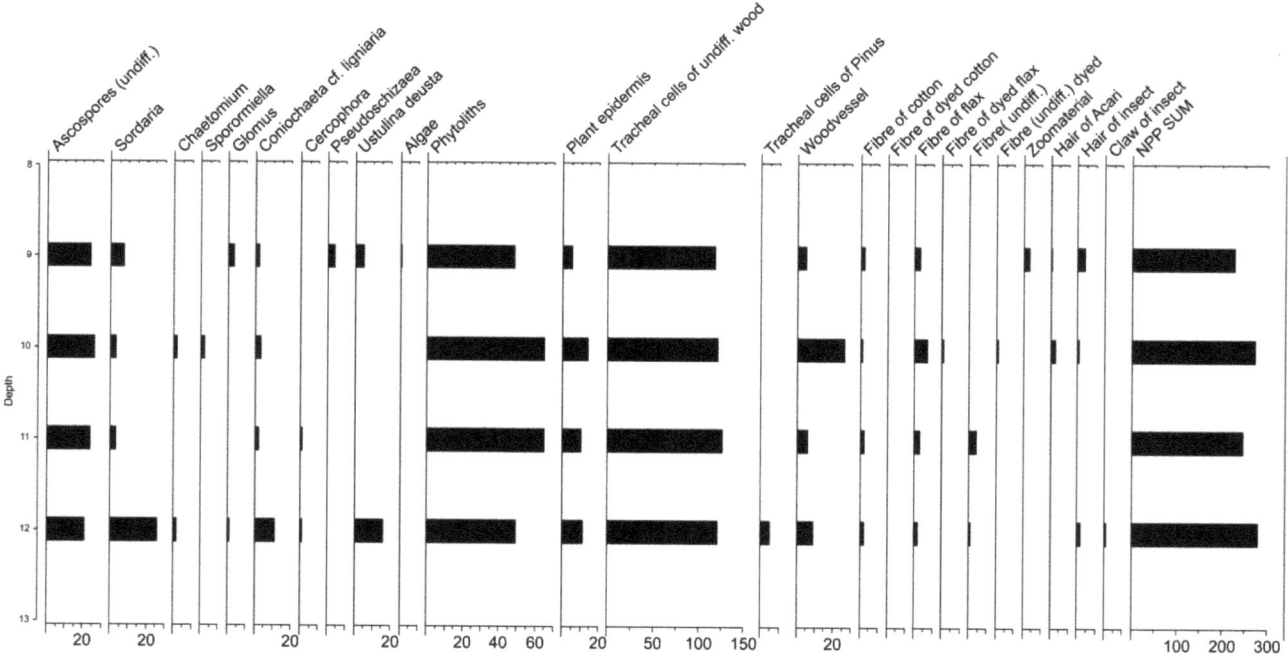

Figure 9.13 Non-pollen palynomorph diagram of the material obtained from Samples 9-12

Sample No 10 was obtained from under the skull of burial **403**. Its palynological spectrum differs from that of the above in that almost no weed pollen have been identified (Figure 9.12); pollen of both wild cereals and those for sowing prevail. The only pollen of arboreal plants identified were pine (*Pinus*), alder (*Alnus*) and zelkova tree (*Zelkova*). There were many spores of forest bracken, especially those of woolly bracken (*Pteridium aquilinum*). Among non-pollen palynomorphs, tracheal and vascular cells of wood predominated, attesting to the existence of a wooden item (probably a coffin) in the burial. Spores of fungus *Coniocheta* were found. There were also many spores of dung fungi: *Sporormiella*, *Sordaria*, and *Chaetomium*. Fibres of flax, cotton and unidentified textile were also identified, of which some were dyed. The sample also included microscopic remains of bird feathers, as well as a small quantity of insect and tick remains (Figure 9.13).

Sample No 11 was obtained from under the skull of burial **406**. The spectra of this sample were characterised by a significant quantity of cereals. Pollen of cultivated species prevailed, while wild species represented a small proportion. Weeds of cereal were well represented, including goosefoot (*Chenopodiaceae*), knot-grass (*Polygonum*), and woolly bracken (*Pteridium aquilinum*). It is worth noting that, in western Georgia, woolly bracken grows along roads, in court-yards and under crops. It is especially prevalent in recently cleared forest. Of arboreal plants only a few pollen of pine were identified. Among non-pollen remains, cells of bark, phytoliths, and epidermis of plants dominated. Spores of the fungus *Coniocheta* are also represented. There were only a few spores of dung fungi *Sordaria* and *Cercophora*. The sample contained the same number of cotton, flax, and unidentified textile fibres. No microscopic remains of ticks and other zoological materials were found in it.

Sample No 12. The palynological spectrum of sample No 12, obtained from around the feet of burial **395**, are shown in Figure 9.12. Their character resembles the palynological spectrum of the sample extracted from the head area of the same burial (Sample 9). Hazel pollen was found in a large quantity. Pollen of chestnut and pine were also represented. Courtyard weeds and spores of forest fern and woolly bracken were found in abundance. Among non-pollen remains, cells of bark, phytoliths, and spores of fungi predominate. In the feet area dung fungi *Sordaria* prevail; spores of other fungi – *Glomus*, *Chaetomium*, *Coniochetae*, and *Ustulina* – are also evidenced, two of which (*Coniochetae*, *Ustulina*) grow on dead bark. The sample contained textile fibres too, including cotton, flax, and unidentified textile. Zoological remains were very few and consisted of single specimens of insect indumenta and claws.

Conclusions

Palynological spectra of residues from kitchenware are of great importance for the definition of palaeodiet and ethnopharmacology. In the Hellenistic period the bulk of the diet of the Nokalakevi population consisted of plants. Cereals prevailed, both cultivated and wild, and various cereal dishes were cooked. Bread was baked, and edible greens (nettle, goosefoot, lime tree leaves, poppy) were widely used.

Many dishes were seasoned with nuts (*Juglans regia*) and hazel (*Corylus*). Meat dishes could also be seasoned with hazelnuts and this might be indicated by finds of its pollen in vessel No 1, together with a significant quantity of bone crystals. Besides hazel, chestnuts, acorns, and pips of beech seem to have also been exploited, since their pollen were identified in the kitchenware of the 4th-2nd centuries BC from Nokalakevi. Though many plants were used simultaneously for both culinary and medicinal purposes, plants used for purely medical purposes were also identified. More likely the inhabitants of Nokalakevi made medicines from them.

The palynological spectra of kitchenware include yarrow, great plantain, absinthe, clover, wild succory, knot-grass, and maidenhair fern from this group of plants. Of arboreal plants lime, alder, joint pine, pine, zelkova, oak, hornbeam, ash, and elm trees also had a medicinal function.

As for burial rites, all the deceased of the early Byzantine period that were studied appear to have been placed in wooden constructions (coffins). This fact is evidenced by a significant quantity of tracheal and vascular cells of bark. A further argument is shaped by the find of pollen of those fungi that settle only on the bark of a dead tree and destroy it. All the deceased studied appear to have been buried during a cold season, since the spectra contained only a small quantity of ticks, insects and microscopical remains of other creatures whose active life is confined to the summer.

Furthermore, the palynological analysis demonstrates that, while cotton was utilised in the Hellenistic period alongside flax and other textiles, by the early Byzantine period this had become more significant and the quantity of cotton fibres found in the later samples is observably greater.

Bibliography

Araujo, A. and Ferreira, I.F. 2000. Paleoparasitology and the antiquity of human host-parasite relationships. *Mem. Inst. Oswaldo Cruz, Rio de Janeiro 95* (Suppl. 1): 89-93

Berg, G. 2002. Last meals: recovering abdominal contents from skeletonized remains. *Journal of Archaeological Science* 29: 1349-1365

Bitadze, L., Kvavadze, E., Lanchava, O., Isakadze, R., Laliashvili, Sh., Vacheishvili, N., Gaprindashvili, P. and Dobrovolskaya, M. 2010. Preliminary report of complex study of burial of a rich lady found in the Bagrati church. *Annales* (6): 280-310

Bitadze, L., Chitanava, D., Laliashvili, Sh., Kvavadze, E. and Zubiashvili, T. 2011. *Problems of ethnic identity of population of Kartli and alteration of anthropological type from the 3rd millennium BC up to the 20th century*. Tbilisi, Meridiano (in Georgian)

Bitadze, L., Shengelia, N., Kvavadze, E. and Laliashvili, Sh. 2011. Development of bioarchaeological studies in Georgia (actuality and prospects). *Annales* (7) 475-49 (in Georgian)

Chaves, S. and Reinhard, K. 2006. Critical analysis of coprolite evidence of medicinal plant use. Piaui, Brazil. *Palaeogeography, Palaeoclimatology, Palaoecology* 237: 110-118

Chikhladze, V. and Kvavadze, E. 2011. Headdress decoration, hair-do and results of palynological study of organic remains. *Annales* (7): 455-473 (in Georgian)

van Geel, B. 2008. Forty years of non-pollen palynomorphs: a state of the art. In Maritan, M. And Miola, A. (ed.) *3rd International Workshop of Quaternary Non Pollen Palynomorphs*. Padova, University of Padova Press: 64-65

van Geel, B. and Aptroot, A. 2006. Fossil ascomycetes in Quaternary deposits. *Nova Hedvigia* (82) 3-4: 313-329

van Geel, B., Buurman, J., Brinkkemper, O., Schelvis, J., Aptroot, A., van Reenen, G. and Hakbijl, T. 2003. Environmental reconstruction of a Roman Period settlement site in Uitgeest (The Netherlands), with special reference to coprophilous fungi. *Journal of Archaeological Science* (30): 873-883

Grossgeim, G.G. 1946. *Rastitelnie resursi Kavkaza* [Plant resources of Caucasus]. Baku, Azerbaijan Acad. Of Science (in Russian)

van Hoeve, M.L. and Hendrikse, M. 1998. *A study of non-pollen objects in pollen slides (the types as described by Dr Bas van Geel and colleagues)*. Utrech

Jamieson, A. and Moenssens, A. 2009. *Wiley encyclopaedia of forensic science*. London, John Wiley & Sons Ltd.

Kvavadze, E. 2011. Reconstruction of paleoecological conditions and life style in the period of archaeological cultures spread in Kartli during the last 5000 years. In Bitadze, L. (ed.) *Reconstruction of paleoecological conditions and life style in the period of archaeological cultures spread in Kartli during the last 5000 years*. Tbilisi, Meridiano: 495-576 (in Georgian)

Kvavadze, E. and Narimanishvili, G. 2010. Paleolandscapes of the Tsalka plateau in the Late Pleistocene and Holocene (in the light of palynological data from archaeological and geological material). In Gamkrelidze, G. (ed.) Rescue Archaeology in Georgia: *Baku-Tbilisi-Ceyhan and south Caucasian pipelines*. Tbilisi, Georgian National Museum: 587-606

Kvavadze, E., Narimanishvili, G., and Bitadze, L. 2010. Textile fibres of flax (Linum), cotton (Gossipium) and animal wool as non-pollen-palynomorphs in the Late Bronze Age burials of Saphar-Kharaba, Southern Georgia. *Vegetation History and Archaeobotany* (19) 5-6: 479-494

Lomitashvili, D., Tvalchrelidze, Z., Kebuladze, N., Murghulia, N., Bokeria, M., Kvavadze, E., Colvin, I., Everill, P., Neil, B. and Timby, J. 2010. Georgian-British expedition at Nokalakevi. Report of archaeological excavations at Nokalakevi in 2008-2009. *Dziebani* (20): 133-152 (in Georgian)

Odisharia, T. and Sabakhtarashvili, Sh. 1992. *Lechebnie rastenia Gruzii i phytoterapevticheskie retsepti* [The medicinal plants of Georgia and phytotherapeutic prescriptions]. Tbilisi, Sinatle (in Russian)

Reinhard, K.J., Hamilton, D.L. and Hevly, R.H. 1991. Use of pollen concentration in paleopharmacology: coprolite evidence of medicinal plants. *Journal of Ethnobiology* (11): 117-134

Reinhard, K. J. and Bryanth, V.M. 2008. Burials: dietary sampling methods. *Encyclopaedia of Archaeology*, Elsevier: 937-944

Sikharulidze, A., Bitadze, L., Kvavadze, E., Asatiani, T. and Dighmelashvili, K. 2012. Results of complex study carried out to define the identity of a lady buried in the yard of the Samtavro monastery. *Annales* (8): 351-377

CHAPTER TEN

Zooarchaeological study of animal remains from Nokalakevi

By Ben Gruwier

Introduction

During the summer of 2010 a zooarchaeological study was made of the faunal remains from two trenches at Nokalakevi. A total of 1,664 animal remains were studied from Trench A and Trench B.

The material came from several contexts: **232**, **235**, **267** and **268** from Trench A; and **397**, **401**, **420** and **423** from Trench B. The majority of the fragments from Trench B (**397**, **420**, **423**) consisted of material of Hellenistic age, the remainder (from **401**) was dated to the early Byzantine period. Most fragments from Trench A were also of Hellenistic age: **232**, **235**, **268**. Context **267** however was dated to the early Byzantine period. The material was divided in two phases for further interpretation: Hellenistic and early Byzantine.

Identifications were made in the field by the author. This was achieved by using a small comparative collection present on site in addition to the identification keys provided by Schmidt (1972), Boessneck (1969) and Cohen *et al* (1996). Measurements were taken where possible, as described in Von den Driesch (1976). Ages of domestic mammals were estimated following Silver (1969).

Taphonomy

As the animal remains were collected by hand, a number of smaller fragments may have been missed during the excavations. The preservation was variable, even within the same context. Some bones were well preserved while others were highly fragmented.

The encountered faunal remains were assigned to different taphonomic groups as described in Gautier (1987). The following groups could be identified in the zooarchaeological record at Nokalakevi: consumption refuse, manufacture refuse and the remains of carcasses.

Based on the presence of several cutmarks and chopmarks on the bones from most contexts, the majority of the animal remains could be interpreted as consumption waste. The exception being the horse remains. As there are no indications of butchery it is more probable that these few remains belonged to animals that died near the site and were later deposited with the rest of the animal remains.

Moreover the presence of multiple gnawing marks and traces of root etching in almost every stratigraphical unit, from both trenches, suggest that most of the animal remains must have been lying on the surface for some time or were buried in shallow deposits (Lyman 1994).

Although it is likely that some of the site's stratigraphic sequence is the result of the gradual deposition of colluvium (see Chapters Two, Four and Five), there were no indications that the faunal remains rolled down from higher ground. It is therefore presumed that the majority of the material was still *in situ* when excavated.

Faunal composition

It is clear that for both periods the majority of the animal remains belonged to the three main domesticates: cattle, sheep/goat and pig (Table 10.1). Where possible there was a distinction made between sheep and goat. Only one fragment could be identified to species level and belonged to sheep. The absence of goat bones might however be due to the relatively small sample.

Cattle and pig seem to be equally represented, while ovicaprids are less frequent in the faunal composition. Although it is presumed that most of the suidae fragments belong to domestic pig, a few large specimens in the assemblage are most likely to be attributed to wild boar.

In general it is accepted by zooarchaeologists that a length of at least 40 mm for the lower third molar is a good indication that a fragment belongs to wild boar (Ervynck and Vanderhoeven 1992). In the Nokalakevi assemblage there were unfortunately no complete lower third molars present where this measurement could be taken.

However, according to a recent biometric study by Albarella *et al* (2009), the modern wild boar from the Caucasus and Central Asia are in general very large animals. Although the sample in this study is not very large, it is noteworthy that the measurements (BT) on the distal part of two humeri from Nokalakevi fall well into the range of the largest specimens that were measured by Albarella and his collegues for the Caucasian and Middle Eastern region. A large right humerus of NOK10/A **267** had a BT of 34.4 mm and a right humerus from NOK10/A **268** had a BT of 40.9 mm. The breadth of the latter even surpasses all modern samples from the region. Besides these two humeri, there were also a few other fragments of impressive size that, although no measurements could be taken, are most likely to be attributed to wild boar. These include a calcaneus from NOK10/A **267**, two male canines and a mandibula from NOK10/A **268** and a

Taxon	A268*	A235	A232	B420*	Total Hellenistic	A267	B401*	Total Early Byzantine
Chicken (*Gallus gallus* f. domestica)	**2				2	1		1
Unidentified birds	4	1			5	2	5	7
Hare (*Lepus europaeus*)			1		1			
Red Deer (*Cervus elaphus*)	3				3			
Roe Deer (*Capreolus capreolus*)	3	1			4			
Aurochs (*Bos primigenius primigenius*)						1		1
Equid (*Equus* sp.)	2			1	3		2	2
Wild boar/ pig (*Sus scrofa/ Sus scrofa* f. domestica)	59	23	20	33	135	30	75	105
Sheep/ goat (*Ovis ammon* f. aries/ *Capra aegagrus* f. hircus)	19	12	6	12	49	20	21	41
Sheep (*Ovis ammon* f. aries)	1				1			
Cattle (*Bos primigenius* f. taurus)	68	36	18	29	151	46	63	109
Unidentified mammal vertebrae	6	6	1		13	3	2	5
Unidentified mammal ribs	16	3	3	5	27	25	20	45
Unidentified mammal	228	214	73	142	657	103	195	298
Total	411	296	122	222	1050	231	383	614

Table 10.1: Animal bone assemblage (*= including other contexts **= with 18 fragments of one individual)

metacarpal and a pair of ulnae (belonging to the same individual) from NOK10/B **401**.

The other wild mammals consisted of hare, red deer and roe deer. Based on the size; a large distal fragment of a humerus could be identified as aurochs. According to the criteria of Degerbol and Fredskild (1970) a distal breadth (BD) of 112.4mm falls well into the range of *Bos primigenius primigenius*. As there is some overlap in the size of small aurochs and large domestic cattle, there is a possibility that this fragment belongs to a large domestic bull. But as the measurement was much larger than that of all other cattle fragments it is more likely to belong to auroch.

A total of five fragments could be identified as equid (*Equus* sp.). Judging by the size of these remains, they probably all belong to domestic horse (*Equus ferus* f. Caballus).

Of the several bird bones that were found, only a few fragments could be identified to species level. Two loose fragments in addition to a sub-complete carcass of chicken were present in the assemblage. The other fragments might belong to wild birds that were caught or that lived around the site.

Interpretation

Palaeoecology

Although the species composition gives little information about the natural environment of Nokalakevi, there are a few species that give some insight into what the landscape must have looked like. The presence of a significant number of cattle from the Hellenistic period onwards indicates that Nokalakevi and its environs had, at least for some part, an open landscape. The bones of hare in the assemblage are also an indication of a more open environment. Red deer, wild boar and roe deer are on the other hand animals indicative of temperate forests (Kurten 2007). This gives the general impression that the landscape around Nokalakevi was of a mixed nature.

The presence of aurochs may perhaps give us some more insight into the environment around the site. Although at present there is still some debate about the exact nature of the original habitat of the aurochs in the Holocene (e.g. Vera 2000), it is clear that even into the Byzantine period there may still have been a climax vegetation present in the vicinity of the site that could support a population of these large ungulates.

As an important part of its diet was composed of grasses, it is presumed that the aurochs had a preference for small open patches in dense forests that would give it the opportunity to graze. Sedge marshes and river valleys would have formed a suitable habitat (Van Vuure 2002). This is in accordance with Hippocrates' description of the vegetation of western Georgia as marshy and wooded during the classical period (Braund 1994).

From a palynological sequence at the nearby site of Ispani 2 it was concluded that cultural change through the various archaeological phases did not have a major impact on land use intensity. It was not until the 20th century that anthropogenic influence on the landscape became more marked (De Klerk *et al* 2009).

Although the animal remains from Nokalakevi do not give us a detailed insight into the region's palaeoenvironment, the presence of domesticated animals alongside a considerable amount of wild animals, including large herbivores like the aurochs, suggest the presence of a mixed landscape with a still significant proportion of woodland.

Today Nokalakevi lies on the border between the Colchian plain, subject to agricultural practice, and the forested foothills that further north develop into the main Caucasus range (De Klerk *et al* 2009). Perhaps its surrounding landscape may have known little change since ancient times, where the plains, when not subject to periodic incursions of the Black Sea and subsequent marshy conditions, were probably used for breeding cattle and ovicaprids, while the nearby forest, still in a more or less "pristine" condition, could be used for hunting and breeding pigs. The gradual degradation of the natural environment seen in Western Europe might have happened at a slower rate in western Georgia.

Palaeoeconomy

It is clear that domestic mammals were the main source of meat at Nokalakevi from the Hellenistic period onwards. Based on the number of remains (Figures 10.1 and 10.2), there seems to have been an emphasis on herds of cattle and pig. Sheep/goat husbandry was probably of less importance.

These relative proportions are generally confirmed when looking at the weight of the fragments of our main domestic species (Figures 10.3 and 10.4). Cattle is followed by pig as the most important species, while sheep/goat seems to have been of less importance. When looking at the weight though, cattle seems to have been much more prominent than pig in comparison with a simple fragment count. As cattle bones are in general larger than the bones of the other two species (and bear more meat on a single bone), the results of the weight method give a more realistic insight compared to the number of remains. Thus cattle seem to have been the most important meat provider by far during both periods.

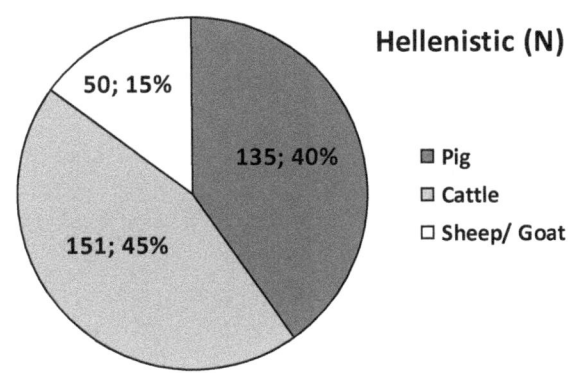

Figure 10.1: Relative importance of the three main domesticates in the Hellenistic period based on the number of remains

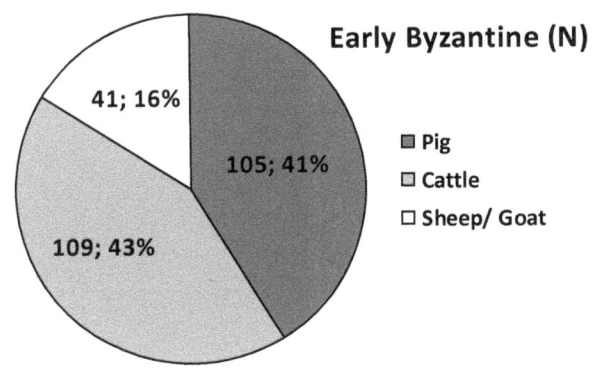

Figure 10.2: Relative importance of the three main domesticates in the Early Byzantine period based on the number of remains

Tsalkin (1966) states that the Greek colonies of the Black Sea region initially had a livestock regime that was primarily based on sheep and goat husbandry. This economic strategy was based on the agricultural practices of the local tribes. As the quantity of sheep/ goat fell through time, the percentage of cattle gradually grew. Perhaps the predominance of cattle in the Hellenistic layers at Nokalakevi can also be seen as a result of this evolution. For pig it is clear that these animals were bred mainly for their meat. But for cattle and sheep the main purpose may have been their secondary products like wool, milk and traction. In terms of cattle there are some indications that this was in fact the case at Nokalakevi. When looking for example at the ages of this species compared with the other two domestic mammals, it is clear, at least for the Hellenistic period, that all cattle fragments had reached the age where the epiphysis and diaphysis fuse together (Table 10.2). For the early Byzantine period this is not the case.

To get a better idea of the demography of the animal herds and their use, the fragments were divided into

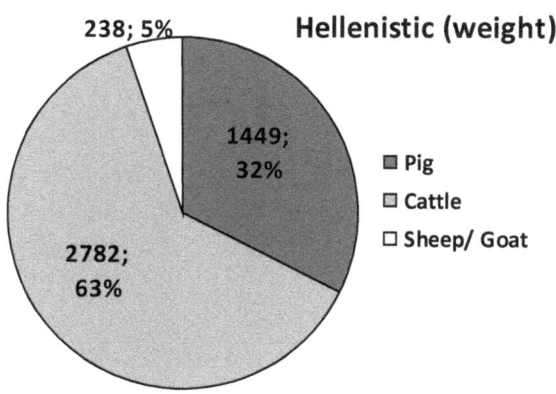

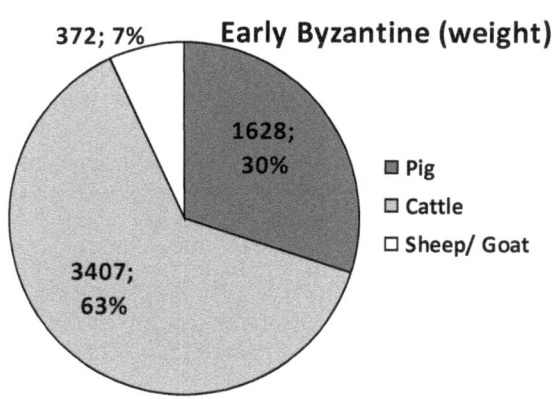

Figure 10.3: Relative importance of the three main domesticates in the Hellenistic period based on the weight of the fragments

Figure 10.4: Relative importance of the three main domesticates in the Early Byzantine period based on the number of remains

Taxon	Hellenistic				Early Byzantine	
	A268*	A235	A232	B420*	A267	B401*
Pig/ Wild Boar						
Mandibula	perinatal					
Scapula	prox f; prox nf		prox f			prox f
Humerus					dist f; dist f; dist fusing	dist f
Radius	prox nf; prox nf	perinatal			dist f	prox f
Ulna	prox nf					perinatal
Femur	dist f					dist nf
Tibia				dist f		dist nf; dist f
Metapodial						dist f
Metacarpus			prox f + dist f			(4x) prox f; (2x) prox f + dist f
Metatarsus						(3x) prox f; (2x) prox f + dist nf
Phalanx I	prox f + dist f; prox f + dist nf				prox nf + dist f; prox f + dist f	(2x) prox fusing; (3x) prox f + dist f
Phalanx II	prox f + dist f					prox f
Sheep/ goat						
Humerus	dist f					
Femur					prox f	prox nf; dist f
Calcaneus		prox nf			prox f	prox f; prox nf
Metapodial		prox f				
Metacarpus					prox f	prox f; dist nf
Phalanx I						prox f + dist f
Phalanx II						prox f + dist nf
Cattle						
Scapulae			prox f			prox f
Humerus			dist f		dist f; dist f	dist nf; dist nf; dist nf
Radius		prox f				
Ulna						prox nf
Femur						dist f; prox f
Tibia						dist nf
Calcaneus					prox nf	prox f
Metacarpus		prox f				prox f; prox f
Metatarsus	prox f; prox f				prox f; prox f	
Metapodial	dist f					dist f; prox f; dist nf
Phalanx I	dist f; prox f + dist f		prox f + dist f		(3x) prox f + dist f	

Table 10.2: Animal bone fragments aged by epiphyseal fusion (= including other associated contexts)*

different age categories for cattle, pig and sheep/goat. Because the sample was small, it was impossible to draw solid conclusions, but the results do give some indications about the possible management of livestock at the site.

The impression is that for pig, the majority of the animals did not survive their third year (Figure 10.5). Only one individual for both periods reaches the age of 42 months. This is not the case for cattle, where the proportion of individuals that survive the age of 36 months is relatively large compared to the younger age groups. A certain number of animals in the herd had, therefore, probably been kept past their optimal age for reasons other than meat production (Figure 10.6).

It is, therefore, likely that part of the cattle herd was primarily used for dairy and/or draught before being killed. The broadening of the proximal articulation of a first phalanx (from NOK10/A **267**) confirms this hypothesis at least for the early Byzantine period. This pathological condition on the joint between the first phalanx and distal epiphysis of the metapodial, can be seen as a skeletal adaptation to load-bearing (Bartosiewicz *et al* 1997).

For sheep and goat there are fewer indications about the demography of the herd as the sample for these species is even smaller than that of the other two (pig and cattle). The results therefore carry less statistical weight (Figure 10.7). The general impression given by the results, however seems to be more indicative of a pattern that looks like that of cattle, where older animals are also well represented. Perhaps these animals were also kept principally for their secondary products.

Very little information about the age of the animals was available from tooth eruption. Only a few mandibles with teeth were recovered. For pig there were four mandibles recovered from the Hellenistic context NOK10/B **401**. A first specimen was aged 17 to 22 months, a second less than 12 to 16 months. The third and the fourth specimens were in the early stages of dental wear described by Grant (1982) and belonged to young animals too. For another Hellenistic context (NOK10/A **232**) two specimens were aged around 17 to 22 months again and a third specimen was estimated older than 17 to 22 months.

For cattle there is even less information available, but the presence of both a deciduous fourth premolar as well as a third molar with severe tooth wear, shows that both young and older animals were present at the site during the later period. The same conclusions can perhaps be drawn for sheep/goat. Two mandibulae in a late stage of tooth wear (from NOK10/A **235** and NOK10/B **401**) show that old animals were present on the site. A mandible with a fourth deciduous premolar (NOK10/A **268**) and a second one with a third molar that had not yet erupted (NOK10/A **235**), demonstrate that young animals were also represented. These fragments came from animals that were not older than 17 to 20 months for the premolar and 18 to 24 months for the molar. Very few additional

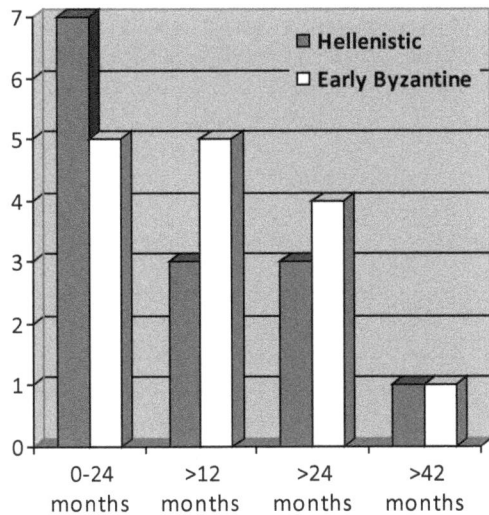

Figure 10.5: Mortuary graph based on the epiphyseal fusion data of pig

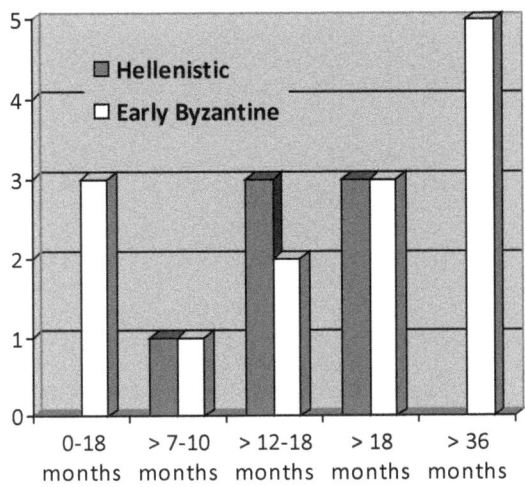

Figure 10.6: Mortuary graph based on the epiphyseal fusion data of cattle

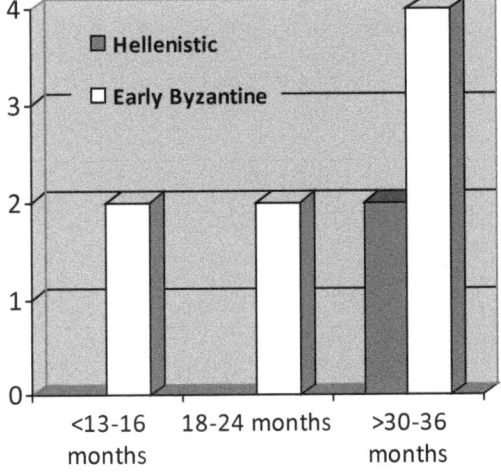

Figure 10.7: Mortuary graph based on the epiphyseal fusion data of sheep/ goat

conclusions can be drawn from the tooth eruption data. Although for pig the same conclusion was reached for the tooth eruption as for the epiphyseal fusion data, nothing further can be said about the other species with any certainty.

The Nokalakevi assemblage also offered an opportunity to evaluate the techniques and tools used to process animal carcasses on the site. Again there was little difference between the two periods. Traces were found on the remains of cattle, pig and sheep/goat and in one case on a chicken coracoid. Judging by the fact that cutmarks

Hellenistic	cutmark	chopmark	other
A272			
SHEEP/ GOAT			
Humerus	1		
A268			
CATTLE			
Phalanx I	1		
SHEEP/ GOAT			
Humerus	1		
PIG			
Axis	1		
Costa	1		
Scapula		1	
Humerus	1	1	
Radius			1*
unidentified		1	
A231			
CATTLE			
Costa		1	
Phalanx I	1		
A232			
CATTLE			
Radius		1	
Thoracic vertebra	1		
PIG			
Mandibula	1		
Scapula	1		
Ulna	1		
B420			
CATTLE			
Humerus	1		
A217			
CATTLE			
Costa	2		
A235			
CATTLE			
Mandibula		2	
Cervical vertebra	1		
Costa	1	1	
Radius + Ulna	1		
Calcaneus	1		
PIG			
Scapula	3		
Femur	1		
A216			
CATTLE			
Humerus		1	

Early Byzantine	cutmark	chopmark	other
A267			
CHICKEN			
Coracoid	1		
CATTLE			
Humerus	1		
Radius			1**
Calcaneus	1		
SHEEP/ GOAT			
Scapula	1		
Humerus	2		
Femur	1		
Calcaneus	1		
PIG			
Humerus	2		
Ulna	1		
B397			
CATTLE			
Humerus	1		
B398			
PIG			
Humerus	1		
Phalanx II	1		
B401			
CATTLE			
Axis	1		
Femur	1		1**
PIG			
Scapula	1		
Ulna	1		
Unidentified		2°	
B424			
PIG			
Cranium			1***
Phalanx I			11***
B414			
PIG			
Costa			2***
Unidentified			15***
B421			
CATTLE			
Humerus	1		
Femur		1	
SHEEP/ GOAT			
Humerus	1		

Table 10.3: Butchery and other modifications (*=perforation, **=shaving mark, ***=burned, °=vertebra)

126

are the most commonly found traces on the animal bones, it seems that a mode of butchery was used that depended mainly on a sharp blade (Table 10.3 and Figures 10.8 and 10.9). A knife was probably used for the initial disarticulation of the animal. The presence of several cutmarks found around the proximal radioulnar joint of a cow give the impression that this type of tool was, for example, used to separate the upper from the lower limb (Fig. 10.10).

The presence of shaving marks on two cattle fragments indicate that a comparable sharp tool was also used for the removal of the meat from the bones. Cleavers were most likely used for the further processing of the bony parts. In two cases there were also found chopmarks on the mandibulae of cattle that are perhaps indications for the extraction of marrow. One pig radius had a perforation through the proximal epiphysis, but it was unclear whether this was intentional or not.

The cutmark on a coracoid of a chicken shows that this animal was also eaten at the site. The other remains of chicken are probably also fragments of animals that were kept for their meat and eggs.

A few fragments give some insight in the appearance of the animals kept at Nokalakevi. A horncore of cattle from the early Byzantine period (NOK10/B **401**) shows that at least during the later period a horned breed of cattle was kept at the site. As there were no complete long bones present in the assemblage, it was impossible to estimate the withers heights of cattle, pig and ovicaprids.

The Hellenistic context NOK10/A **263** contained a sub-complete carcass of a chicken that was associated with a human skeleton (NOK10/A **261**). On the humerus, tibiotarsus and tarsometatarsus it was possible to take measurements that give an idea of the size of the animal. When comparing the Nokalakevi individual with the size variations described in the work of Thesing (1977), it can be concluded that a small breed of domestic fowl was kept at Nokalakevi in the Hellenistic period.

Game was poorly represented in the Nokalakevi assemblage and hunting was probably almost irrelevant to the economy of the site. However, the hunting of both small and large game did take place, including that of hare, red deer and roe deer.

On a humerus of wild boar (NOK10/A **267**) and on the humerus of the aurochs there were cutmarks on the distal epiphysis indicating that these animals were also hunted. As hunting was insignificant from an economic point of view, it might perhaps have had a social function. Hunting wild boar and especially aurochs must have been very dangerous (Van Vuuren 2002) and catching one of these animals must have added greatly to one's social status.

A proportion of the unidentified bird remains probably also belong to wild animals that may have been hunted.

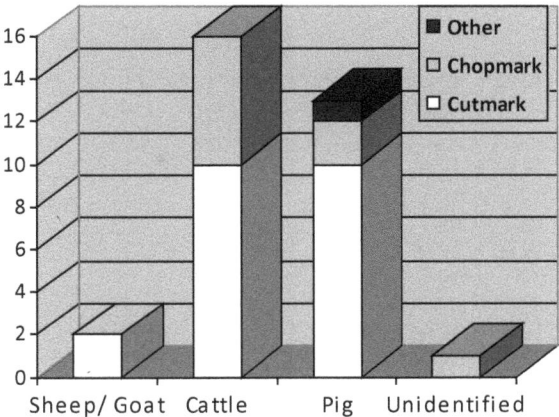

Figure 10.8: Butchery traces from the Hellenistic period

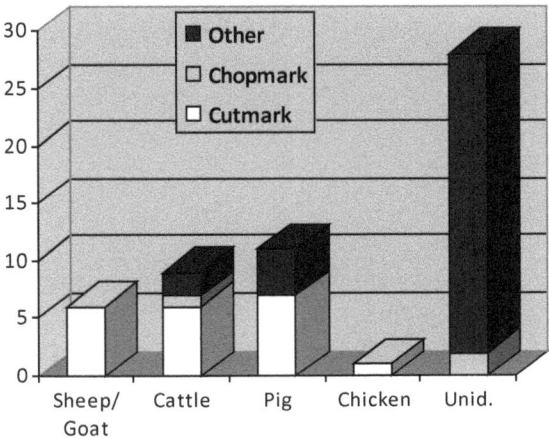

Figure 10.9: Butchery traces from the Early Byzantine period

Figure 10.10: Cutmarks on cattle radioulna

127

Ritual use of animals

There are a few indications that some animal remains were not just consumption waste, but that their deposition also had a certain ritual significance. This might perhaps have been the case for the chicken carcass. As this animal was found in close proximity to a human skeleton (NOK10/A **261**) it might have represented a sacrificial meal.

The burned fragments (mostly of pig) from NOK10/B **414** and NOK10/B **424** were perhaps also part of a ritual. Pigs are well known to have been sacrificed in antiquity. According to Plinius, in his *Naturalis Historia*, piglets were ready for sacrifice from their fifth day (Wilkins 2004). The presence of a roe deer antler in NOK10/A **268** may also point in this direction. As no other traces of antler were found on the site, and apparently no bone working took place, the antler may also have had a ritual significance. As this was a fragment that had naturally shed from the animals skull, it was probably found somewhere in the forest and brought to the site. It cannot be seen as consumption waste, as it did not belong to an animal that was hunted.

Conclusion

The majority of the animal remains at Nokalakevi consisted of primary consumption waste. From this data, information about the economy of the site during the Hellenistic and early Byzantine period was inferred. It was clear that cattle was the most important species followed by pig. Sheep and goat were less significant. Pig husbandry clearly took place for the production of meat, while cattle was probably in the first place bred for its secondary products like dairy and traction. Chicken was the only domestic bird that was found (and clearly also eaten) at the site.

After the animals were killed, their carcasses were butchered and the meat removed mainly by making use of a sharp blade. The bony parts may later have been chopped up with the use of a cleaver.

Besides the domesticated mammals, there were also a few fragments of wild animals. These remains, with the exception of roe deer, probably belong to hunted animals. Both small and big game were present. Hare, red deer, roe deer, wild boar and aurochs were identified. Some of the unidentified bird remains may also belong to hunted wild fowl.

The environment around Nokalakevi was probably of a mixed nature. Areas of the adjoining plain must have been cleared for agricultural/ pastoral purposes, while at the same time a significant part of the landscape must have remained forested.

Bibliography

Albarella, U., Dobney, K. and Rowley-Conwey, P. 2009. Size and shape of the Eurasian wild boar (Sus scrofa), with a view to the reconstruction of its Holocene history. *Environmental Archaeology* 14 (2): 103-136

Bartosiewicz, L., Van Neer, W., Lentacker, A. and Fabis, M. 1997. Draught Cattle: their osteological identification and history. *Annales Sciences Zoologiques* 218. Musée Royal de l'Afrique Centrale, Tervuren

Boessneck, J. 1969. Osteological Differences between Sheep (Ovis aries Linné) and Goat (Capra hircus Linné). In Brothwell, D., and Higgs, E., (ed.) *Science in Archaeology*. London, Thames and Hudson: 331-358

Braund, D. 1994. *Georgia in Antiquity: a History of Colchis and Transcaucasian Iberia 550 BC-AD 562*. Oxford, Oxford University Press

Cohen, A. and Sergeantson, B. 1996. *A manual for the identification of bird bones from archaeological sites*. London, Archetype Publications

De Klerk, P., Haberl, A., Kaffke, A., Krebs, M., Matchutadze, I., Minke, M., Schulz, J., and Joosten, H. 2009. Vegetation history and environmental development since ca 6000 cal yr BP in and around Ispani 2 (Kolkheti lowlands, Georgia). *Quaternary science review* 28: 890-910

Degerbol, M and Fredskild B. 1970. The Urus (Bos primigenius Boj.) and Neolithic domesticated cattle in Denmark. *Det Kongelige Danske Videnskabernes Selskab, Biologiske Skrifter* 17. Munksgaard, Kobenhavn

Ervynck, A. and Vanderhoeven, A. 1992. Het dierenbot. In Vanderhoeven A., Vynckier G., Ervynck, A. & Cooremans, B. (ed) *Het oudheidkundige bodemonderzoek aan de Kielenstraat te Tongeren (prov. Limburg): Interimverslag 1990-1993. Archeologie in Vlaanderen* II: 89-146

Grant, A. 1982. The use of tooth wear as a guide to the age of domestic ungulates. In Wilson, B., Grigson, C. & Payne, S. (ed) *Ageing and sexing animal bones from Archaeological Sites*. British Archaeological Reports 109: 91-108

Kurtén, B. 2007. *Pleistocene mammals of Europe*. Transaction Publishers, London

Lyman, R. L. 1994. *Vertebrate taphonomy*. Cambridge University Press Cambridge

Schmidt, E. 1972. *Atlas of Animal Bones*. Elsevier, Amsterdam

Silver, I. A. 1969. The ageing of domestic animals. In Brothwell, D. and Higgs E.S. (eds.). *Science in Archaeology*. Thames and Hudson, London: 283–302

Thesing, R. 1977. *Die Großentwicklung des haushuhns in vor- und frühgeschichtlicher Zeit*. Unpublished doctoral dissertation, Munich University

Tsalkin V.I. 1966. The early animal husbandry of the tribes of Eastern Europe and Central Asia. *Materialy I issledovaniya po arkheologii SSSR* 135

Van Vuure, C. T. 2002. History, morphology and ecology of the Aurochs (*Bos taurus primigenius*). *Lutra* 45-1: 1-16

Von den Driesch, A. 1976. *A guide to the measurement of animal bones from archaeological sites. Peabody Museum Bulletin 1*. Cambridge, Massachusetts, Harvard University Press

Von den Driesch, A. and Boessneck, J. 1974. Kritische Anmerkungen zur Widerristhöhenberechnung aus Längenmaßen vor- und frühgeschichtlicher Tierknochen. *Saugetierkundliche Mitteilungen* 22: 325-348

Wilkins, B. 2004. Roman suovitaurilia and its predecessors. In O'day, S.J., van Neer, W. & Ervynck, A. (ed) *Behaviour behind bones. 9th Icaz conference, Durham (2002)*, Oxbow Books, Oxford: 73-76

Lightning Source UK Ltd.
Milton Keynes UK
UKHW021847270322
400676UK00002B/5

9 781407 312439